T0301597

Mathematical Methods for Finance

The Frank J. Fabozzi Series

Mathematical Methods for Finance

Tools for Asset and Risk Management

SERGIO M. FOCARDI
FRANK J. FABOZZI
TURAN G. BALI

WILEY

To the memory of my parents
SMF

*To my wife, Donna,
and my children, Patricia, Karly, and Francesco*
FJF

*To my wife, Mehtap,
and my son, Kaan*
TGB

Contents

Preface

Since the pioneering work of Harry Markowitz in the 1950s, mathematical tools drawing from the fields of standard and stochastic calculus, set theory, probability theory, stochastic processes, matrix algebra, optimization theory, and differential equations have increasingly made their way into finance. Some of these tools have been used in the development of financial theory, such as asset pricing theory and option pricing theory, as well as like theories in the practice of asset management, risk management, and financial modeling.

Different areas of finance call for different mathematics. For example, asset management, also referred to as investment management and money management, is primarily concerned with understanding hard facts about financial processes. Ultimately, the performance of an asset manager is linked to an understanding of risk and return. This implies the ability to extract information from time series data that are highly noisy and appear nearly random. Mathematical models must be simple, but with a deep economic meaning. In other areas, the complexity of instruments is the key driver behind the growing use of sophisticated mathematics in finance. There is the need to understand how relatively simple assumptions on the probabilistic behavior of basic quantities translate into the potentially very complex probabilistic behavior of financial products. Examples of such products include option-type financial derivatives (such as options, swaptions, caps, and floors), credit derivatives, bonds with embedded option-like payoffs (such as callable bonds and convertible bonds), structured notes, and mortgage-backed securities.

One might question whether all this mathematics is justified in finance. The field of finance is generally considered much less accurate and viable than the physical sciences. Sophisticated mathematical models of financial markets and market agents have been developed but their accuracy is questionable to the point that the recent global financial crisis is often blamed on unwarranted faith on faulty mathematical models. However, we believe that the mathematical handling of finance is reasonably successful and models are not to be blamed for this crisis. Finance does not study laws of nature but complex human artifacts—the financial markets—that are designed to be largely uncertain. We could make financial markets less uncertain and, thereby, mathematical models more faithful by introducing more rules and collecting more data. Collectively, we have decided not to do so and, therefore, models can only be moderately accurate. Still, they offer a valuable design tool to engineer our financial systems. Nevertheless, the mathematics of finance cannot be that of physics. It is the mathematics of learning and complexity, similar to the mathematics used in studying biological and ecological systems.

In 1960, the physicist Eugene Wigner, recipient of the 1962 Nobel Prize in Physics, wrote his now famous paper "The Unreasonable Effectiveness of Mathematics in the Natural Sciences." Wigner argued that the success of mathematics in describing natural phenomena is so extraordinary that it is in itself a phenomenon that needs explanation.[1] Mathematics in finance is reasonably effective and the reasons why it is reasonably effective deserve an explanation. Recently, the world went through the worst financial and economic crisis since the Great Depression. Many have pointed their fingers at the growing use of mathematics in finance and the resulting mathematical models. We would argue that mathematics does not have much to do with that crisis. In a nutshell, we believe that mathematics is reasonably effective in finance because we apply it to study large engineered artifacts—financial markets—that have been designed to have a lot of freedom. Modern financial systems are designed to be relatively unpredictable and uncontrolled in order to leave possibilities of changes and innovations. The level of unpredictability and control is different in different systems. Some systems are prone to crises. Mathematics does a reasonably good job to describe these systems. But the mathematics involved is not the same as that of physics. It is the mathematics of learning and complexity. Mathematics can be perceived as ineffective in finance only if we insist on comparing it with physics.

There are differences between finance and the physical sciences. In the three centuries following the publication of Newton's *Principia* in 1687, physics has developed into an axiomatic theory. Physical theories are axiomatic in the sense that that the entire theory can be derived through mathematical deduction from a small number of fundamental laws. Physics is not yet completely unified but the different disciplines that make the body of physics are axiomatic. Even more striking is the fact that physical phenomena can be approximately represented by computational structures, so that physical reality can be mimicked by a computer program.

---

[1] E. Wigner, "The Unreasonable Effectiveness of Mathematics in the Natural Sciences," *Communications in Pure and Applied Mathematics* 13 (1960): 1–14.

Though it is clear that finance has made progress and will make additional progress only by adopting the scientific method of empirical science, it should be clear that there are significant differences between finance and physics. We can identify, albeit with some level of arbitrariness, four major differences between finance and the physical sciences:

1. Finance must study a global financial system without the possibility of studying simplified subsystems.
2. Finance is an empirical science, but the ability to conduct experiments in finance is limited when compared with the experimental facilities built in the physical sciences.
3. Finance does not study laws of nature, but it studies a human artifact that is subject to changes due to human decisions.
4. Finance systems are self-reflecting in the sense that the knowledge accumulated on the system changes the system itself.

None of the above four points is in itself an objection to the scientific study of finance as a mathematical science. However, it should be clear that the methods of scientific investigations and the findings of finance might be conceptually different from those of the physical sciences. It would probably be a mistake to expect in finance the same type of generalized axiomatic laws that we find in physics.

One of the major sources of the progress made by physics is due to the ability to isolate elementary subsystems, to come out with laws that apply to these subsystems, and then to recover macroscopic laws by a mathematical process. For example, the study of mechanics was greatly simplified by the study of the material point, a subsystem without structure identified by a small number of continuous variables. After identifying the laws that govern the motion of a material point, the motion of any physical body can be recovered by a process of mathematical integration. Simplifications of this type allow one to both simplify the mathematics and to perform empirical tests in a simplified environment.

In financial economics, however, we cannot study idealized subsystems because we cannot identify subsystems with a simplified behavior. This is not to say that attempts have not been made. Drawing on the principles of microeconomics, financial economics attempts to study the behavior of individuals as the elementary units of the financial system. The real problem, however, is that the study of individuals as economic "atoms" cannot produce simple laws because it is the study of a human financial decision-making process, which is very complex in itself. In addition, we cannot perform experiments. Instead, we have to rely on how the only financial system we know develops in itself.

Note that the possibility to study elementary subsystems does not co-incide with the existence of fundamental laws. For example, consider the Schrödinger equation of quantum mechanics formulated in 1926 by the physicist Erwin Schrödinger. The equation is a partial differential equation describing how in some physical system a quantum state evolves over time. Although the Schrödinger equation is indeed a fundamental law, it applies to any system and not only to microscopic entities. Fundamental laws are not necessarily microscopic laws. We might be able to find fundamental laws of finance even if we are unable to isolate elementary subsystems.

There is a strong connection between fundamental laws and the ability to make experiments. By their nature, fundamental laws are very general and can be applied, albeit after difficult mathematical manipulations, to any phenomena. Therefore, after discovering a fundamental law it is generally possible to design experiments specific to test that same law. In many instances in the history of physics, crucial experiments have suggested rejection of a theory in favor of a new competing theory. However, in finance the ability to conduct experiments is limited though important research in this field has been carried on. In the 1970s, Daniel Kahneman and Amos Tversky performed groundbreaking research on cognitive biases in decision making. Vernon Smith studied different types of market organization, in particular auctions. This type of research has changed the perspective of finance as an empirical science. Still, we cannot make a close parallel between experimental finance and experimental physics where we can design experiments to decide between theories.

Perhaps the deepest difference between finance and physics is the fact that finance studies a human artifact which is subject to change in function of human decisions. Physics aims at discovering fundamental physical laws while finance determines laws that apply to a specific artifact. The level of generality of finance is intrinsically lower than that of physics. In addition, financial systems tend to change in function of the knowledge accumulated so that the object of inquiry is not stable.

As a result of all the above, it is unlikely that the kind of mathematics used in physics is appropriate to the study of financial theories. For example, we cannot expect to find any simple law that might be expressed with a closed formula. Hence, empirical testing cannot be done by comparing the results of closed-form solutions with experiments but more likely by comparing the results of long calculations. Thus the mathematical description of financial systems was delayed until researchers in finance had high-performance computers to perform the requisite large number of calculations. Nor can we expect a great level of accuracy in our descriptions of financial phenomena. If we want to compare finance to the natural sciences, we have to compare our knowledge of finance with our knowledge of the laws that govern macrosystems. While physicists have been able to determine extremely precise laws that govern subsystems such as atoms, their ability to predict macroscopic phenomena such as earthquakes or weather remains quite limited. Parallels between finance and the natural sciences are to be found more in the theory of complex systems than in fundamental physics.

In this book, special emphasis has been put on describing concepts and mathematical techniques, leaving aside lengthy demonstrations, which, while the substance of mathematics, are of limited interest to the practitioner and student of financial economics. From the practitioner's point of view, what is important is to have a firm grasp of the concepts and techniques so as to understand the appropriate application. There is no prerequisite mathematical knowledge for reading this book: all mathematical concepts used in the book are explained, starting from ordinary calculus and matrix algebra. It is, however, a demanding book given the breadth and depth of concepts covered. Each chapter begins with a brief description of how the tool it covers is used in finance, which is then followed by the learning objectives for the chapter. Each chapter concludes with its key points.

In writing this book, special attention was given to bridging the gap between the intuition of the practitioner and academic mathematical analysis. Often there are simple compelling reasons for adopting sophisticated concepts and techniques that are obscured by mathematical details. That said, whenever possible, we tried to give the reader an understanding of the reasoning behind these concepts. The book has many examples of how quantitative analysis is used in the practice of asset management.

SERGIO M. FOCARDI
FRANK J. FABOZZI
TURAN G. BALI

About the Authors

Sergio M. Focardi is a Visiting Professor at Stony Brook University, SUNY, where he holds a joint appointment in the College of Business and the Department of Applied Mathematics and Statistics. Prior to that, he was a Professor of Finance at the EDHEC Business School in Nice. Professor Focardi is a founding partner of the Paris-based consulting firm The Intertek Group. A member of the editorial board of the *Journal of Portfolio Management*, he has authored numerous articles and books on financial modeling and risk management including the following Wiley books: *Probability and Statistics for Finance* (2010), *Quantitative Equity Investing: Techniques and Strategies* (2010), *Robust Portfolio Optimization and Management* (2007), *Financial Econometrics* (2007), *Financial Modeling of the Equity Market* (2006), *The Mathematics of Financial Modeling and Investment Management* (2004), *Risk Management: Framework, Methods and Practice* (1998), and *Modeling the Markets: New Theories and Techniques* (1997). He also coauthored three monographs published by the Research Foundation of the CFA Institute: *Challenges in Quantitative Equity Management* (2008), *The Impact of the Financial Crisis on the Asset Management Industry* (2010), *Trends in Quantitative Finance* (2006). His research interests include the econometrics of large equity portfolios and the modeling of regime changes. Professor Focardi holds a degree in Electronic Engineering from the University of Genoa and a PhD in Mathematical Finance and Financial Econometrics from the University of Karlsruhe.

Frank J. Fabozzi is Professor of Finance at EDHEC Business School and a member of the EDHEC Risk Institute. He has held various professorial positions at Yale and MIT. In 2013–2014 he will hold the position of James Wei Visiting Professor in Entrepreneurship at Princeton University. Since the 2011–2012 academic year, he has been a Visiting Fellow in the Department of Operations Research and Financial Engineering at Princeton University. A trustee for the BlackRock family of closed-end funds, Professor Fabozzi has authored and edited many books in asset management and quantitative finance. In addition to his position as editor of the *Journal of Portfolio Management* and editorial board member of *Quantitative Finance*, he serves on the advisory board of The Wharton School's Jacobs Levy Equity Management Center for Quantitative Financial Research, the Q Group Selection Committee, and from 2003 to 2011 on the Council for the Department of Operations Research and Financial Engineering at Princeton University. He is a Fellow of of the International Center for Finance at Yale University. He is the CFA Institute's 2007 recipient of the C. Stewart Sheppard Award and an inductee into the Fixed Income Analysts Society Hall of Fame. Professor Fabozzi earned a PhD in Economics in September 1972 from the City University of New York and holds the professional designations of Chartered Financial Analyst (1977) and Certified Public Accountant (1982). In 1994, he was awarded an Honorary Doctorate of Humane Letter from Nova Southeastern University.

Turan G. Bali is the Robert S. Parker Chair Professor of Finance at the McDonough School of Business at Georgetown University. Before joining Georgetown University, Professor Bali was the David Krell Chair Professor of Finance at Baruch College and the Graduate School and University Center of the City University of New York. He also held visiting faculty positions at New York University and Princeton University. Professor Bali specializes in asset pricing, risk management, fixed income securities, and financial derivatives. A founding member of the Society for Financial Econometrics, he has worked on consulting projects sponsored by major financial institutions and government organizations in the United States and other countries. In addition, he currently serves as an Associate Editor for the following journals: *Journal of Banking and Finance*, *Journal of Futures Markets*, *Journal of Portfolio Management*, *Review of Financial Economics*, and *Journal of Risk*. He served on the review committee of several research foundations such as the National Science Foundation, Research Grants Council of Hong Kong, Scientific and Technological Research Council of Turkey, and Social Sciences and Humanities Research Council of Canada. With more than 50 published articles in economics and finance journals, Professor Bali's work has appeared in the *Journal of Finance*, *Journal of Financial Economics*, *Review of Financial Studies*, *Journal of Monetary Economics*, *Management Science*, *Review of Economics and Statistics*, *Journal of Business*, and *Journal of Financial and Quantitative Analysis*.

CHAPTER 1

Basic Concepts

Sets, Functions, and Variables

In mathematics, sets, functions, and variables are three fundamental concepts. First, a **set** is a well-defined collection of objects. A set is a gathering together into a whole of definite, distinct objects of our perception, which are called elements of the set. Sets are one of the most fundamental concepts in mathematics. Set theory is seen as the foundation from which virtually all of mathematics can be derived. For example, structures in abstract algebra, such as groups, fields, and rings, are sets closed under one or more operations. One of the main applications of set theory is constructing relations. Second, a **function** is a relation between a set of inputs and a set of permissible outputs with the property that each input is related to exactly one output. Functions are the central objects of investigation in most fields of modern mathematics. There are many ways to describe or represent a function. Some functions may be defined by a formula or algorithm that tells how to compute the output for a given input. Others are given by a picture, called the **graph of the function**. A function can be described through its relationship with other functions, for example, as an inverse function or as a solution of a differential equation. Finally, a **variable** is a value that may change within the scope of a given problem or set of operations. In contrast, a **constant** is a value that remains unchanged, though often unknown or undetermined. Variables are further distinguished as being either a dependent variable or an independent variable. Independent variables are regarded as inputs to a system and may take on different values freely. Dependent variables are those values that change as a consequence of changes in other values in the system.

The concepts of sets, functions, and variables are fundamental to many areas of finance and its applications. Starting with the mean-variance portfolio theory of Harry Markowitz in 1952, then the capital asset pricing model of William Sharpe in 1964, the option pricing model of Fischer Black and Myron Scholes in 1973, and the more recent developments in financial econometrics, financial risk management and asset pricing, financial economists constantly use the concepts of sets, functions, and variables. In this chapter we discuss these concepts.

What you will learn after reading this chapter:

- The notion of sets and set operations
- How to define empty sets, union of sets, and intersection of sets.
- The elementary properties of sets.
- How to describe the dynamics of quantitative phenomena.
- The concepts of distance and density of points.
- How to define and use functions and variables.

INTRODUCTION

In this chapter we discuss three basic concepts used throughout this book: sets, functions, and variables. These concepts are used in financial economics, financial modeling, and financial econometrics.

SETS AND SET OPERATIONS

The basic concept in calculus and in probability theory is that of a **set**. A set is a collection of objects called **elements**. The notions of both elements and set should be considered primitive. Following a common convention, let's denote sets with capital Latin or Greek letters: $A, B, C, \Omega \ldots$ and elements with small Latin or Greek letters: a, b, ω. Let's then consider collections of sets. In this context, a set is regarded as an element at a higher level of aggregation. In some instances, it might be useful to use different alphabets to distinguish between sets and collections of sets.[1]

Proper Subsets

An element a of a set A is said to belong to the set A written as $a \in A$. If every element that belongs to a set A also belongs to a set B, we say that A is contained in B and write: $A \subset B$. We will distinguish whether A is a **proper subset** of B (i.e., whether there is at least one element that belongs to B but not to A) or if the two sets might eventually coincide. In the latter case we write $A \subseteq B$.

In the United States there are indexes that are constructed based on the price of a subset of common stocks from the universe of all common stock in the country. There are three types of common stock (equity) indexes:

1. Produced by stock exchanges based on all stocks traded on the particular exchanges (the most well known being the New York Stock Exchange Composite Index).
2. Produced by organizations that subjectively select the stocks included in the index (the most popular being the Standard & Poor's 500).
3. Produced by organizations where the selection process is based on an objective measure such as market capitalization.

The Russell equity indexes, produced by Frank Russell Company, are examples of the third type of index. The Russell 3000 Index includes the 3,000 largest U.S. companies based on total market capitalization. It represents approximately 98% of the investable U.S. equity market. The Russell 1000 Index includes 1,000 of the largest companies in the Russell 3000 Index while the Russell 2000 Index includes the 2,000 smallest companies in the Russell 3000 Index. The Russell Top 200 Index includes the 200 largest companies in the Russell 1000 Index and the Russell Midcap Index includes the 800 smallest companies in the Russell 1000 Index. None of the indexes include non-U.S. common stocks.

---

[1]In this book we consider only the elementary parts of set theory which is generally referred to as naive set theory. This is what is needed to understand the mathematics of calculus. However, set theory has evolved into a separate mathematical discipline which deals with the logical foundations of mathematics.

Let us introduce the notation:

A = all companies in the United States that have issued common stock

I_{3000} = companies included in the Russell 3000 Index

I_{1000} = companies included in the Russell 1000 Index

I_{2000} = companies included in the Russell 2000 Index

I_{Top200} = companies included in the Russell Top 200 Index

I_{Midcap} = companies included in the Russell Midcap 200 Index

We can then write the following:

$I_{3000} \subset A$	(every company that is contained in the Russell 3000 Index is contained in the set of all companies in the United States that have issued common stock)
$I_{1000} \subset I_{3000}$	(the largest 1,000 companies contained in the Russell 1000 Index are contained in the Russell 3000 Index)
$I_{Midcap} \subset I_{1000}$	(the 800 smallest companies in the Russell Midcap Index are contained in the Russell 1000 Index)

$I_{Top200} \subset I_{1000} \subset I_{3000} \subset A$
$I_{Midcap} \subset I_{1000} \subset I_{3000} \subset A$

Throughout this book we will make use of the convenient logic symbols $\forall$ and $\exists$ that mean respectively, "for any element" and "an element exists such that." We will also use the symbol $\Rightarrow$ that means "implies." For instance, if A is a set of real numbers and $a \in A$, the notation $\forall a: a < x$ means "for any number a smaller than x" and $\exists a: a < x$ means "there exists a number a smaller than x."

Empty Sets

Given a subset B of a set A, the complement of B with respect to A written as B^C is formed by all elements of A that do not belong to B. It is useful to consider sets that do not contain any elements called **empty sets**. The empty set is usually denoted by $\emptyset$. For example, stocks with negative prices form an empty set.

Union of Sets

Given two sets A and B, their **union** is formed by all elements that belong to either A or B. This is written as $C = A \cup B$. For example,

$I_{1000} \cup I_{2000} = I_{3000}$ (the union of the companies contained in the Russell 1000 Index and the Russell 2000 Index is the set of all companies contained in the Russell 3000 Index)

$I_{\text{Midcap}} \cup I_{\text{Top200}} = I_{1000}$ (the union of the companies contained in the Russell Midcap Index and the Russell Top 200 Index is the set of all companies contained in the Russell 1000 Index)

    Let $I_{\text{Long lived}}$ be those stocks that existed in the last 30 years.

Intersection of Sets

Given two sets A and B, their **intersection** is formed by all elements that belong to both A and B. This is written as $C = A \cap B$. For example, let

$$I_{\text{S\&P}} = \text{companies included in the S\&P 500 Index}$$

The S&P 500 is a stock market index that includes 500 widely held common stocks representing about 77% of the New York Stock Exchange market capitalization. (**Market capitalization** for a company is the product of the market value of a share and the number of shares outstanding.) Call $I_{\text{Long lived}}$ those stocks that existed in the last 30 years. Then

$I_{\text{S\&P}} \cap I_{\text{Long lived}} = C$ (the stocks contained in the S&P 500 Index that existed for the last 30 years)

We can also write:

$I_{1000} \cap I_{2000} = \emptyset$ (companies included in both the Russell 2000 and the Russell 1000 Index is the empty set since there are no companies that are in both indexes)

Elementary Properties of Sets

Suppose that the set Ω includes all elements that we are presently considering (i.e., that it is the total set). Three elementary properties of sets are given below:

> *Property 1.* The complement of the total set is the empty set and the complement of the empty set is the total set:

$$\Omega^C = \emptyset, \emptyset^C = \Omega$$

Property 2. If A, B, C are subsets of Ω, then the distribution properties of union and intersection hold:

$$A \cup (B \cap C) = (A \cup B) \cap (A \cup C)$$
$$A \cap (B \cup C) = (A \cap B) \cup (A \cap C)$$

Property 3. The complement of the union is the intersection of the complements and the complement of the intersection is the union of the complements:

$$(B \cup C)^C = B^C \cap C^C$$
$$(B \cap C)^C = B^C \cup C^C$$

DISTANCES AND QUANTITIES

Calculus describes the dynamics of quantitative phenomena. This calls for equipping sets with a metric that defines distances between elements. Though many results of calculus can be derived in abstract metric spaces, standard calculus deals with sets of *n*-tuples of real numbers. In a quantitative framework, real numbers represent the result of observations (or measurements) in a simple and natural way.

n-tuples

An *n*-tuple, also called an *n*-dimensional vector, includes n components: $(a_1, a_2, \ldots, a_n)$. The set of all *n*-tuples of real numbers is denoted by R^n. The R stands for real numbers.

For example, suppose the monthly rates of return on a hedge fund portfolio in 2011 are as shown in Table 1.1 with the actual return for the S&P 500 (the benchmark index for the hedge fund portfolio manager).[2]

Then the monthly returns, r_{port}, for the hedge fund portfolio can be written as a 12-tuple and has the following 12 components:

$$r_{\text{port}} = \begin{bmatrix} 0.41\%, 1.23\%, 0.06\%, 1.48\%, -1.20\%, -1.18\% \\ 0.23\%, -3.21\%, -3.89\%, 2.67\%, -1.29\%, -0.43\% \end{bmatrix}$$

---

[2]The monthly rate of return on the S&P 500 is computed as follows:

$$\frac{\text{Dividends paid on all the stock in the index} + \text{Change in the index value for the month}}{\text{Value of the index at the beginning of the period}} - 1$$

TABLE 1.1 Monthly Returns for the Hedge Fund
Composite and S&P 500 Indexes

Month	Hedge Fund Portfolio	S&P 500
January	0.41%	2.26%
February	1.23%	3.20%
March	0.06%	−0.10%
April	1.48%	2.85%
May	−1.20%	−1.35%
June	−1.18%	−1.83%
July	0.23%	−2.15%
August	−3.21%	−5.68%
September	−3.89%	−7.18%
October	2.67%	10.77%
November	−1.29%	−0.51%
December	−0.43%	0.85%

Similarly, the return $r_{S\&P}$ on the S&P 500 can be expressed as a 12-tuple as follows:

$$r_{S\&P} = \begin{bmatrix} 2.26\%, 3.20\%, -0.10\%, 2.85\%, -1.35\%, -1.83\% \\ -2.15\%, -5.68\%, -7.18\%, 10.77\%, -0.51\%, 0.85\% \end{bmatrix}$$

One can perform standard operations on n-tuples. For example, consider the hedge fund portfolio returns in the two 12-tuples. The 12-tuple that expresses the deviation of the hedge fund portfolio's performance from the benchmark S&P 500 index is computed by subtracting from each component of the return 12-tuple from the corresponding return on the S&P 500. That is,

$$r_{port} - r_{S\&P}$$
$$= \begin{bmatrix} 0.41\%, 1.23\%, 0.06\%, 1.48\%, -1.20\%, -1.18\% \\ 0.23\%, -3.21\%, -3.89\%, 2.67\%, -1.29\%, -0.43\% \end{bmatrix}$$
$$- \begin{bmatrix} 2.26\%, 3.20\%, -0.10\%, 2.85\%, -1.35\%, -1.83\% \\ -2.15\%, -5.68\%, -7.18\%, 10.77\%, -0.51\%, 0.85\% \end{bmatrix}$$
$$= \begin{bmatrix} -1.86\%, -1.96\%, 0.17\%, -1.37\%, 0.15\%, 0.65\% \\ 2.37\%, 2.46\%, 3.29\%, -8.10\%, -0.78\%, -1.29\% \end{bmatrix}$$

It is the resulting 12-tuple that is used to compute the **tracking error** of a portfolio—the standard deviation of the variation of the portfolio's return from its benchmark index's return.

Coming back to the portfolio return, one can compute a logarithmic return for each month by adding 1 to each component of the 12-tuple and then taking the natural logarithm of each component. One can then obtain a geometric average, called the **geometric return**, by multiplying each component of the resulting vector and taking the 12th root.

Distance

Consider the real line R^1 (i.e., the set of real numbers). Real numbers include rational numbers and irrational numbers. A **rational number** is one that can be expressed as a fraction, c/d, where c and d are integers and $d \neq 0$. An **irrational number** is one that cannot be expressed as a fraction. Three examples of irrational numbers are

$$\sqrt{2} \cong 1.4142136$$

Ratio between diameter and circumference

$$= \pi \cong 3.141592653589793238462$6$$

Natural logarithm $= e \cong 2.718281828459045235360287471352$6

On the real line, distance is simply the absolute value of the difference between two numbers $|a - b|$ which also can be written as

$$\sqrt{(a - b)^2}$$

R^n is equipped with a natural metric provided by the Euclidean distance between any two points

$$d[(a_1, a_2, \ldots, a_n), (b_1, b_2, \ldots, b_n)] = \sqrt{\sum (a_i - b_i)^2}$$

Given a set of numbers A, we can define the least upper bound of the set. This is the smallest number s such that no number contained in the set exceeds s. The quantity s is called the **supremum** and written as $s = \sup A$. More formally, the supremum is that number, if it exists, that satisfies the following properties:

$$\forall a : a \in A, s \geq a$$
$$\forall \varepsilon > 0, \exists a : s - a \leq \varepsilon$$

where ε is any real positive number. The supremum need not belong to the set A. If it does, it is called the **maximum**.

Similarly, **infimum** is the greatest lower bound of a set *A*, defined as the greatest number *s* such that no number contained in the set is less than *s*. If infimum belongs to the set it is called the **minimum.**

Density of Points

A key concept of set theory with a fundamental bearing on calculus is that of **density of points**. In fact, in financial economics we distinguish between discrete and continuous quantities. **Discrete quantities** have the property that admissible values are separated by finite distances. **Continuous quantities** are such that one might go from one to any of two possible values passing through every possible intermediate value. For instance, the passing of time between two dates is considered to occupy every possible instant without any gap.

The fundamental continuum is the set of real numbers. A **continuum** can be defined as any set that can be placed in a one-to-one relationship with the set of real numbers. Any continuum is an **infinite non-countable set**; a proper subset of a continuum can be a continuum. It can be demonstrated that a finite interval is a continuum as it can be placed in a one-to-one relationship with the set of all real numbers.

The intuition of a continuum can be misleading. To appreciate this, consider that the set of all rational numbers (i.e., the set of all fractions with integer numerator and denominator) has a dense ordering, that is, has the property that given any two different rational numbers a,b with $a < b$, there are infinite other rational numbers in between. However, rational numbers have the cardinality of natural numbers. That is to say rational numbers can be put into a one-to-one relationship with natural numbers. This can be seen using a clever construction that we owe to the seventeenth-century Swiss mathematician Jacob Bernoulli.

Using Bernoulli's construction, we can represent rational numbers as fractions of natural numbers arranged in an infinite two-dimensional table in which columns grow with the denominators and rows grow with the numerators. A one-to-one relationship with the natural numbers can be established following the path: (1,1) (1,2) (2,1) (3,1) (2,2) (1,3) (1,4) (2,3) (3,2) (4,1) and so on (see Table 1.2).

TABLE 1.2 Bernoulli's Construction to Enumerate Rational Numbers

1/1	1/2	1/3	1/4
2/1	2/2	2/3	2/4
3/1	3/2	3/3	3/4
4/1	4/2	4/3	4/4

Bernoulli thus demonstrated that there are as many rational numbers as there are natural numbers. Though the set of rational numbers has a dense ordering, rational numbers do not form a continuum as they cannot be put in a one-to-one correspondence with real numbers.

Given a subset A of R^n, a point $a \in A$ is said to be an **accumulation point** if any sphere centered in a contains an infinite number of points that belong to A. A set is said to be "closed" if it contains all of its own accumulation points and "open" if it does not.

FUNCTIONS

The mathematical notion of a function translates the intuitive notion of a relationship between two quantities. For example, the price of a security is a function of time: to each instant of time corresponds a price of that security.

Formally, a **function** f is a mapping of the elements of a set A into the elements of a set B. The set A is called the **domain** of the function. The subset $R = f(A) \subseteq B$ of all elements of B that are the mapping of some element in A is called the **range** R of the function f. R might be a proper subset of B or coincide with B.

The concept of function is general: the sets A and B might be any two sets, not necessarily sets of numbers. When the range of a function is a set of real numbers, the function is said to be a **real function** or a **real-valued function**.

Two or more elements of A might be mapped into the same element of B. Should this situation never occur, that is, if distinct elements of A are mapped into distinct elements of B, the function is called an **injection**. If a function is an injection and $R = f(A) = B$, then f represents a one-to-one relationship between A and B. In this case the function f is invertible and we can define the **inverse function** $g = f^{-1}$ such that $f(g(a)) = a$.

Suppose that a function f assigns to each element x of set A some element y of set B. Suppose further that a function g assigns an element z of set C to each element y of set B. Combining functions f and g, an element z in set C corresponds to an element x in set A. This process results in a new function, function h, and that function takes an element in set A and assigns it to set C. The function h is called the composite of functions g and f, or simply a **composite function**, and is denoted by $h(x) = g[f(x)]$.

VARIABLES

In applications in finance, one usually deals with functions of numerical variables. Some distinctions are in order. A **variable** is a symbol that represents any element in a given set. For example, if we denote time with a variable t, the letter t represents any possible moment of time. **Numerical variables** are symbols that represent numbers. These numbers might, in turn, represent the elements of another set. They might be thought of as numerical indexes which are in a one-to-one relationship with the elements of a set. For example, if we represent time over a given interval with a variable t, the letter t represents any of the numbers in the given interval. Each of these numbers in turn represents an instant of time. These distinctions might look pedantic but they are important for the following two reasons.

First, we need to consider **numeraire** or units of measure. Suppose, for instance, that we represent the price P of a security as a function of time t: $P = f(t)$. The function f links two sets of numbers that represent the physical quantities price and time. If we change the time scale or the currency, the numerical function f will change accordingly though the abstract function that links time and price will remain unchanged.

Variables can be classified as qualitative or quantitative. Qualitative (or categorical) variables take on values that are names or labels. Examples of qualitative variables would include the color of a ball (e.g., red, green, blue) or a dummy variable (also known as an indicator variable) taking the values 0 or 1. Quantitative variables are numerical. They represent a measurable quantity. For example, when we speak of the population of a city, we are talking about the number of people in the city, which is a measurable attribute of the city. Therefore, population would be a quantitative variable.

Variables can also be classified as deterministic or random. In probability and statistics, a random variable, or stochastic variable, is a variable that can take on a set of possible different values, each with an associated probability. For example, when a coin is tossed 10 times, the random variable is the number of tails (or heads) that are noted. X can only take the values 0, 1, ..., 10, so in this example X is a discrete random variable. Variables might represent phenomena that evolve over time. A deterministic variable evolves according to fixed rules, for example an investment that earns a fixed compound interest rate that grows as an exponential function of time. A random variable might evolve according to chance.

One important type of function is a sequence. A **sequence** is a mapping of the set of natural numbers into real numbers.

KEY POINTS

- A set is a collection of objects called elements.
- Empty sets are sets that do not contain any elements.
- The union of two sets is formed by all elements that belong to either of the two sets.

- The intersection of two sets is formed by all elements that belong to both of the sets.
- Calculus describes the dynamics of quantitative phenomena.
- Real numbers represent the result of observations (or measurements) in a simple and natural way.
- Discrete quantities have the property that admissible values are separated by finite distances.
- Continuous quantities are such that one might go from one to any of two possible values passing through every possible intermediate value.
- A function is a relation between a set of inputs and a set of permissible outputs with the property that each input is related to exactly one output.
- A variable is a value that may change within the scope of a given problem or set of operations.
- Numerical variables are symbols that represent numbers.
- A deterministic variable is a variable whose value is not subject to variations due to chance.
- A random variable or stochastic variable is a variable whose value is subject to variations due to chance or randomness.

CHAPTER **2**

Differential Calculus

Financial market instruments can be divided into two groups. The first group includes cash market instruments, such as stocks, bonds, commodities, and foreign currencies, which are referred to as the **primary set of assets**. The second group includes financial derivatives, such as options, futures, forwards, and swaps, which are written on the primary set of assets. Financial derivatives are claims that promise some payment or delivery in the future contingent on the underlying asset's behavior. Differential calculus is useful to understand and investigate the changes in prices and riskiness of these financial instruments. Using differential calculus, one can:

- Determine the sensitivity of bonds to changes in interest rates.
- Measure the sensitivity of an individual stock (or stock market index) to changes in cash flows (e.g., dividend yields).
- Investigate the sensitivity of an individual stock (or stock market index) to changes in discount rates (e.g., expected returns).
- Estimate the sensitivity of an individual stock (or stock market index) to changes in discount rates (e.g., expected returns).
- Estimate the sensitivity of bonds and individual stocks (or stock market indexes) to changes in macroeconomic variables (e.g., default spread, term spread, inflation rate, growth rate of industrial production, and consumption-to-wealth ratio).
- Investigate how the prices of options change as a result of changes in the price of the underlying asset.
- Investigate how the prices of options change as a result of changes in the volatility of the underlying asset return.
- Determine the optimal value of a function (minimum or maximum) faced by an investor.

What you will learn after reading this chapter:

- The notion of limit.
- The essentials of limit theorems.
- The common definitions linking relevant conditions to limits of functions and sequences.
- The concept of continuity and total variation.
- Differentiation and commonly used rules for computing first-order derivatives.
- Computing second-order and higher-order derivatives.
- The Chain rule.
- Taylor series expansion.
- Financial applications of differential calculus.
- Duration and convexity of bonds.

INTRODUCTION

Invented in the seventeenth century independently by the British physicist Isaac Newton and the German philosopher G. W. Leibnitz, calculus—or infinitesimal calculus to use its first name—was a major mathematical breakthrough that made possible the modern development of the physical sciences. Calculus introduced two key ideas:

- The concept of instantaneous rate of change.
- A framework and rules for linking together quantities and their instantaneous rates of change.

Suppose that a quantity such as the price of a financial instrument varies as a function of time. Given a finite interval, the rate of change of that quantity is the ratio between the amount of change and the length of the time interval. Graphically, the rate of change is the steepness of the straight line that approximates the given curve.[1] In general, the rate of change will vary as a function of the length of the time interval.

What happens when the length of the time interval gets smaller and smaller? Calculus made the concept of infinitely small quantities precise with the notion of **limit**. If the rate of change can get arbitrarily close to a definite

---

[1]The rate of change should not be confused with the return on an asset, which is the asset's percentage price change.

number by making the time interval sufficiently small, that number is the instantaneous rate of change. The **instantaneous rate of change** is the limit of the rate of change when the length of the interval gets infinitely small. This limit is referred to as the **derivative of a function**, or simply, **derivative**. Graphically, the derivative is the steepness of the tangent to a curve.

Starting from this definition and with the help of a number of rules for computing a derivative, it was shown that the instantaneous rate of change of a number of functions—such as polynomials, exponentials, logarithms, and many more—can be explicitly computed as a closed formula. For example, the rate of change of a polynomial is another polynomial of a lower degree.

The process of computing a derivative, referred to as **derivation** or **differentiation**, solves the problem of finding the steepness of the tangent to a curve and is the subject of this chapter. The process of **integration** solves the problem of finding the area below a given curve and is the subject of the next chapter. The reasoning is similar. The area below a curve is approximated as the sum of rectangles and is defined as the limit of these sums when the rectangles get arbitrarily small.

As explained in the next chapter, a key result of calculus is the discovery that integration and differentiation are inverse operations: Integrating the derivative of a function yields the function itself.

LIMITS

The notion of **limit** is fundamental in calculus. It applies to both functions and sequences. Consider an infinite sequence S of real numbers

$$S \equiv (a_1, a_2, \ldots, a_i, \ldots)$$

If, given any real number $\varepsilon > 0$, it is always possible to find a natural number $i(\varepsilon)$ such that

$$i \geq i(\varepsilon) \text{ implies } |a_i - a| < \varepsilon$$

then we write

$$\lim_{n \to \infty} a_n = a$$

and say that the sequence S tends to a when n tends to infinity, or that a is the limit of the sequence S.

Two aspects of this definition should be noted. First, ε can be chosen arbitrarily small. Second, for every choice of ε, the difference in absolute value, between the elements of the sequence S and the limit a is smaller than ε for every index i above $i(\varepsilon)$. This translates the notion that the sequence S gets arbitrarily close to a as the index i grows.

We can now define the concept of limit for functions. Suppose that a real function $y = f(x)$ is defined over an open interval (a,b), that is, an interval that excludes its end points. If, for a real number c in the interval (a,b), there is a real number d such that, given any real number $\varepsilon > 0$, it is always possible to find a positive real number $r(\varepsilon)$ such that

$$|x - c| < r(\varepsilon) \text{ implies } | f(x) - d| < \varepsilon$$

then we write

$$\lim_{x \to c} f(x) = d$$

and say that the function f tends to the limit d when x tends to c.

These basic definitions can be easily modified to cover all possible cases of limits: infinite limits, limits from the left or from the right or finite limits when the variable tends to infinity. Figure 2.1 presents in graphical form

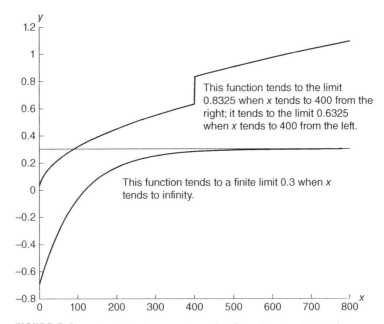

FIGURE 2.1   Graphical Presentation of Infinite Limits, Limits from the Left or Right, and Finite Limits

TABLE 2.1   Most Common Definitions Associating the Relevant Condition to Each Limit

The sequence tends to a finite limit	$\lim\limits_{n \to \infty} a_n = a$	$\forall \varepsilon > 0, \ \exists i(\varepsilon) : \ |a_n - a| < \varepsilon$ for $n > i(\varepsilon)$
The sequence tends to plus infinity	$\lim\limits_{n \to \infty} a_n = +\infty$	$\forall D > 0, \ \exists i(D) : \ a_n > D$ for $n > i(\varepsilon)$
The sequence tends to minus infinity	$\lim\limits_{n \to \infty} a_n = -\infty$	$\forall D < 0, \ \exists i(D) : \ a_n < D$ for $n > i(\varepsilon)$
Finite limit of a function	$\lim\limits_{x \to c} f(x) = d$	$\forall \varepsilon > 0, \ \exists r(\varepsilon) : \ |f(x) - d| < \varepsilon$ for $|x - c| < r(\varepsilon)$
Finite left limit of a function	$\lim\limits_{x \to c^-} f(x) = d$	$\forall \varepsilon > 0, \ \exists r(\varepsilon) : \ |f(x) - d| < \varepsilon$ for $|x - c| < r(\varepsilon), \ x < c$
Finite right limit of a function	$\lim\limits_{x \to c^+} f(x) = d$	$\forall \varepsilon > 0, \ \exists r(\varepsilon) : \ |f(x) - d| < \varepsilon$ for $|x - c| < r(\varepsilon), \ x > c$
Finite limit of a function when x tends to plus infinity	$\lim\limits_{x \to +\infty} f(x) = d$	$\forall \varepsilon > 0, \ \exists R(\varepsilon) > 0 : \ |f(x) - a| < \varepsilon$ for $x > R(\varepsilon)$
Finite limit of a function when x tends to minus infinity	$\lim\limits_{x \to -\infty} f(x) = d$	$\forall \varepsilon > 0, \ \exists R(\varepsilon) > 0 : \ |f(x) - a| < \varepsilon$ for $x < -R(\varepsilon)$
Infinite limit of a function	$\lim\limits_{x \to c} |f(x)| = \infty$	$\forall D > 0, \ \exists r(D) : \ |f(x)| > D$ for $|x - c| < r(D)$
Infinite limit of a function when x tends to plus infinity	$\lim\limits_{x \to +\infty} f(x) = +\infty$	$\forall D > 0, \ \exists R(D) : \ f(x) > D$ for $x > r(D)$

these cases. Table 2.1 lists the most common definitions, associating the relevant condition to each limit.

Note that the notion of limit can be defined only in a continuum. In fact, the limit of a sequence of rational numbers is not necessarily a rational number.

CONTINUITY

Continuity is a property of functions, a continuous function being a function that does not make jumps. Intuitively, a continuous function might be considered one that can be represented through an uninterrupted line in a Cartesian diagram. Its formal definition relies on limits.

A function f is said to be **continuous** at the point c if

$$\lim_{x \to c} f(x) = f(c)$$

This definition does not imply that the function f is defined in an interval; it requires only that c be an accumulation point for the domain of the function f.

A function can be **right continuous** or **left continuous** at a given point if the value of the function at the point c is equal to its right or left limit respectively. A function f that is right or left continuous at the point c can make a jump provided that its value coincides with one of the two right or left limits. (See Figure 2.2.) A function $y = f(x)$ defined on an open interval (a,b) is said to be continuous on (a,b) if it is continuous for all $x \in (a,b)$.

A function can be **discontinuous** at a given point for one of two reasons: (1) either its value does not coincide with any of its limits at that point or (2) the limits do not exist. For example, consider a function f defined in the interval $[0,1]$ that assumes the value 0 at all rational points in that interval, and the value 1 at all other points. Such a function is not continuous at any point of $[0,1]$ as its limit does not exist at any point of its domain.

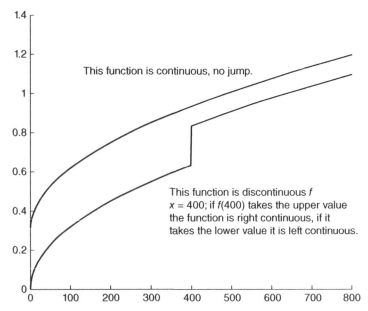

FIGURE 2.2   Graphical Illustration of Right Continuous and Left Continuous

TOTAL VARIATION

Consider a function $f(x)$ defined over a closed interval $[a,b]$. Then consider a partition of the interval $[a,b]$ into n disjoint subintervals defined by $n + 1$ points: $a = x_0 < x_1 < \ldots < x_{n-1} < x_n = b$ and form the sum

$$T = \sum_{i=1}^{n} |f(x_i) - f(x_{i-1})|$$

The supremum of the sum T over all possible partitions is called the **total variation** of the function f on the interval $[a,b]$. If the total variation is finite, the function f is said to have **bounded variation** or **finite variation**. Note that a function can be of infinite variation even if the function itself remains bounded. For example, the function that assumes the value 1 on rational numbers and 0 elsewhere is of infinite variation in any interval, though the function itself is finite.

Continuous functions might also exhibit infinite variation. The following function is continuous but with infinite variation in the interval $[0,1]$:

$$f(x) = \begin{cases} 0 \text{ for } x = 0 \\[2mm] x \, \sin\left(\dfrac{\pi}{x}\right) \text{ for } 0 < x \le 1 \end{cases}$$

THE NOTION OF DIFFERENTIATION

Given a function $y = f(x)$ defined on the open interval (a,b), consider its increments around a generic point x consequent to an increment h of the variable $x \in (a,b)$

$$\Delta y = f(x + h) - f(x)$$

Consider now the ratio $\Delta y/h$ between the increments of the dependent variable y and the independent variable x. Called the **difference quotient**, this quantity measures the average rate of change of y in some interval around x. For instance, if y is the price of a security and t is time, the difference quotient

$$\Delta y = \frac{y(t + h) - y(t)}{h}$$

represents the average price change per unit of time over the interval $[t, t + h]$. The ratio $\Delta y/h$ is a function of h. We can therefore consider its limit when h tends to zero.

If the limit

$$f'(x) = \lim_{h \to 0} \frac{f(x+h) - f(x)}{h}$$

exists, we say that the function f is differentiable at x and that its derivative is f', also written as

$$\frac{df}{dx} \quad \text{or} \quad \frac{dy}{dx}$$

The derivative of a function represents its instantaneous rate of change. If the function f is differentiable for all $x \in (a,b)$, then we say that f is differentiable in the open interval (a,b).

The notation dy/dx has proved useful because it suggests that the derivative is the ratio between two infinitesimal quantities and that calculations can be performed with infinitesimal quantities as well as with discrete quantities. When first invented, calculus was thought of as the "calculus of infinitesimal quantities" and was therefore called "infinitesimal calculus." Only at the end of the nineteenth century was calculus given a sound logical basis with the notion of the limit. The infinitesimal notation remained, however, as a useful mechanical device to perform calculations. The danger in using the infinitesimal notation and computing with infinitesimal quantities is that limits might not exist. Should this be the case, the notation would be meaningless.

In fact, not all functions are differentiable; that is to say, not all functions possess a derivative. A function might be differentiable in some domain and not in others or be differentiable in a given domain with the exception of a few singular points. A prerequisite for a function to be differentiable at a point x is that it is continuous at the point.

However, continuity is not sufficient to ensure differentiability. This can be easily illustrated. Consider the Cartesian plot of a function f. Derivatives have a simple geometric interpretation: The value of the derivative of f at a point x equals the angular coefficient of the tangent of its plot in the same point (see Figure 2.3). A continuous function does not make jumps, while a differentiable function does not change direction by discrete amounts (i.e., it does not have cusps). A function can be continuous but not differentiable at some points. For example, the function $y = |x|$ at $x = 0$ is continuous but not differentiable. However, there are examples of functions that defy visual intuition; in fact, it is possible to demonstrate that there are functions that are continuous in a given interval but never differentiable. One such example is the path of a Brownian motion which we will discuss in Chapter 10.

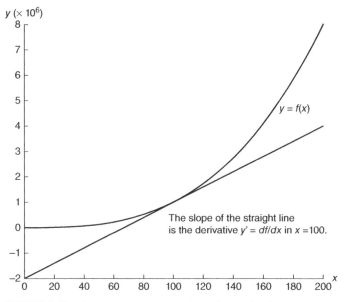

FIGURE 2.3   Geometric Interpretation of a Derivative

COMMONLY USED RULES FOR COMPUTING DERIVATIVES

There are rules for computing derivatives. These rules are mechanical rules that apply provided that all derivatives exist. The proofs are provided in all standard calculus books. The *basic rules* are:

Rule 1: $\frac{d}{dx}(c) = 0$, where c is a real constant.

Rule 2: $\frac{d}{dx}(bx^n) = nbx^{n-1}$, where b is a real constant.

Rule 3: $\frac{d}{dx}(af(x) + bg(x)) = a\frac{d}{dx}f(x) + b\frac{d}{dx}g(x)$, where a and b are real constants.

Rule 3 is called the rule of termwise differentiation and shows that differentiation is a linear operation.

Let's apply the basic rules to the following function:

$$y = a + b_1x + b_2x^2 + b_3x^3 + \cdots + b_kx^n$$

where $a, b_1, b_2, b_3, \ldots, b_n$ are the constants.

The first term is just a and as per Rule 1 the derivative is zero. The derivative of $b_1 x$ by Rule 2 is b_1. For each term $b_i x^i$ by Rule 2 the derivative is $ib_i x^{i-1}$. Thus, the derivative of

$$
\begin{array}{ll}
b_2 x^2 & \text{is} \quad 2b_2 x^1 \\
b_3 x^3 & \text{is} \quad 3b_3 x^2 \\
b_4 x^4 & \text{is} \quad 4b_4 x^3 \\
\text{etc.}
\end{array}
$$

Therefore, the derivative of y is

$$\frac{dy}{dx} = b_1 + 2b_2 x^1 + 3b_3 x^2 + 4b_4 x^3 + \cdots + nb_n x^{n-1}$$

There is a special rule for a **composite function**. Consider a composite function: $h(x) = f[g(x)]$. Provided that h and g are differentiable at the point x and that f is derivable at the point $s = g(x)$, then the following rule, called the **chain rule**, applies:

$$
\begin{aligned}
h'(x) &= f'(g(x))g'(x) \\
h(x) &= f(g(x)) \\
\frac{dh}{dx} &= \left(\frac{df}{dg}\right)\left(\frac{dg}{dx}\right)
\end{aligned}
$$

Let's take the first derivative of the following composite function:

$$y = \left(a + b_1 x + b_2 x^2 + b_3 x^3 + \cdots + b_n x^n\right)^m$$

where

$$g(x) = a + b_1 x + b_2 x^2 + b_3 x^3 + \cdots + b_n x^n$$

and

$$h(x) = f(g(x)) = g(x)^m$$

Applying the chain rule gives

$$
\begin{aligned}
h'(x) &= f'(g(x)) \cdot g'(x) \\
\frac{dy}{dx} &= m\left(a + b_1 x + b_2 x^2 + b_3 x^3 + \cdots + b_n x^n\right)^{m-1} \\
&\quad \times \left(b_1 + 2b_2 x + 3b_3 x^2 + \cdots + nb_n x^{n-1}\right)
\end{aligned}
$$

Table 2.2 shows the **sum rule, product rule, quotient rule,** and **chain rule** for calculating derivatives in both standard and infinitesimal notation. In Table 2.2, it is assumed that a,b are real constants (i.e., fixed real numbers), that f, g, and h are functions defined in the same domain, and that all functions are differentiable at the point x. Table 2.3 lists (without proof) a number of commonly used derivatives.

Rule 3 or sum rule is explained in the earlier example. We now provide an example for the product rule.

$$y = \left(a + b_1 x + b_2 x^2 + b_3 x^3 + \cdots + b_n x^n\right) \cdot \left(c + d_1 x + d_2 x^2 + d_3 x^3 + \cdots + d_n x^n\right)$$

where

$$f(x) = \left(a + b_1 x + b_2 x^2 + b_3 x^3 + \cdots + b_n x^n\right)$$

$$g(x) = \left(c + d_1 x + d_2 x^2 + d_3 x^3 + \cdots + d_n x^n\right)$$

and

$$h(x) = f(x) \cdot g(x)$$

Applying the product rule gives

$$h'(x) = f'(x) \cdot g(x) + f(x) \cdot g'(x)$$
$$\frac{dy}{dx} = \left(b_1 + 2b_2 x + 3b_3 x^2 + \cdots + nb_n x^{n-1}\right)$$
$$\cdot \left(c + d_1 x + d_2 x^2 + d_3 x^3 + \cdots + d_n x^n\right)$$
$$+ \left(a + b_1 x + b_2 x^2 + b_3 x^3 + \cdots + b_n x^n\right)$$
$$\cdot \left(d_1 + 2d_2 x + 3d_3 x^2 + \cdots + nd_n x^{n-1}\right)$$

We now use the same functions, $f(x)$ and $g(x)$, to illustrate the quotient rule:

$$y = \frac{\left(a + b_1 x + b_2 x^2 + \cdots + b_n x^n\right)}{\left(c + d_1 x + d_2 x^2 + \cdots + d_n x^n\right)}$$

where

$$h(x) = \frac{f(x)}{g(x)}$$

TABLE 2.2 Commonly Used Rules of Derivation

	Function	Standard Notation		Infinitesimal Notation
Termwise differentiation	$h(x) = af(x) + bg(x)$	$h'(x) = af'(x) + bg'(x)$	or	$\dfrac{dh}{dx} = a\dfrac{df}{dx} + b\dfrac{dg}{dx}$
Product rule	$h(x) = f(x)g(x)$	$h'(x) = f'(x)g(x) + f(x)g'(x)$	or	$\dfrac{dh}{dx} = \dfrac{df}{dx}g + f\dfrac{dg}{dx}$
Quotient rule	$h(x) = \dfrac{f(x)}{g(x)}$	$h'(x) = \dfrac{f'(x)\cdot g(x) - f(x)\cdot g'(x)}{g(x)^2}$	or	$\dfrac{dh}{dx} = \dfrac{\dfrac{df}{dx}g - f\dfrac{dg}{dx}}{g^2}$
Reciprocal rule	$h(x) = \dfrac{1}{g(x)}$	$h'(x) = -\dfrac{g'(x)}{(g(x))^2}$	or	$\dfrac{dh}{dx} = -\dfrac{1}{(g(x))^2}\dfrac{dg}{dx}$
Chain rule	$h(x) = f(g(x))$	$h'(x) = f'(g(x))g'(x)$		$\dfrac{dh}{dx} = \dfrac{df}{dg}\dfrac{dg}{dx}$

TABLE 2.3   Commonly Used Derivatives

$f(x)$	$\dfrac{df}{dx}$	Domain of P
x^n	nx^{n-1}	R, $x \neq 0$ if $n < 0$
x^α	$ax^{\alpha-1}$	$x > 0$
$\sin x$	$\cos x$	R
$\cos x$	$-\sin x$	R
$\tan x$	$\dfrac{1}{\cos^2(x)}$	$-\dfrac{\pi}{2} + n\dfrac{\pi}{2} < x < \dfrac{\pi}{2} + n\dfrac{\pi}{2}$
$\ln x$	$\dfrac{1}{x}$	$x > 0$
e^x	e^x	R
$\log(f(x))$	$\dfrac{f'(x)}{f(x)}$	$f(x) \neq 0$

Note: Where R denotes real numbers.

Applying the quotient rule gives

$$h'(x) = \frac{f'(x) \cdot g(x) - f(x) \cdot g'(x)}{g(x)^2}$$

$$\frac{dy}{dx} = \frac{\begin{aligned} &\left(b_1 + 2b_2 x + \cdots + nb_n x^{n-1}\right) \cdot \left(c + d_1 x + d_2 x^2 + \cdots + d_n x^n\right) \\ &- \left(a + b_1 x + b_2 x^2 + \cdots + b_n x^n\right) \cdot \left(d_1 + 2d_2 x + \cdots + nd_n x^{n-1}\right) \end{aligned}}{\left(c + d_1 x + d_2 x^2 + \cdots + d_n x^n\right)^2}$$

Given a function $f(x)$, its derivative $f'(x)$ represents its instantaneous rate of change. The logarithmic derivative

$$\frac{d}{dx} \ln P(x) = \frac{f'(x)}{f(x)}$$

for all x such that $P(x) \neq 0$, represents the instantaneous percentage change. In finance, the function $p = p(t)$ represents prices; its logarithmic derivative represents the instantaneous returns.

Given a function $y = f(x)$, its increments $\Delta f = f(x + \Delta x) - f(x)$ can be approximated by

$$\Delta f(x) = f'(x)\Delta x$$

The quality of this approximation depends on the function itself.

HIGHER-ORDER DERIVATIVES

Suppose that a function $f(x)$ is differentiable in an interval D and its derivative is given by

$$f'(x) = \frac{df(x)}{dx}$$

The derivative might in turn be differentiable. The derivative of a derivative of a function is called a **second-order derivative** and is denoted by

$$f''(x) = \frac{d^2 f(x)}{dx^2} = \frac{d\left(\frac{df(x)}{dx}\right)}{dx}$$

Provided that the derivatives exist, this process can be iterated, producing derivatives of any order. A derivative of order n is written in the following way:

$$f^{(n)}(x) = \frac{d^n f(x)}{dx^n} = \frac{d\left(\frac{df^{n-1}(x)}{dx^{n-1}}\right)}{dx}$$

Let's take the first, second, and third derivatives of the polynomial function:

$$y = f(x) = a + b_1 x + b_2 x^2 + b_3 x^3 + \cdots + b_n x^n$$

$$f'(x) = \frac{dy}{dx} = b_1 + 2b_2 x + 3b_3 x^2 + \cdots + nb_n x^{n-1}$$

$$f''(x) = \frac{d^2 y}{dx^2} = 2b_2 + 6b_3 x + \cdots + n(n-1)b_n x^{n-2}$$

$$f'''(x) = \frac{d^3 y}{dx^3} = 6b_3 x + \cdots + n(n-1)(n-2)b_n x^{n-3}$$

Application to Bond Analysis

Two concepts used in bond portfolio management, duration and convexity, provide an illustration of derivatives. A bond is a contract that provides a predetermined stream of positive cash flows at fixed dates assuming that the issuer does not default nor prepay the bond issue prior to the stated maturity date. If the interest rate is the same for each period, the present value of a risk-free bond has the following expression:

$$V = \frac{C}{(1+i)^1} + \frac{C}{(1+i)^2} + \cdots + \frac{C+M}{(1+i)^N}, \quad i = 1, \cdots, N$$

where V is the value of the bond, C is the coupon interest, M is the bond's maturity value, i is the interest rate required by investors, and N is the time until the bond's maturity.

If interest rates are different for each period, the previous formula becomes

$$V = \frac{C}{(1+i_1)^1} + \frac{C}{(1+i_2)^2} + \cdots + \frac{C+M}{(1+i_N)^N}, \ i = 1, \cdots, N$$

In Chapter 10, we introduce the concept of continuous compounding. With continuous compounding, if the short-term interest rate is constant, the bond valuation formula becomes[2]

$$V = \frac{C}{e^{1i}} + \frac{C}{e^{2i}} + \cdots + \frac{C+M}{e^{Ni}}$$

Application of the First Derivative   The sensitivity of the bond price V to a change in interest rates is given by the first derivative of V with respect to the interest rate i. The first derivative of V with respect to the interest rate i is called *dollar duration*. We can compute dollar duration in each case using the derivation formulas defined thus far. In the discrete-time case we can write

$$
\begin{aligned}
\frac{dV(i)}{di} &= \frac{d}{di}\left(\frac{C}{(1+i)^1} + \frac{C}{(1+i)^2} + \cdots + \frac{C+M}{(1+i)^N}\right) \\
&= \frac{d}{di}\left[\frac{C}{(1+i)^1}\right] + \cdots + \frac{d}{di}\left[\frac{C+M}{(1+i)^N}\right] \\
&= C\frac{d}{di}\left[\frac{1}{(1+i)^1}\right] + \cdots + (C+M)\frac{d}{di}\left[\frac{1}{(1+i)^N}\right]
\end{aligned}
$$

We can use the quotient rule

$$\frac{d}{dx}\left[\frac{1}{f(x)}\right] = -\frac{1}{f^2(x)}f'(x)$$

to compute the derivatives of the generic summand as follows:

$$\frac{d}{di}\left[\frac{1}{(1+i)^i}\right] = -\frac{1}{(1+i)^{2i}}i(1+i)^{i-1} = -i\frac{1}{(1+i)^{i+1}}$$

---

[2]If the short-term rate is variable:

$$V = Ce^{-\int_0^1 i(s)ds} + Ce^{-\int_0^2 i(s)ds} + \cdots + (C+M)e^{-\int_0^N i(s)ds}$$

Therefore, the derivative of the bond value V with respect to the interest rates is

$$\frac{dV}{di} = -(1+i)^{-1}[C(1+i)^{-1} + 2C(1+i)^{-2} + \cdots + N(C+M)(1+i)^{-N}]$$

Using a similar reasoning, we can slightly generalize this formula, allowing the interest rates to be different for each period. Call i_t the interest rate for period t. The sequence of values is called the yield curve.

Now suppose that interest rates are subject to a parallel shift. In other words, let's assume that the interest rate for period t is $(i_t + x)$. If we compute the first derivative with respect to x for $x = 0$, we obtain

$$\left.\frac{dV(i)}{dx}\right|_{x=0} = \left.\frac{d}{dx}\left(\frac{C}{(1+i_1+x)^1} + \frac{C}{(1+i_2+x)^2} + \cdots + \frac{C}{(1+i_N+x)^N}\right)\right|_{x=0}$$

$$= -[C(1+i_1)^{-2} + 2C(1+i_2)^{-3} + \cdots + N(C+M)(1+i_N)^{-N-1}]$$

In this case, we cannot factorize any term as interest rates are different in each period. Obviously, if interest rates are constant, the yield curve is a straight line and a change in the interest rates can be thought of as a parallel shift of the yield curve.

In the continuous-time case, assuming that interest rates are constant, the dollar duration is[3]

$$\frac{dV}{di} = \frac{d[Ce^{-1i} + Ce^{-2i} + \cdots + (C+M)e^{-Ni}]}{di}$$

$$= -1Ce^{-1i} - 2Ce^{-2i} - \cdots - N(C+M)e^{-Ni}$$

---

[3]When interest rates are deterministic but time-dependent, the derivative dV/di is computed as follows. Assume that interest rates experience a parallel shift $i(t) + x$ and compute the derivative with respect to x evaluated at $x = 0$. To do this, we need to compute the following derivative:

$$\frac{d}{dx}e^{-\int_0^t [i(s)+x]ds} = \frac{d}{dx}\left[e^{-\int_0^t i(s)ds}e^{-\int_0^t xds}\right] = e^{-\int_0^t i(s)ds}\frac{d}{dx}(e^{-xt})$$

$$= -te^{-xt}e^{-\int_0^t i(s)ds}$$

$$\left.\frac{d}{dx}e^{-\int_0^t [i(s)+x]ds}\right|_{x=0} = -te^{-xt}e^{-\int_0^t i(s)ds}\Big|_{x=0} = -te^{-\int_0^t i(s)ds}$$

Therefore, we can write the following:

$$\left.\frac{dV}{dx}\right|_{x=0} = -Ce^{-\int_0^1 i(s)ds} - 2Ce^{-\int_0^2 i(s)ds} - \cdots - N(C+M)e^{-\int_0^N i(s)ds}$$

For $i = $ constant we find again the formula established above.

where we make use of the rule

$$\frac{d}{dx}(e^x) = e^x$$

Application of the Chain Rule

The above formulas express dollar duration, which is the derivative of the price of a bond with respect with the interest rate and which approximates price changes due to small parallel interest rate shifts. Practitioners, however, are more interested in the percentage change of a bond price with respect to small parallel changes in interest rates. The percentage change is the price change divided by the bond value:

$$\frac{dV}{di}\frac{1}{V}$$

The percentage price change is approximated by *duration,* which is the derivative of a bond's value with respect to interest rates divided by the value itself. Recall from the formulas for derivatives that the latter is the logarithmic derivative of a bond's price with respect to interest rates:

$$\text{Duration} = \frac{dV}{di}\frac{1}{V} = \frac{d(\log V)}{di}$$

Based on the above formulas, we can write the following formulas for duration:

Duration for constant interest rates in discrete time:

$$\frac{dV}{di}\frac{1}{V} = -\frac{1}{V(1+i)}\left[\frac{C}{(1+i)} + \frac{2C}{(1+i)^2} + \cdots + \frac{N(C+M)}{(1+i)^N}\right]$$

Duration for variable interest rates in discrete time:

$$\frac{dV}{dx}\frac{1}{V} = -\frac{1}{V}\left[\frac{C}{(1+i_1)^2} + \frac{2C}{(1+i_2)^3} + \cdots + \frac{N(C+M)}{(1+i_N)^{N+1}}\right]$$

Duration for continuously compounding constant interest rate in discrete time:[4]

$$\frac{dV}{di}\frac{1}{V} = -\frac{1}{V}[Ce^{-i} + 2Ce^{-2i} + \cdots + N(C+M)e^{-Ni}]$$

We will now illustrate the chain rule of derivation by introducing the concept of effective duration. The bond valuation we presented earlier is for an option-free bond. But when a bond has an embedded option, such as a call option, it is more complicated to value. Similarly, the sensitivity of the value of a bond to changes in interest rates is more complicated to assess when there is an embedded call option. Intuitively, we know that the sensitivity of the value of a bond with an embedded option would be sensitive to not only how changes in interest rates affect the present value of the cash flows as shown above for an option-free bond, but also how they would affect the value of the embedded option.

We use the following notation to assess the sensitivity of a callable bond's value (i.e., a bond with an embedded call option) to a change in interest rates. The value of an option-free bond can be decomposed as follows:

$$V_{ofb} = V_{cb} + V_{co}$$

where

V_{ofb} = value of an option-free bond
V_{cb} = value of a callable bond
V_{co} = value of a call option on the bond

The above equation says that an option-free bond's value depends on the sum of the value of a callable bond's value and a call option on that option-free bond. The equation can be rewritten as follows:

$$V_{cb} = V_{ofb} - V_{co}$$

That is, the value of a callable bond is found by subtracting the value of the call option from the value of the option-free bond. Both components on the right side of the valuation equation depend on the interest rate i.

---

[4]The duration for continuously compounding variable interest rate in discrete time is

$$\frac{dV}{di}\frac{1}{V} = -\frac{1}{V}\left[Ce^{-\int_0^1 i(s)ds} + 2Ce^{-\int_0^2 i(s)ds} + \cdots + N(C+M)e^{-\int_0^N i(s)ds}\right]$$

Using linearity to compute the first derivative of the valuation equation with respect to i and dividing both sides of the equation by the callable bond's value gives

$$\frac{dV_{cb}}{di}\frac{1}{V_{cb}} = \frac{dV_{ofb}}{di}\frac{1}{V_{cb}} - \frac{dV_{co}}{di}\frac{1}{V_{cb}}$$

Multiplying the numerator and denominator of the right-hand side by the value of the option-free bond and rearranging terms gives

$$\frac{dV_{cb}}{di}\frac{1}{V_{cb}} = \frac{dV_{ofb}}{di}\frac{1}{V_{ofb}}\frac{V_{ofb}}{V_{cb}} - \frac{dV_{co}}{di}\frac{1}{V_{ofb}}\frac{V_{ofb}}{V_{cb}}$$

The above equation is the sensitivity of a callable bond's value to changes in interest rates. That is, it is the duration of a callable bond, which we denote by Dur_{cb}.[5] The component given by

$$\frac{dV_{ofb}}{di}\frac{1}{V_{ofb}}$$

is the duration of an option-free bond's value to changes in interest rates, which we denote by Dur_{ofb}. Thus, we can have

$$Dur_{cb} = Dur_{ofb}\frac{V_{ofb}}{V_{cb}} - \frac{dV_{co}}{di}\frac{1}{V_{ofb}}\frac{V_{ofb}}{V_{cb}}$$

Now let's look at the derivative, which is the second term in the above equation. The change in the value of an option when the price of the under-lying changes is called the option's *delta*. In the case of an option on a bond, as explained above, changes in interest rates change the value of a bond. In turn, the change in the value of the bond changes the value of the embedded option. Here is where we see a function of a function and the need to apply the chain rule. That is,

$$V_{co}(i) = f[V_{ofb}(i)]$$

---

[5]Actually, it is equal to $-Dur_{cb}$, but because we will be omitting the negative sign for the durations on the right-hand side, this will not affect our derivation.

This tells us that the value of the call option on an option-free bond depends on the value of the option-free bond and the value of the option-free bond depends on the interest rate. Now let's apply the chain rule. We get

$$\frac{dV_{co}(i)}{di} = \frac{df}{dV_{ofb}}\frac{dV_{ofb}}{di}$$

The first term on the right-hand side of the equation is the change in the value of the call option for a change in the value of the option-free bond. This is the delta of the call option, Δ_{co}. Thus,

$$\frac{dV_{co}(i)}{di} = -\Delta_{co}\frac{dV_{ofb}}{di}$$

Substituting this equation into the equation for the duration and rearranging terms we get

$$Dur_{cb} = Dur_{ofb}\frac{V_{ofb}}{V_{cb}}(1 - \Delta_{co})$$

This equation tells us that the duration of the callable bond depends on the following three quantities. The first quantity is the duration of the corresponding option-free bond. The second quantity is the ratio of the value of the option-free bond to the value of the callable bond. The difference between the value of an option-free bond and the value of a callable bond is equal to the value of the call option. The greater (smaller) the value of the call option, the higher (lower) the ratio. Thus, we see that the duration of the callable bond will depend on the value of the call option. Basically, this ratio indicates the leverage effectively associated with the position. The third and final quantity is the delta of the call option. The duration of the callable bond as given by the above equation is called the *option-adjusted duration* or *effective duration*.

Application of the Second Derivative   We can now compute the second derivative of the bond value with respect to interest rates. Assuming cash flows do not depend on interest rates, this second derivative is called *dollar convexity*. Dollar convexity divided by the bond's value is called *convexity*. In the discrete-time fixed interest rate case, the computation of convexity is based on the second derivatives of the generic summand:

$$\frac{d^2}{di^2}\left[\frac{1}{(1+i)^t}\right] = \frac{d}{di}\left\{\frac{d}{di}\left[\frac{1}{(1+i)^t}\right]\right\} = \frac{d}{di}\left[-t\frac{1}{(1+i)^{t+1}}\right]$$

$$= -t\frac{d}{di}\left[\frac{1}{(1+i)^{t+1}}\right] = t(1+t)\frac{1}{(1+i)^{t+2}}$$

Therefore, dollar convexity assumes the following expression:

$$
\begin{aligned}
\frac{d^2 V(i)}{di^2} &= \frac{d^2}{di^2}\left[\frac{C}{(1+i)^1} + \frac{C}{(1+i)^2} + \cdots + \frac{C+M}{(1+i)^N}\right] \\
&= C\frac{d^2}{di^2}\left[\frac{1}{(1+i)^1}\right] + \cdots + (C+M)\frac{d^2}{di^2}\left[\frac{1}{(1+i)^N}\right] \\
&= [2C(1+i)^{-3} + 2\cdot 3C(1+i)^{-4} + \cdots \\
&\quad + N(N+1)(C+M)(1+i)^{-(N+2)}]
\end{aligned}
$$

Using the same reasoning as before, in the variable interest rate case, dollar convexity assumes the following expression:

$$
\begin{aligned}
\frac{d^2 V(i)}{dx^2}\bigg|_{x=0} &= [2C(1+i_1)^{-3} + 2\cdot 3\cdot C(1+i_2)^{-4} \\
&\quad + \cdots + N(N+1)(C+M)(1+i_N)^{-N-2}]
\end{aligned}
$$

This scheme changes slightly in the continuous-time case, where, assuming that interest rates are constant, the expression for convexity is[6]

$$
\begin{aligned}
\frac{d^2 V}{di^2} &= \frac{d^2[Ce^{-i} + Ce^{-2i} + \cdots + (C+M)e^{-Ni}]}{di^2} \\
&= 1^2\cdot Ce^{-i} + 2^2\cdot Ce^{-2i} + \cdots + N^2\cdot (C+M)e^{-Ni}
\end{aligned}
$$

where we make use of the rule

$$
\frac{d^2}{dx^2}(e^x) = e^x
$$

We can now write the following formulas for convexity:
Convexity for constant interest rates in discrete time:

$$
\frac{dV^2}{di^2}\frac{1}{V} = \frac{1}{V(1+i)^2}\left[\frac{2C}{(1+i)} + \frac{(3)(2)C}{(1+i)^2} + \cdots + \frac{N(N+1)(C+M)}{(1+i)^N}\right]
$$

---

[6]For variable interest rates this expression becomes

$$
\frac{dV}{dx}\bigg|_{x=0} = 1^2 Ce^{-\int_0^1 i(s)ds} + 2^2 Ce^{-\int_0^2 i(s)ds} + \cdots + N^2(C+M)e^{-\int_0^N i(s)ds}
$$

Convexity for variable interest rates in discrete time:

$$\frac{d^2 V}{dx^2}\frac{1}{V} = \frac{1}{V}\left[\frac{2C}{(1+i_1)^3} + \frac{(3)(2)C}{(1+i_2)^4} + \cdots + \frac{N(N+1)(C+M)}{(1+i_N)^{N+2}}\right]$$

Convexity for continuously compounding constant interest rate in discrete time:[7]

$$\frac{d^2 V}{di^2}\frac{1}{V} = \frac{1}{V}[Ce^{-i} + 2^2 Ce^{-2i} + \cdots + N^2(C+M)e^{-Ni}]$$

TAYLOR SERIES EXPANSION

An important relationship used in economics and finance theory to approximate how the value of a function, such as a price function, will change is the **Taylor series expansion**. We begin by establishing **Taylor's theorem**. Consider a continuous function with continuous derivatives up to order n in the closed interval $[a,b]$ and differentiable with continuous derivatives in the open interval (a,b) up to order $n + 1$. It can be demonstrated that there exists a point $\xi \in (a,b)$ such that

$$f(b) = f(a) + f'(a)(b-a) + \frac{f''(a)(b-a)^2}{2!} + \cdots + \frac{f^{(n)}(a)(b-a)^n}{n!} + R_n$$

where the residual R_n can be written in either of the following forms:

$$\textit{Lagrange's form:} \quad R_n = \frac{f^{(n+1)}(\xi)(b-a)^{n+1}}{(n+1)!}$$

$$\textit{Cauchy's form:} \quad R_n = \frac{f^{(n+1)}(\xi)(b-\xi)^n(b-a)}{n!}$$

---

[7]The convexity for continuously compounding variable interest rate in discrete time is

$$\frac{d^2 V}{di^2}\frac{1}{V} = \frac{1}{V}\left[Ce^{-\int_0^1 i(s)ds} + 2^2 Ce^{-\int_0^2 i(s)ds} + \cdots + N^2(C+M)e^{-\int_0^N i(s)ds}\right]$$

In general, the point $\xi \in (a,b)$ is different in the two forms. This result can be written in an alternative form as follows. Suppose x and x_0 are in (a,b). Then, using Lagrange's form of the residual, we can write

$$f(x) = f(x_0) + f'(x)(x - x_0) + \frac{f''(x)(x - x_0)^2}{2!} + \cdots + \frac{f^{(n)}(x)(x - x_0)^n}{n!}$$
$$+ \frac{f^{(n+1)}(\xi)(x - x_0)^{n+1}}{(n+1)!}$$

If the function f is infinitely differentiable, that is, it admits derivatives of every order and if

$$\lim_{n \to \infty} R_n = 0$$

the infinite series obtained is called a **Taylor series expansion** (or simply **Taylor series**) for $f(x)$. If $x_0 = 0$, the series is called a **Maclaurin series**.

Such series, called a **power series**, generally converge in some interval, called the **interval of convergence**, and diverge elsewhere.

The Taylor series expansion is a powerful analytical tool. To appreciate its importance, consider that a function that can be expanded in a power series is represented by a denumerable set of numbers even if it is a continuous function. Consider also that the action of any linear operator on the function f can be represented in terms of its action on powers of x.

The Maclaurin expansion of the exponential and of trigonometric functions are given by:

$$e^x = 1 + x + \frac{x^2}{2!} + \cdots + \frac{x^n}{n!} + R_n$$
$$\sin x = x - \frac{x^3}{3!} + \frac{x^5}{5!} + \cdots + \frac{(-1)^n x^{2n+1}}{(2n+1)!} + R_n$$
$$\cos x = 1 - \frac{x^2}{2!} + \frac{x^4}{4!} + \cdots + \frac{(-1)^n x^{2n}}{(2n)!} + R_n$$

Application to Bond Analysis

Let's illustrate a Taylor and Maclaurin power series by computing a second-order approximation of the changes in the present value of a bond due to a parallel shift of the yield curve. This information is important to portfolio managers and risk managers to control the interest rate risk exposure of a position in bonds. In bond portfolio management, the first two terms of the

Taylor expansion series are used to approximate the change in an option-free bond's value when interest rates change. An approximation based on the first two terms of the Taylor series is called a **second order approximation**, because it considers only first and second powers of the variable.

We begin with the bond valuation equation, again assuming a single discount rate. We first compute dollar duration and convexity, that is, the first and second derivatives with respect to x evaluated at $x = 0$, and we expand in Maclaurin power series. We obtain

$$V(x) = V(0) - (\text{Dollar duration})x + \frac{1}{2}(\text{Dollar convexity})x^2 + R_3$$

where R_3 is the residual in the Lagrange form as defined above. The subscript 3 means that it is the residual after the first two terms.

We can write this expression explicitly as

$$
\begin{aligned}
V(x) = {} & \frac{C}{(1+i)^1} + \frac{C}{(1+i)^2} + \cdots + \frac{C+M}{(1+i)^N} \\
& - x\left[\frac{C}{(1+i)^2} + \frac{C}{(1+i)^3} + \cdots + \frac{N(C+M)}{(1+i)^{N+1}} \right] \\
& + \frac{1}{2}x^2\left[\frac{2C}{(1+i)^3} + \frac{3\cdot 2\cdot C}{(1+i)^4} + \cdots + \frac{(N(N+1))(C+M)}{(1+i)^{N+2}} \right] \\
& - \frac{1}{3\cdot 2}x^3\left[\frac{3\cdot 2\cdot C}{(1+i+\xi)^4} + \frac{4\cdot 3\cdot 2\cdot C}{(1+i+\xi)^5} + \cdots \right. \\
& \left. + \frac{N(N+1)(N+2)(C+M)}{(1+i+\xi)^{N+3}} \right]
\end{aligned}
$$

Bond portfolio managers, however, are primarily interested in percentage price change. We can now compute the percentage price change as follows:

$$
\begin{aligned}
\frac{\Delta V}{V} = {} & \frac{V(x) - V(0)}{V(0)} \\
= {} & -x\left[\left[\frac{C}{(1+i)^2} + \frac{C}{(1+i)^3} + \cdots + \frac{N(C+M)}{(1+i)^{N+1}} \right] \right. \\
& \left. \times \frac{1}{\dfrac{C}{(1+i)^1} + \dfrac{C}{(1+i)^2} + \cdots + \dfrac{C+M}{(1+i)^N}} \right] \\
& + \frac{1}{2}x^2\left[\left[\frac{2\cdot C}{(1+i)^3} + \frac{3\cdot 2\cdot C}{(1+i)^4} + \cdots + \frac{N(N+1)\,(C+M)}{(1+i)^{N+2}} \right] \right.
\end{aligned}
$$

$$\times \frac{1}{\left[\dfrac{C}{(1+i)^1} + \dfrac{C}{(1+i)^2} + \cdots + \dfrac{C+M}{(1+i)^N}\right]}$$

$$-\frac{1}{3\cdot 2}x^3 \left[\left[\frac{3\cdot 2\cdot C}{(1+i+\xi)^4} + \cdots + \frac{N(N+1)(N+2)\,(C+M)}{(1+i+\xi)^{N+3}}\right]\right.$$

$$\times \frac{1}{\left[\dfrac{C}{(1+i)^1} + \dfrac{C}{(1+i)^2} + \cdots + \dfrac{C+M}{(1+i)^N}\right]}$$

The first term in the square brackets on the right-hand side of the equation is the first approximation and is the approximation based on the duration of the bond. The second term in the square brackets on the right-hand side is the second derivative, the convexity measure, multiplied by one half. The third term is the residual. Its size is responsible for the quality of the approximation.

The residual is proportional to the third power of the interest rate shift x. The term in the square bracket of the residual is a rather complex function of C,M,N, and i. A rough approximation of this term is $N(N+1)(N+2)$. In fact, in the case of zero-coupon bonds, that is, $C = 0$, the residual can be written as

$$R_3 = -\frac{1}{3\times 2}x^3 \left[\left(\frac{N(N+1)(N+2)M}{(1+i+\xi)^{N+3}}\right)\frac{1}{\left[\dfrac{M}{(1+i)^N}\right]}\right]$$

$$= N(N+1)\,(N+2)\frac{(1+i)^N}{(1+i+\xi)^{N+3}}$$

which is a third order polynomial in N.

Therefore, the error of the second order approximation is of the order $[1/(3 \times 2)](xN)^3$. For instance, if $x = 0.01$ and $N = 20$ years, the approximation error is of the order 0.001. The following numerical example will clarify these derivations.

In our illustration to demonstrate how to use the Taylor series, we use an option-free bond with a coupon rate of 9% that pays interest semiannually and has 20 years to maturity. Suppose that the initial yield is 6%. In terms of our bond valuation equation, this means $C = \$4.5$, $M = \$100$, and $i = 0.06$. Substituting these values into the bond valuation equation, the price of the bond is $134.6722.

Suppose that we want to know the approximate percentage price change if the interest rate (i.e., i) increases instantaneously from 6% to 8%. In the bond market, a change in interest rates is referred to in terms of basis points. One basis point is equal to 0.0001 and, therefore, 1 percentage point is 100 basis points. In our illustration, we are looking at an instantaneous change in interest rates of 200 basis points. We will use the two terms of the Taylor series to show the approximate percentage change in the bond's value for a 200 basis point increase in interest rates.

We do know what the answer is already. The initial value for this bond is \$134.6722. If the interest rate is 8%, the value of this bond would be \$109.8964. This means that the bond's value declines by 18.4%. Let's see how well the Taylor series using only two terms approximates this change.

The first approximation is the estimate using duration. The duration for this bond is 10.66 found by using the formula above for duration. The convexity measure for this bond is 164.11 The change in interest rates, di, is 200 basis points. Expressed in decimal it is 0.02. The first term of the Taylor series gives

$$-10.66 \times (0.02) = -0.2132 = -21.32\%$$

Notice that this approximation overestimates the actual change in value, which is -18.4% and means that the estimated new value for the bond is underestimated.

Now we add the second approximation. The second term of the Taylor series gives

$$\frac{1}{2}(164.11) \times (0.02)^2 = 3.28\%$$

The approximate percentage change in the bond's value found by using the first term of the Taylor series and the second term of the Taylor series is $-21.32\% + 3.28\% = -18.0\%$. The actual percentage change in value is -18.4%. Thus the two terms of the Taylor series do an excellent job of approximating the percentage change in value.

Let's look at what would happen if the change in interest rates is a decline from 6% to 4%. The exact percentage change in value is $+25.04\%$ (from 134.6722 to 168.3887). Now the change in interest rates di is -0.02. Notice that the approximate change in value due to duration is the same except for a change in sign. That is, the approximate change based on the first term (duration) is $+21.32\%$. Since the percentage price change is underestimated, the new value of the bond is underestimated. The change due to the second term of the Taylor series is the same in magnitude and sign since when -0.02 is squared, it gives a positive value. Thus, the approximate change is $21.32\% + 3.28\% = 24.6\%$. Using the terms of the Taylor series does a good job of estimating the change in the bond's value.

We used a relatively large change in interest rates to see how well the two terms of the Taylor series approximate the percentage change in a bond's value. For a small change in interest rates, duration does an effective job. For example, suppose that the change in interest rates is 10 basis points. That is, di is 0.001. For an increase in interest rates from 6% to 6.1% the actual change in the bond's value would be -1.06% ($134.6722 to $133.2472). Using just the first term of the Taylor series, the approximate change in the bond's value gives the precise change:

$$-10.66 \times 0.001 = -1.066\%$$

For a decrease in interest rates by 10 basis points, the result would be 1.066%.

What this illustration shows is that for a small change in a variable, a linear approximation does a good job of estimating the change in the value of the price function of a bond. A different interpretation, however, is possible. Note that in general convexity is computed as a number, which is a function of the term structure of interest rates as follows:

$$\text{Dollar convexity} = [2C(1 + i_1)^{-3} + 2 \cdot 3 \cdot C(1 + i_2)^{-4} + \cdots \\ + N \cdot (N + 1) \cdot (C + M)(1 + i_N)^{-N-2}]$$

This expression is a nonlinear function of all the yields. It is sensitive to changes of the curvature of the term structure. In this sense, it is a measure of the convexity of the term structure.

Let's suppose now that the term structure experiences a change that can be represented as a parallel shift plus a change in slope and curvature. In general both duration and convexity will change. The previous Maclaurin expansion, which is valid for parallel shifts of the term structure, will not hold. However, we can still attempt to represent the change in a bond's value as a function of duration and convexity. In particular, we could represent the changes in a bond's value as a linear function of duration and convexity. This idea is exploited in more general terms by assuming that the term structure changes are a linear combination of factors.

CALCULUS IN MORE THAN ONE VARIABLE

The previous concepts of calculus can be extended to a multivariate environment, that is, they can be extended to functions of several variables. Given a function of n variables, $y = f(x_1, \ldots, x_n)$, we can define n **partial derivatives**

$$\frac{\partial f(x_1, \ldots, x_n)}{\partial x_i}$$

$i = 1, \ldots, n$ holding constant $n - 1$ variables and then using the definition for derivatives of univariate functions:

$$\frac{\partial f(x_1, \ldots, x_n)}{\partial x_i} = \lim_{h \to 0} \frac{f(x_1, \ldots, x_i + h, \ldots, x_n) - f(x_1, \ldots, x_i, \ldots, x_n)}{h}$$

Repeating this process we can define partial derivatives of any order. Consider, for example, the following function of two variables:

$$f(x, y) = e^{-(x^2 + \sigma xy + y^2)}$$

Its partial derivatives up to order 2 are given by the following formulas:

$$\frac{\partial f}{\partial x} = -(2x + \sigma y)e^{-(x^2 + \sigma xy + y^2)}$$

$$\frac{\partial f}{\partial y} = -(2y + \sigma x)e^{-(x^2 + \sigma xy + y^2)}$$

$$\frac{\partial^2 f}{\partial x^2} = -2e^{-(x^2 + \sigma xy + y^2)} + (2x + \sigma y)^2 \, e^{-(x^2 + \sigma xy + y^2)}$$

$$\frac{\partial^2 f}{\partial y^2} = -2e^{-(x^2 + \sigma xy + y^2)} + (2y + \sigma x)^2 \, e^{-(x^2 + \sigma xy + y^2)}$$

$$\frac{\partial^2 f}{\partial x \partial y} = (2x + \sigma y)(2y + \sigma x) \, e^{-(x^2 + \sigma xy + y^2)} - \sigma e^{-(x^2 + \sigma xy + y^2)}$$

In bond analysis, we can also compute partial derivatives in the case where each interest rate is not the same for each time period in the bond valuation formula. In that case, derivatives can be computed for each time period's interest rate. When the percentage price sensitivity of a bond to a change in the interest rate for a particular time period is computed, the resulting measure is called **rate duration** or **partial duration**.[8]

KEY POINTS

■ Through the concept of the limit, calculus has rendered precise the notion of infinitesimally small and infinitely large.

■ A sequence or a function tends to a finite limit if there is a number to which the sequence or the function can get arbitrarily close; a sequence or a function tends to infinity if it can exceed any given quantity. Starting from these simple concepts, rules for computing limits can be established and limits computed.

■ A derivative of a function is the limit of its incremental ratio when the interval tends to zero. Derivatives represent the rate of change of quantities.

■ The derivative of the product of a constant and a function is the product of the constant and the derivative of the function.

■ The derivative of a sum of functions is the sum of derivatives and called termwise differentiation.

■ The derivative of a product of functions is the derivative of the first function times the second plus the first function times the derivative of the second and is called the product rule.

■ The derivative of a function of functions is the product of the outer function with respect to the inner function times the derivative of the inner function and is called the chain rule.

■ A derivative of order n of a function is defined as the function that results from applying the operation of derivation n times.

■ A function that is differentiable to any order at a given point a can be represented as a series of the powers of $(x - a)$ times the n-th derivative at a times the reciprocal of $n!$; this expansion is called a Taylor series expansion.

■ A Taylor series expansion series is used to approximate the value of a function.

■ Taylor series truncated to the first or second terms are called first- and second-order approximations, respectively.

---

[8]There is a technical difference between rate duration and partial duration but the difference is not important here.

- A special case of the Taylor series is a Maclaurin series. The McLaurin series is the Taylor series computed around $x = 0$.
- Differentiation can be extended to functions of more than one variable.
- A function of n variables has n first derivatives, n-square second derivatives, and so on.

CHAPTER 3

Integral Calculus

Integration is an important concept in mathematics and, together with its inverse, differentiation, is one of the two main operations in calculus—and the term *integral* can also refer to the notion of the anti-derivative. Using integral calculus, one can compute the area under an explicit function or approximate the area under highly nonlinear functions:

- Integral calculus is useful for pricing financial derivatives.
- The price of a derivatives contract is calculated as the present value of expected future payoffs that depend on the future asset price distribution.
- To deal with the non-normality features of asset return distributions, one has to use integral calculus to approximate the area under a skewed fat-tailed density function when computing option prices.
- Integral calculus is useful for Monte Carlo simulations that are widely used for pricing derivative instruments with option-type features.
- When pricing options with Monte Carlo simulation, it is necessary to generate a large sample of possible future asset prices that will produce possible future payoffs. To do so, one has to draw a large number of random variables from a specific distribution. From random number generator, one may have to rely on integral calculus depending on the choice of a probability distribution for underlying assets.

What you will learn after reading this chapter:

- The meaning of integration and its relationship to differentiation.
- What a Riemann integral is and its properties.
- What a Lebesque-Stieltjes integral is and its relationship to a Riemann integral.
- What are indefinite and proper integrals.
- That the fundamental theorem of calculus is that integration is the inverse operation of derivation.
- What integral, Laplace, and Fourier transforms are and how they are used.

INTRODUCTION

As explained in the previous chapter, differentiation addresses the problem of defining the instantaneous rate of change. **Integration**, the subject of this chapter, addresses the problem of calculating the area of an arbitrary figure. Areas are easily defined for rectangles and triangles, and any plane figure that can be decomposed into these objects. While formulas for computing the area of polygons have been known since antiquity, a general solution of the problem was arrived at first in the seventeenth century with the development of calculus.

RIEMANN INTEGRALS

Let's begin by defining the integral in the sense of Riemann, so called after the German mathematician Bernhard Riemann who introduced it. Consider a bounded function $y = f(x)$ defined in some domain which includes the interval $[a,b]$. Consider the partition of the interval $[a,b]$ into n disjoint subintervals $a = x_0 < x_1 < \ldots < x_{n-1} < x_n = b$, and form the sums

$$S_n^U = \sum_{i=1}^{n} f^M(x_i)(x_i - x_{i-1})$$

where $f^M(x_i) = \sup f(x), x \in [x_{i-1}, x_i]$, and

$$S_n^L = \sum_{i=1}^{n} f_m(x_i)(x_i - x_{i-1})$$

where $f_m(x_i) = \inf f(x)$ and $x \in [x_{i-1}, x_i]$

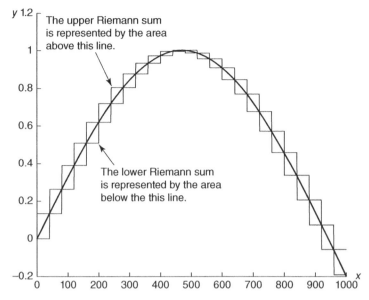

FIGURE 3.1 Riemann Sums

Figure 3.1 illustrates this construction. S_n^U, S_n^L are called, respectively, the **upper Riemann sum** and **lower Riemann sum**. Clearly an infinite number of different sums S_n^U, S_n^L can be formed depending on the choice of the partition. Intuitively, each of these sums approximates the area below the curve $y = f(x)$, the upper sums from above, the lower sums from below. Generally speaking, the more refined the partition the more accurate the approximation.

Consider the sets of all the possible sums $\{S_n^U\}$ and $\{S_n^L\}$ for every possible partition. If the supremum of the set $\{S_n^L\}$ (which in general will not be a maximum) and the infimum of the set $\{S_n^U\}$ (which in general will not be a minimum) exist, respectively, and if the minimum and the supremum coincide, the function f is said to be "Riemann integrable in the interval (a,b)."

If the function f is Riemann integrable in $[a,b]$, then

$$I = \int_a^b f(x)dx = \sup\{S_n^L\} = \inf\{S_n^U\}$$

is the proper integral of f on $[a,b]$ in the sense of Riemann.

An alternative definition of the proper integral in the sense of Riemann is often given as follows. Consider the Riemann sums

$$S_n = \sum_{i=1}^{n} f(x_i^*)(x_i - x_{x-1})$$

where x_i^* is an arbitrary point in the interval $[x_1, x_{i-1}]$. Call $\Delta x_i = (x_i - x_{i-1})$ the length of the ith interval. The proper integral I between a and b in the sense of Riemann can then be defined as the limit (if the limit exists) of the sums S_n when the maximum length of the subintervals tends to zero:

$$I = \lim_{\max \Delta x_i \to 0} S_n$$

In the above, the limit operation has to be defined as the limit for any sequence of sums S_n as for each n there are infinitely many sums. Note that the function f need not be continuous to be integrable. It might, for instance, make a finite number of jumps. However, every function that is integrable must be of bounded variation.

Properties of Riemann Integrals

Let's now introduce a number of properties of the integrals (we will state these without proof). These properties are simple mechanical rules that apply provided that all integrals exist. Suppose that a, b, c are fixed real numbers, that f, g, h are functions defined in the same domain, and that they are all integrable on the same interval (a, b). The following properties apply:

Properties of Riemann Integrals

　　Property 1: $\int_b^a f(x)dx = 0$

　　Property 2: $\int_a^c f(x)dx = \int_a^b f(x)dx + \int_b^c f(x)dx, \quad a \leq b \leq c$

　　Property 3: $h(x) = \alpha f(x) + \beta g(x) \Rightarrow \int_a^b h(x)dx = \alpha \int_a^b f(x)dx$
　　$+\beta \int_a^b g(x)dx$

　　Property 4: $\int_a^b f'(x)g(x)dx = f(x)g(x) \big|_a^b - \int_a^b f(x)g'(x)dx$

- Properties 1 and 2 establish that integrals are additive with respect to integration limits.
- Property 3 is the statement of the linearity of the operation of integration.
- Property 4 is the rule of integration by parts.

Now consider a composite function: $h(x) = f(g(x))$. Provided that g is integrable on the interval (a, b) and that f is integrable on the interval corresponding to all the points $s = g(x)$, the following rule, known as the **chain rule of integration**, applies:

$$\int_a^b f(y)dy = \int_{g^{-1}(a)}^{g^{-1}(b)} f(g(x))g'(x)dx$$

Integrals compute the area under a function for a specific interval. To illustrate, we now compute the integral of $f(x) = \sqrt{x}$ from 0 to 1:

$$\int_0^1 \sqrt{x}dx$$

The fundamental theorem of calculus is the fundamental link between the operations of differentiating and integrating. Applied to the square root curve, $f(x) = x^{1/2}$, it says to look at the antiderivative $F(x) = (2/3)\,x^{3/2}$, and simply take $F(1) - F(0)$, where 0 and 1 are the boundaries of the interval [0,1]. So, the exact value of the area under the curve is computed as

$$\int_0^1 \sqrt{x}dx = \int_0^1 x^{1/2}dx = \left(\frac{2}{3}\right) x^{3/2}\Big|_0^1 = F(1) - F(0)$$

$$= \left(\frac{2}{3}\right)(1^{3/2} - 0^{3/2}) = \frac{2}{3}$$

If we generalize, the integral of $f(x) = x^n$ with $n \neq -1$, is computed as

$$\int_a^b x^n dx = \left(\frac{x^{n+1}}{n+1}\right)\Big|_a^b = \left(\frac{b^{n+1} - a^{n+1}}{n+1}\right)$$

LEBESGUE-STIELTJES INTEGRALS

Most applications of calculus require only the integral in the sense of Riemann. However, a number of results in probability theory with a bearing on economics and finance theory can be properly established only in the framework of the **Lebesgue-Stieltjes integral**. Let's therefore extend the definition of integrals by introducing the Lebesgue-Stieltjes integral.

The integral in the sense of Riemann takes as a measure of an interval its length, also called the **Jordan measure**. The definition of the integral can be extended in the sense of Lebesgue-Stieltjes by defining the integral with respect to a more general **Lebesgue-Stieltjes measure**.

Consider a nondecreasing, left-continuous function $g(x)$ defined on a domain which includes the interval $[x_i - x_{i-1}]$ and form the differences $m_{Li} = g(x_i) - g(x_{i-1})$. These quantities are a generalization of the concept of length. They are called **Lebesgue measures**. Suppose that the interval (a,b) is divided into a partition of n disjoint subintervals by the points $a = x_0 < x_1 < \ldots < x_n = b$ and form the Lebesgue-Stieltjes sums

$$S_n = \sum_{i=1}^{n} f(x_i^*) m_{Li}, x_i^* \in (x_i, x_{i-1})$$

where x_i^* is any point in ith subinterval of the partition.

Consider the set of all possible sums $\{S_n\}$. These sums depend on the partition and the choice of the midpoint in each subinterval. We define the integral of $f(x)$ in the sense of Lebesgue-Stieltjes as the limit, if the limit exists, of the Lebesgue-Stieltjes sums $\{S_n\}$ when the maximum length of the intervals in the partition tends to zero. We write, as in the case of the Riemann integral,

$$I = \int_a^b f(x) dg(x) = \lim S_n$$

The integral in the sense of Lebesgue-Stieltjes can be defined for a broader class of functions than the integral in the sense of Riemann. If f is an integrable function and g is a differentiable function, the two integrals coincide. In the following chapters, all integrals are in the sense of Riemann unless explicitly stated to be in the sense of Lebesgue-Stieltjes.

INDEFINITE AND IMPROPER INTEGRALS

To this point, we have defined the integral as a real number associated with a function on an interval (a,b). If we allow the upper limit b to vary, then the integral defines a function

$$F(x) = \int_a^x f(u) du$$

which is called an **indefinite integral**.

Given a function f, there is an indefinite integral for each starting point. From the definition of integral, it can be seen that any two indefinite integrals of the same function differ only by a constant. In fact, given a function f, consider the two indefinite integrals:

$$F_a(x) = \int_a^x f(u)du, \ F_b(x) = \int_b^x f(u)du$$

If $a < b$, we can write

$$F_a(x) = \int_a^x f(u)du = \int_a^b f(u)du + \int_b^x f(u)du = \text{constant} + F_b(x)$$

We can now extend the definition of proper integrals by introducing improper integrals. **Improper integrals** are defined as limits of indefinite integrals either when the integration limits are infinite or when the integrand diverges to infinity at a given point. Consider the improper integral

$$\int_a^\infty f(x)dx$$

This integral is defined as the limit

$$\int_a^\infty f(x)dx = \lim_{x \to \infty} \int_a^x f(u)du$$

if the limit exists. Consider now a function f that goes to infinity as x approaches the upper integration limit b. We define the improper integral

$$\int_a^b f(x)dx$$

as the left limit

$$\int_a^b f(x)dx = \lim_{x \to b^-} \int_a^x f(u)du$$

A "proper" Riemann integral assumes the integrand is defined and finite on a closed and bounded interval, bracketed by the limits of integration. An improper integral occurs when one or more of these conditions are not satisfied. In some cases, such integrals may be defined by considering the limit of a sequence of proper Riemann integrals on progressively larger intervals.

Consider, for example, the function $1/((x+1)\sqrt{x})$ integrated from 0 to ∞. At the lower bound, as x goes to 0 the function goes to ∞, and the upper bound is itself ∞, though the function goes to 0. Thus, it is a doubly improper integral. Integrated, say, from 1 to 3, an ordinary Riemann sum suffices to produce a result of $\pi/6$. To integrate from 1 to ∞, a Riemann sum is not possible. However, any finite upper bound, say t (with $t > 1$), gives a well-defined result, $2\arctan(\sqrt{t}) - \pi/2$. This has a finite limit as t goes to infinity, namely $\pi/2$. Similarly, the integral from 1/3 to 1 allows a Riemann sum as well, coincidentally again producing $\pi/6$. Replacing 1/3 by an arbitrary positive value s (with $s < 1$) is equally safe, giving $\pi/2 - 2\arctan(\sqrt{t})$. This, too, has a finite limit as s goes to zero, namely $\pi/2$. Combining the limits of the two fragments, the result of this improper integral is π:

$$\int_0^\infty \frac{dx}{(x+1)\sqrt{x}} = \lim_{s \to 0} \int_s^1 \frac{dx}{(x+1)\sqrt{x}} + \lim_{t \to \infty} \int_1^t \frac{dx}{(x+1)\sqrt{x}}$$

$$= \lim_{s \to 0} \left(\frac{\pi}{2} - 2\arctan\sqrt{s}\right) + \lim_{t \to \infty} \left(2\arctan\sqrt{t} - \frac{\pi}{2}\right)$$

$$= \frac{\pi}{2} + \left(\pi - \frac{\pi}{2}\right) = \pi$$

This process does not guarantee success; a limit may fail to exist, or may be unbounded. For example, over the bounded interval 0 to 1, the integral of $1/x$ does not converge; and over the unbounded interval 1 to ∞, the integral of $1/\sqrt{x}$ does not converge.

The improper integral

$$\int_{-1}^1 \frac{dx}{x^{2/3}} = 6$$

is unbounded internally, but both left and right limits exist. It may also happen that an integrand is unbounded at an interior point, in which case the integral must be split at that point, and the limit integrals on both sides must exist and must be bounded. Thus,

$$\int_{-1}^1 \frac{dx}{x^{2/3}} = \lim_{s \to 0} \int_{-1}^s \frac{dx}{x^{2/3}} + \lim_{t \to 0} \int_t^1 \frac{dx}{x^{2/3}}$$

$$= \lim_{s \to 0} 3\left(1 - s^{1/3}\right) + \lim_{t \to 0} 3\left(1 - t^{1/3}\right)$$

$$= 3 + 3 = 6$$

A similar definition can be established for the lower integration limit. Improper integrals exist only if these limits exist. For instance, the integral

$$\int_0^1 \frac{1}{x}dx = \lim_{x \to 0^+} \left[-\frac{1}{x^2} \right]_0^1 = \lim_{x \to 0^+} \left(\frac{1}{x^2} - 1 \right) = \infty$$

does not exist.

THE FUNDAMENTAL THEOREM OF CALCULUS

The **fundamental theorem of calculus** shows that integration is the inverse operation of derivation; it states that, given a continuous function f, any of its indefinite integrals F is a differentiable function and the following relationship holds:

$$\frac{dF(x)}{dx} = \frac{d \int_a^x f(u)du}{dx} = f(x)$$

If the function f is not continuous, then the fundamental theorem still holds, but in any point of discontinuity the derivative has to be replaced with the left or right derivative dependent on whether or not the function f is left or right continuous at that point.

Given a continuous function f, any function F such that

$$\frac{dF(x)}{dx} = f(x)$$

is called a **primitive** or an **indefinite integral of the function** f. It can be demonstrated that any two primitives of a function f differ only by a constant. Any primitive of a function f can therefore be represented generically as an indefinite integral plus a constant.

As an immediate consequence of the fundamental theorem of calculus we can now state that, given a primitive F of a function f, the definite integral

$$\int_a^b f(x)dx$$

can be computed as

$$\int_a^b f(x)dx = F(b) - F(a)$$

TABLE 3.1   Commonly Used Integrals

$f(x)$	$\int f(x)dx$	Domain
x^n	$\dfrac{1}{n+1}x^{n+1}$	$n \neq -1,\ R, x \neq 0$ if $n < 0$
x^α	$\dfrac{1}{\alpha+1}x^{\alpha+1}$	$x > 0$
$\sin x$	$-\cos x$	R
$\cos x$	$\sin x$	R
$\dfrac{1}{x}$	$\log x$	$x > 0$
e^x	e^x	R
$\dfrac{f'(x)}{f(x)}$	$\log [f(x)]$	$f(x) > 0$

All three properties—the linearity of the integration operation, the chain rule, and the rule of integration by parts—hold for indefinite integrals:

$$h(x) = af(x) + bg(x) \Rightarrow \int h(x)dx = a \int f(x)dx + b \int g(x)dx$$

$$\int f'(x)g(x)dx = f(x)g(x) - \int f(x)g'(x)dx$$

$$y = g(x) \Rightarrow \int f(y)dy = \int f(x)g'(x)dx$$

The differentiation formulas established in the previous chapter can now be applied to integration.

Table 3.1 lists a number of commonly used integrals.

INTEGRAL TRANSFORMS

Integral transforms are operations that take any function $f(x)$ into another function $F(s)$ of a different variable s through an improper integral

$$F(s) = \int_{-\infty}^{\infty} G(s, x) f(x)dx$$

The function $G(s,x)$ is referred to as the **kernel of the transform**. The association is one-to-one so that f can be uniquely recovered from its transform

F. For example, linear processes can be studied in the time domain or in the frequency domain: The two are linked by integral transforms. We will see how integral transforms are applied to several applications in finance. The two most important types of integral transforms are the **Laplace transform** and **Fourier transform**. We discuss both in this section.

Laplace Transforms

Given a real-valued function f, its **one-sided Laplace transform** is an operator that maps f to the function $L(s) = \mathscr{L}(f(x))$ defined by the improper integral

$$L(s) = \mathscr{L}[f(x)] = \int_{0}^{\infty} e^{-sx} f(x) dx$$

if it exists.

The Laplace transform of a real-valued function is thus a real-valued function. The one-sided transform is the most common type of Laplace transform used in physics and engineering. However, in probability theory, Laplace transforms are applied to density functions. As these functions are defined on the entire real axis, the two-sided Laplace transforms are used. In probability theory, the two-sided Laplace transform is called the **moment generating function**. The **two-sided Laplace transform** is defined by

$$L(s) = \mathscr{L}[f(x)] = \int_{-\infty}^{\infty} e^{-sx} f(x) dx$$

if the improper integral exists.

Laplace transforms "project" a function into a different function space, that of their transforms. Laplace transforms exist only for functions that are sufficiently smooth and decay to zero sufficiently rapidly when $x \to \infty$. The following conditions ensure the existence of the Laplace transform:

- $f(x)$ is piecewise continuous.
- $f(x)$ is of exponential order as $x \to \infty$, that is, there exist positive real constants K, a, and T, such that $|f(x)| \le K e^{ax}$, for $x > T$.

Note that the above conditions are sufficient but not necessary for Laplace transforms to exist. It can be demonstrated that, if they exist, Laplace transforms are unique in the sense that if two functions have the same Laplace transform they coincide pointwise. As a consequence, the

Laplace transforms are invertible in the sense that the original function can be fully recovered from its transform. In fact, it is possible to define the in-verse **Laplace transform** as the operator $\mathcal{L}^{-1}(F(s))$ such that

$$\mathcal{L}^{-1}[L(s)] = f(x)$$

The inverse Laplace transform can be represented as a **Bromwich inte-gral**, that is, an integral defined on a contour in the complex plane that leaves all singularities of the transform to the left:

$$f(X) = \frac{1}{2\pi i} \int\limits_{\gamma-i\infty}^{\gamma+i\infty} e^{sx} L(s) ds$$

The following conditions ensure the existence of an inverse Laplace transform:

$$\lim_{s \to \infty} F(s) = 0$$

$$\lim_{s \to \infty} s F(s) \text{ is finite}$$

We now demonstrate (without proof) some key properties of Laplace transforms; and both the one-sided and two-sided Laplace transforms have these similar properties. The Laplace transform is a linear operator in the sense that, if f, g are real-valued functions that have Laplace transforms and a, b are real-valued constants, then the following property holds:

$$L[af(x) + bg(x)] = \int\limits_{-\infty}^{\infty} e^{-sx}(af(x) + bg(x))dx$$

$$= a \int\limits_{-\infty}^{\infty} e^{-sx} f(x)dx + b \int\limits_{-\infty}^{\infty} e^{-sx} g(x)dx$$

$$= a\mathcal{L}[f(x)] + b\mathcal{L}[g(x)]$$

Laplace transforms turn differentiation, integration, and convolution (defined below) into algebraic operations. For derivatives the following property holds for the two-sided transform:

$$\mathcal{L}\left[\frac{df(x)}{dx}\right] = s\mathcal{L}[f(x)]$$

and

$$\mathcal{L}\left[\frac{df(x)}{dx}\right] = s\mathcal{L}[f(x)] - f(0)$$

for the one-sided transform. For higher derivatives, the following formula holds for the two-sided transform:

$$\mathcal{L}[f^{(n)}(x)] = s^n\mathcal{L}[f(x)] - s^{n-1} f(0) - s^{n-2} f'(0) - \ldots - f^{(n-1)}(0)$$

An analogous property holds for integration for one-sided transforms:

$$\mathcal{L}\left[\int_0^t f(x)\right] = \frac{1}{s}\mathcal{L}[f(x)] \text{ for the one-sided transform}$$

$$\mathcal{L}\left[\int_0^t f(x)\right] = \frac{1}{s}\mathcal{L}[f(x)] \text{ for the two-sided transform}$$

Consider now the convolution. Given two functions f and g, their **convolution** $h(x) = f(x) * g(x)$ is defined as the integral

$$h(x) = (f * g)(x) = \int_{-\infty}^{\infty} f(x - t)g(t)dt$$

It can be demonstrated that the following property holds:

$$\mathcal{L}[h(x)] = \mathcal{L}[f * g] = \mathcal{L}[f(x)]\mathcal{L}[g(x)]$$

As we will see in Chapter 9 when we cover differential equations, these properties are useful in solving differential equations, turning them into algebraic equations. These properties are also used in representing probability distributions of sums of variables.

The Laplace transform can be used to solve a differential equation. Consider the following first-order linear differential equation:

$$\frac{dN}{dt} = -\lambda N$$

where λ is a decay constant. Rearranging the equation to one side, we have

$$\frac{dN}{dt} + \lambda N = 0$$

Next, we take the Laplace transform of both sides of the equation

$$\left(s\tilde{N}(s) - N_0\right) + \lambda\tilde{N}(s) = 0$$

where $\tilde{N}(s) = L\{N(t)\}$ and $N_0 = N(0)$. Solving, we find

$$\tilde{N}(s) = \frac{N_0}{s + \lambda}$$

Finally, we take the inverse Laplace transform to find the general solution

$$N(t) = L^{-1}\{\tilde{N}(s)\} = L^{-1}\left\{\frac{N_0}{s + \lambda}\right\} = N_0 e^{-\lambda t}$$

Fourier Transforms

Fourier transforms are similar in many respects to Laplace transforms. Given a function f, its Fourier transform $\hat{f}(\omega) = \mathcal{F}[f(x)]$ is defined as the integral

$$\hat{f}(\omega) = \mathcal{F}[f(x)] = \int_{-\infty}^{+\infty} e^{-2\pi i \omega x} f(x) dx$$

if the improper integral exists, where i is the imaginary unity. The Fourier transform of a real-valued function is thus a complex-valued function. For a large class of functions the Fourier transform exists and is unique, so that the original function, f, can be recovered from its transform, $\hat{f}$.

The following conditions are sufficient but not necessary for a function to have a forward and inverse Fourier transform:

- $\int_{-\infty}^{\infty} |f(x)| dx$ exists.
- The function $f(x)$ is piecewise continuous.
- The function $f(x)$ has bounded variation.

The inverse Fourier transform can be represented as

$$f(x) = \mathscr{F}^{-1}[\hat{f}(\omega)] = \int\limits_{-\infty}^{\infty} e^{2\pi i \omega x} \hat{f}(\omega) d\omega$$

Fourier transforms are linear operators. The Fourier transform of the convolutions is the product of Fourier transforms; the Fourier transform of derivatives and integrals have similar properties to the Laplace transform.

CALCULUS IN MORE THAN ONE VARIABLE

The definition of the integral can be obtained in the same way as in the one variable case. The integral is defined as the limit of sums of multidimensional rectangles. Multidimensional integrals represent the ordinary concept of volume in three dimensions and n-dimensional hypervolume in more than three dimensions. A more general definition of the integral that includes both the Riemann and the Riemann-Stieltjes as special cases, will be considered in Chapter 5 where we cover the basics of probability.

KEY POINTS

- Integrals represent the area below a curve; they are the limit of sums of rectangles that approximate the area below the curve. Furthermore, integrals can generally be used to represent cumulated quantities, such as cumulated gains.
- The fundamental theorem of calculus proves that integrals and derivatives are inverse operations insofar as the derivative of the integral of a function returns the function.
- The integral of the product of a constant and a function is the product of the constant and the integral of the function.
- The integral of a sum of functions is the sum of the integrals.
- An integral transform is a particular kind of mathematical operator.
- There are numerous useful integral transforms. Each is specified by a choice of the kernel function.
- An integral transform maps an equation from its original domain into another domain.
- Manipulating and solving an equation in the target domain can be much easier than manipulating and solving in the original domain. The

solution is then mapped back to the original domain with the inverse of the integral transform.

■ Laplace and Fourier transforms of a function are the integral of that function times an exponential.

■ Laplace and Fourier transforms are useful because they transform differentiation and integration into algebraic operations, thereby providing a method for solving linear differential equations.

■ Integration can be extended to functions of more than one variable.

CHAPTER 4

Matrix Algebra

I n mathematics, a **matrix** is a rectangular array of numbers, symbols, or expressions, arranged in rows and columns. Matrix algebra generalizes classical analytical notions such as derivatives and exponentials to higher dimensions. Matrix algebra collects the various partial derivatives of a single function with respect to many variables, and of a multivariate function with respect to a single variable, into vectors and matrices that can be treated as single entities. This greatly simplifies operations, such as finding the maximum or minimum of a multivariate function and solving systems of differential equations. Calculations in portfolio theory, financial economics, and financial econometrics rely on the use of matrix algebra because of the need to manipulate large data inputs.

- Matrix algebra is used for optimal portfolio selection.
- Matrix algebra is useful for computing expected return of a portfolio that contains many assets.
- Matrix algebra is useful for computing the variance (or risk) of a portfolio that contains many assets.
- Optimal portfolio weights are calculated by maximizing the risk-adjusted return of a portfolio or by maximizing expected utility of a risk-averse investor. For either case, matrix algebra is useful for determining optimal asset allocation.
- Matrix algebra is used in financial risk management.
- A matrix is used to describe the outcomes or payoff of an investment or venture.
- Matrix algebra is used for computing value-at-risk and expected shortfall of a portfolio that contains many assets.

- More generally, matrix algebra is used in financial econometrics that has many applications to asset pricing, risk management, and option pricing.
- Matrix algebra is used in finance theory to define a complete market in which the complete set of possible gambles on future states-of-the-world can be constructed with existing assets without friction.
- In complete markets, every agent is able to exchange every good, directly or indirectly, with every other agent without transaction costs. In this setting, goods are state-contingent; that is, a good includes the time and state of the world in which it is consumed. To test whether a particular market is complete or not, one generally needs matrix algebra.

What you will learn after reading this chapter:

- Basic concepts and essentials of vectors and matrices.
- Square matrices and their different types.
- Definitions of identity and diagonal matrices and their properties.
- How to compute the determinant of a matrix.
- The concepts of linear independence and rank.
- How to compute the rank of a matrix.
- Explanations of vector and matrix operations such as transpose, addition, and multiplication of matrices.
- How to compute eigenvalues and eigenvectors.

INTRODUCTION

Ordinary algebra deals with operations such as addition and multiplication performed on individual numbers. In many applications in finance, however, it is useful to consider operations performed on ordered **arrays** of numbers. This is the domain of matrix algebra. Ordered arrays of numbers are called **vectors** and **matrices** while individual numbers are called **scalars**. In this chapter, we will discuss the basics of matrix algebra.

VECTORS AND MATRICES DEFINED

Let's now define precisely the concepts of a vector and a matrix.

Vectors

An **n-dimensional vector** is an ordered array of n numbers. Vectors are generally indicated with boldface lowercase letters. Thus a vector $\mathbf{x}$ is an array of the form

$$\mathbf{x} = [x_1 \ldots x_n]$$

The numbers x_i are called the **components** of the vector $\mathbf{x}$.

A vector is identified by the set of its components. Consider the vectors $\mathbf{x} = [x_1 \ldots x_n]$ and $\mathbf{y} = [y_1 \ldots y_m]$. Two vectors are said to be **equal** if and only if they have the same dimensions $n = m$ and the same components:

$$\mathbf{x} = \mathbf{y} \Leftrightarrow x_i = y_i, \ i = 1, \ldots, \ n$$

Vectors can be **row vectors** or **column vectors**. If the vector components appear in a horizontal row, then the vector is a row vector, such as, for instance, the vector

$$\mathbf{x} = [1 \quad 2 \quad 8 \quad 7]$$

Here are two examples. Suppose that we let w_n be a risky asset's weight in a portfolio. Assume that there are N risky assets. Then the following vector, $\mathbf{w}$, is a row vector that represents a portfolio's holdings of the N risky assets:

$$\mathbf{w} = [w_1 \ w_2 \ldots\ldots\ldots w_N]$$

As a second example of a row vector, suppose that we let r_n be the excess return for a risky asset. (The **excess return** is the difference between the return on a risky asset and the risk-free rate.) Then the following row vector is the excess return vector:

$$\mathbf{r} = [r_1 \ r_2 \ \ldots\ldots\ldots \ r_N]$$

If the vector components are arranged in a column, then the vector is called a column vector. For example, in finance a portfolio's excess return is assumed to be affected by what can be different characteristics or attributes or, more popularly, factors that affect all asset prices. A few examples would be the price-earnings ratio, book-to-value ratio, market capitalization, and industry. We can denote for a particular factor a column vector, **f**, that shows the exposure of each risky asset's excess return to that factor:

$$\mathbf{f} = \begin{bmatrix} f_1 \\ f_2 \\ \cdot \\ \cdot \\ f_N \end{bmatrix}$$

where f_n is the exposure of asset n to factor f.

Vector components can be either real or complex numbers. In most finance applications, vector components are real numbers. Returning to the row vector **w** of a portfolio of holdings, a positive value for w_n would mean that risky asset n is held in the portfolio. This is referred to as a long position. A value of zero would mean that risky asset n is not held in the portfolio. If the value of w_n is negative, this means that there is a short position in risky asset n.

The (Euclidean) **length** of a vector **x**, also called the **norm** of a vector, denoted as $\|\mathbf{x}\|$, is defined as the square root of the sum of the squares of its components:

$$\|\mathbf{x}\| = \sqrt{x_1^2 + \cdots + x_n^2}$$

Matrices

An $n \times m$ **matrix** is a bidimensional ordered array of $n \times m$ numbers. Matrices are usually indicated with boldface uppercase letters. Thus, the generic matrix **A** is an $n \times m$ array of the form

$$\mathbf{A} = \begin{bmatrix} a_{1,1} & \cdot & a_{1,j} & \cdot & a_{1,m} \\ \cdot & \cdot & \cdot & \cdot & \cdot \\ a_{i,1} & \cdot & a_{i,j} & \cdot & a_{i,m} \\ \cdot & \cdot & \cdot & \cdot & \cdot \\ a_{n,1} & \cdot & a_{n,j} & \cdot & a_{n,m} \end{bmatrix}$$

Note that the first subscript indicates rows, while the second subscript indicates columns. The entries a_{ij}—called the **elements** of the matrix **A**—are the numbers at the crossing of the ith row and the jth column. The commas between the subscripts of the matrix entries are omitted when there is no risk of confusion: $a_{i,j} \equiv a_{ij}$. A matrix **A** is often indicated by its generic element between brackets:

$$\mathbf{A} = \{a_{ij}\}_{nm} \quad \text{or} \quad \mathbf{A} = [a_{ij}]_{nm}$$

where the subscripts nm are the **dimensions** of the matrix.

We assume that elements are real numbers unless explicitly stated otherwise. If the matrix entries are real numbers, the matrix is called a **real matrix**.

Two matrices are said to be equal if they are of the same dimensions and have the same elements. Consider two matrices $A = \{a_{ij}\}_{nm}$ and $B = \{b_{ij}\}_{nm}$ of the same order $n \times m$:

$$A = B \text{ means } \{a_{ij}\}_{nm} = \{b_{ij}\}_{nm}$$

SQUARE MATRICES

There are several types of matrices. First there is a broad classification of square and rectangular matrices. A **rectangular matrix** can have a different numbers of rows and columns; a **square matrix** is a matrix with the same number n of rows as of columns.

Diagonals and Antidiagonals

An important concept for a square matrix is the **diagonal**. The diagonal includes the elements that run from the first row, first column to the last row, last column. For example, consider the following square matrix:

$$A = \begin{bmatrix} a_{1,1} & \cdot & a_{1,j} & \cdot & a_{1,n} \\ \cdot & \cdot & \cdot & \cdot & \cdot \\ a_{i,1} & \cdot & a_{i,j} & \cdot & a_{i,n} \\ \cdot & \cdot & \cdot & \cdot & \cdot \\ a_{n,1} & \cdot & a_{n,j} & \cdot & a_{n,n} \end{bmatrix}$$

The diagonal terms are the $a_{j,j}$ terms.

The **antidiagonals** of a square matrix are the other diagonals that do not run from the first row, first column to the last row, last column. For example, consider the following 4×4 square matrix:

$$\begin{bmatrix} 5 & 9 & 14 & 8 \\ 2 & 6 & 12 & 11 \\ 17 & 21 & 42 & 2 \\ 19 & 73 & 7 & 8 \end{bmatrix}$$

The diagonal terms include 5, 6, 42, 8. One antidiagonal is 2, 9. Another antidiagonal is 17, 6, 14. Note that there are antidiagonal terms in rectangular matrices.

Identity Matrix

The $n \times n$ **identity matrix**, denoted by $\mathbf{I}_n$, is a square matrix whose diagonal elements are equal to one while all other terms are zero:

$$\mathbf{I}_n = \begin{bmatrix} 1 & 0 & \cdot & \cdot & \cdot & 0 \\ 0 & 1 & \cdot & \cdot & \cdot & 0 \\ \cdot & & \cdot & & & \cdot \\ \cdot & & & \cdot & & \cdot \\ \cdot & & & & \cdot & \cdot \\ 0 & 0 & \cdot & \cdot & \cdot & 1 \end{bmatrix}$$

A matrix whose entries are all zero is called a **zero matrix**.

Diagonal Matrix

A **diagonal matrix** is a square matrix whose elements are all zero except the ones on the diagonal:

$$\mathbf{A} = \begin{bmatrix} a_{11} & 0 & \cdot & \cdot & \cdot & 0 \\ 0 & a_{22} & \cdot & \cdot & \cdot & 0 \\ \cdot & & \cdot & & & \cdot \\ \cdot & & & \cdot & & \cdot \\ \cdot & & & & \cdot & \cdot \\ 0 & 0 & \cdot & \cdot & \cdot & a_{nn} \end{bmatrix}$$

Given a square $n \times n$ matrix $\mathbf{A}$, the matrix dg $\mathbf{A}$ is the diagonal matrix extracted from $\mathbf{A}$. The diagonal matrix dg $\mathbf{A}$ is a matrix whose elements are all zero except the elements on the diagonal that coincide with those of the matrix $\mathbf{A}$:

$$\mathbf{A} = \begin{bmatrix} a_{11} & a_{12} & \cdot & \cdot & \cdot & a_{1n} \\ a_{21} & a_{22} & \cdot & \cdot & \cdot & a_{2n} \\ \cdot & \cdot & \cdot & & & \cdot \\ \cdot & \cdot & & \cdot & & \cdot \\ \cdot & \cdot & & & \cdot & \cdot \\ a_{n1} & a_{n2} & \cdot & \cdot & \cdot & a_{nn} \end{bmatrix} \Rightarrow \text{dg } \mathbf{A} = \begin{bmatrix} a_{11} & 0 & \cdots & 0 \\ 0 & a_{22} & \cdots & 0 \\ \cdot & & \cdot & \cdot \\ \cdot & & \cdot & \cdot \\ \cdot & & & \cdot \\ 0 & 0 & \cdots & a_{nn} \end{bmatrix}$$

The **trace** of a square matrix $\mathbf{A}$ is the sum of its diagonal elements:

$$\text{tr } \mathbf{A} = \sum_{i=1}^{n} a_{ii}$$

A square matrix is said to be a **symmetric matrix** if the elements above the diagonal are equal to the corresponding elements below the diagonal: $a_{ij} = a_{ji}$. A matrix is called **skew-symmetric** if the diagonal elements are zero and the elements above the diagonal are the opposite of the corresponding elements below the diagonal: $a_{ij} = -a_{ji}$, $i \neq j$, $a_{ii} = 0$.

The most commonly used symmetric matrix in finance and econometrics is the **covariance matrix**, also referred to as the **variance-covariance matrix**.[1] For example, suppose that there are N risky assets and that the variance of the excess return for each risky asset and the covariances between each pair of risky assets are estimated. As the number of risky assets is N there are N^2 elements, consisting of N variances (along the diagonal) and $N^2 - N$ covariances (the antidiagonal terms). Symmetry restrictions reduce the number of independent elements. In fact the covariance $\sigma_{ij}(t)$ between risky asset i and risky asset j will be equal to the covariance between risky asset j and risky asset i. We can therefore arrange the variances and covariances in the following square matrix **V**:

$$\mathbf{V} = \begin{bmatrix} \sigma_{1,1} & \cdot & \sigma_{1,i} & \cdot & \sigma_{1,N} \\ \cdot & \cdot & \cdot & \cdot & \cdot \\ \sigma_{1,i} & \cdot & \sigma_{i,i} & \cdot & \sigma_{i,N} \\ \cdot & \cdot & \cdot & \cdot & \cdot \\ \sigma_{1,N} & \cdot & \sigma_{i,N} & \cdot & \sigma_{N,N} \end{bmatrix}$$

Notice that **V** is a symmetric matrix.

Upper and Lower Triangular Matrix

A matrix **A** is said to be an **upper triangular matrix** if $a_{ij} = 0$, $i > j$. In other words, an upper triangular matrix is a matrix whose elements in the triangle below the diagonal are all zero as is illustrated below:

$$\mathbf{A} = \begin{bmatrix} a_{1,1} & \cdot & a_{1,i} & \cdot & a_{1,n} \\ \cdot & \cdot & \cdot & \cdot & \cdot \\ 0 & \cdot & a_{i,i} & \cdot & a_{i,n} \\ \cdot & \cdot & \cdot & \cdot & \cdot \\ 0 & \cdot & 0 & \cdot & a_{n,n} \end{bmatrix} \text{ [upper triangular]}$$

---

[1]Variances and covariances are described in Chapter 6.

A matrix $\mathbf{A}$ is called **lower triangular** if $a_{ij} = 0$, $i < j$. In other words, a lower triangular matrix is a matrix whose elements in the triangle above the diagonal are zero as is illustrated below:

$$\mathbf{A} = \begin{bmatrix} a_{1,1} & \cdot & 0 & \cdot & 0 \\ \cdot & \cdot & \cdot & \cdot & \cdot \\ \cdot & \cdot & a_{i,i} & \cdot & 0 \\ \cdot & \cdot & \cdot & \cdot & \cdot \\ a_{n,1} & \cdot & a_{n,i} & \cdot & a_{n,n} \end{bmatrix} \quad \text{[lower triangular]}$$

DETERMINANTS

Consider a square, $n \times n$, matrix $\mathbf{A}$. The **determinant** of $\mathbf{A}$, denoted $|\mathbf{A}|$, is defined as follows:

$$|\mathbf{A}| = \sum (-1)^{t(j_1, \cdots, j_n)} \prod_{i=1}^{n} a_{ij}$$

where the sum is extended over all permutations $(j_1, \ldots, j_n)$ of the set $(1, 2, \ldots, n)$ and $t(j_1, \ldots, j_n)$ is the number of transpositions (or inversions of positions) required to go from $(1, 2, \ldots, n)$ to $(j_1, \ldots, j_n)$.

Otherwise stated, a determinant is the sum of all different products formed by taking exactly one element from each row with each product multiplied by

$$(-1)^{t(j_1, \cdots, j_n)}$$

Consider, for instance, the case $n = 2$, where there is only one possible transposition: $1,2 \Rightarrow 2,1$. The determinant of a 2×2 matrix is therefore computed as follows:

$$|\mathbf{A}| = (-1)^0 a_{11}a_{22} + (-1)^1 a_{12}a_{21} = a_{11}a_{22} - a_{12}a_{21}$$

The determinant of a 3×3 matrix is calculated as follows:

$$\begin{vmatrix} a_{11} & a_{12} & a_{13} \\ a_{21} & a_{22} & a_{23} \\ a_{31} & a_{32} & a_{33} \end{vmatrix} = a_{11} \begin{vmatrix} a_{22} & a_{23} \\ a_{32} & a_{33} \end{vmatrix} - a_{12} \begin{vmatrix} a_{21} & a_{23} \\ a_{31} & a_{33} \end{vmatrix} + a_{13} \begin{vmatrix} a_{21} & a_{22} \\ a_{31} & a_{32} \end{vmatrix}$$

$$= a_{11}(a_{22}a_{33} - a_{23}a_{32}) - a_{12}(a_{21}a_{33} - a_{23}a_{31})$$
$$+ a_{13}(a_{21}a_{32} - a_{22}a_{31})$$

Consider a square matrix $\mathbf{A}$ of order n. Consider the matrix $\mathbf{M}_{ij}$ obtained by removing the ith row and the jth column. The matrix $\mathbf{M}_{ij}$ is a square matrix of order $(n-1)$. The determinant $|\mathbf{M}_{ij}|$ of the matrix $\mathbf{M}_{ij}$ is called the **minor** of a_{ij}. The signed minor

$$(-1)^{(i+j)}|\mathbf{M}_{ij}|$$

is called the **cofactor** of a_{ij} and is generally denoted as α_{ij}. The r-minors of the $n \times m$ rectangular matrix $\mathbf{A}$ are the determinants of the matrices formed by the elements at the crossing of r different rows and r different columns of $\mathbf{A}$.

A square matrix $\mathbf{A}$ is called **singular** if its determinant is equal to zero. An $n \times m$ matrix $\mathbf{A}$ is of **rank** r if at least one of its (square) r-minors is different from zero while all $(r+1)$-minors, if any, are zero. A nonsingular square matrix is said to be of **full rank** if its rank r is equal to its order n.

The easiest way to compute the rank of a matrix A is given by the Gauss elimination method. The row-echelon form of A produced by the Gauss algorithm has the same rank as A, and its rank can be read off as the number of nonzero rows.

Consider for example the 4×4 matrix

$$A = \begin{pmatrix} 2 & 4 & 1 & 3 \\ -1 & -2 & 1 & 0 \\ 0 & 0 & 2 & 2 \\ 3 & 6 & 2 & 5 \end{pmatrix}$$

We see that the second column is twice the first column, and that the fourth column equals the sum of the first and the third. The first and the third columns are linearly independent, so the rank of A is two. It produces the following row echelon form of A:

$$A = \begin{pmatrix} 1 & 2 & 0 & 1 \\ 0 & 0 & 1 & 1 \\ 0 & 0 & 0 & 0 \\ 0 & 0 & 0 & 0 \end{pmatrix}$$

which has two nonzero rows. Hence, the rank of A is two.

SYSTEMS OF LINEAR EQUATIONS

A system of n linear equations in m unknown variables is a set of n simultaneous equations of the following form:

$$a_{1,1}x_1 + \cdots + a_{1,m}x_m = b_1$$
$$\dots\dots\dots\dots\dots\dots\dots\dots$$
$$a_{n,1}x_1 + \cdots + a_{1,m}x_m = b_m$$

The $n \times m$ matrix

$$\mathbf{A} = \begin{bmatrix} a_{1,1} & \cdot & a_{1,j} & \cdot & a_{1,m} \\ \cdot & \cdot & \cdot & \cdot & \cdot \\ a_{i,1} & \cdot & a_{i,j} & \cdot & a_{i,m} \\ \cdot & \cdot & \cdot & \cdot & \cdot \\ a_{n,1} & \cdot & a_{n,j} & \cdot & a_{n,m} \end{bmatrix}$$

formed with the coefficients of the variables is called the **coefficient matrix**. The terms b_i are called the **constant terms**.

The **augmented matrix [A b]**—formed by adding to the coefficient matrix a column formed with the constant term—is represented below:

$$[\mathbf{A}\ \mathbf{b}] = \begin{bmatrix} a_{1,1} & \cdot & a_{1,j} & \cdot & a_{1,m}b_1 \\ \cdot & \cdot & \cdot & \cdot & \cdot \\ a_{i,1} & \cdot & a_{i,j} & \cdot & a_{i,m}b_i \\ \cdot & \cdot & \cdot & \cdot & \cdot \\ a_{n,1} & \cdot & a_{n,j} & \cdot & a_{n,m}b_n \end{bmatrix}$$

If the constant terms on the right side of the equations are all zero, the system is called **homogeneous**. If at least one of the constant terms is different from zero, the system is called **nonhomogeneous**.

A system is called **consistent** if it admits a solution, that is, if there is a set of values of the variables that simultaneously satisfy all the equations. A system is called **inconsistent** if there is no set of numbers that satisfy the system equations.

Let's first consider the case of nonhomogeneous linear systems. The fundamental theorems of linear systems state that:

Theorem 1. A system of n linear equations in m unknowns is consistent (i.e., it admits a solution) if and only if the coefficient matrix and the augmented matrix have the same rank.

Theorem 2. If a consistent system of n equations in m variables is of rank $r < m$, it is possible to choose $n-r$ unknowns so that the coefficient matrix of the remaining r unknowns is of rank r. When these $m-r$ variables are assigned any arbitrary value, the value of the remaining variables is uniquely determined.

An immediate consequence of the fundamental theorems is that (1) a system of n equations in n unknown variables admits a solution; and (2) the solution is unique if and only if both the coefficient matrix and the augmented matrix are of rank n.

Let's now examine homogeneous systems. The coefficient matrix and the augmented matrix of a homogeneous system always have the same rank and thus a homogeneous system is always consistent. In fact, the trivial solution $x_1 = \ldots = x_m = 0$ always satisfies a homogeneous system.

Consider now a homogeneous system of n equations in n unknowns. If the rank of the coefficient matrix is n, the system has only the trivial solution. If the rank of the coefficient matrix is $r < n$, then Theorem 2 ensures that the system has a solution other than the trivial solution.

LINEAR INDEPENDENCE AND RANK

Consider an $n \times m$ matrix **A**. A set of p columns extracted from the matrix **A**

$$
\begin{bmatrix}
\cdot & a_{1,i_1} & \cdot & a_{1,i_p} & \cdot \\
\cdot & \cdot & \cdot & \cdot & \cdot \\
\cdot & \cdot & \cdot & \cdot & \cdot \\
\cdot & \cdot & \cdot & \cdot & \cdot \\
\cdot & a_{n,i_1} & \cdot & a_{n,i_p} & \cdot
\end{bmatrix}
$$

is said to be linearly independent if it is not possible to find p constants $\beta_s, s = 1, \ldots, p$ such that the following n equations are simultaneously satisfied:

$$
\beta_1 a_{1,i_1} + \cdots + \beta_p a_{1,i_p} = 0
$$
$$
\ldots\ldots\ldots\ldots\ldots\ldots\ldots
$$
$$
\beta_1 a_{n,i_1} + \cdots + \beta_p a_{n,i_p} = 0
$$

Analogously, a set of q rows extracted from the matrix $\mathbf{A}$ are said to be linearly independent if it is not possible to find q constants λ_s, $s = 1, \ldots, q$, such that the following m equations are simultaneously satisfied:

$$\lambda_1 a_{i_1,1} + \cdots + \lambda_q a_{i_q,1} = 0$$
$$\cdots\cdots\cdots\cdots\cdots\cdots$$
$$\lambda_1 a_{i_1,m} + \cdots + \lambda_q a_{i_q,m} = 0$$

It can be demonstrated that in any matrix the number p of linearly independent columns is the same as the number q of linearly independent rows. This number is equal, in turn, to the rank r of the matrix. Recall that an $n \times m$ matrix $\mathbf{A}$ is said to be of **rank r** if at least one of its (square) r-minors is different from zero while all $(r + 1)$-minors, if any, are zero. The constant, p, is the same for rows and for columns. We can now give an alternative definition of the rank of a matrix:

Given an $n \times m$ matrix $\mathbf{A}$, its **rank**, denoted rank $(\mathbf{A})$, is the number r of linearly independent rows or columns. This definition is meaningful because the row rank is always equal to the column rank.

HANKEL MATRIX

In financial econometrics, a technique called an **autoregressive integrated moving average** (ARIMA) is often estimated in studying time series data. To understand this technique, it is important to understand a special type of matrix, a Hankel matrix. A **Hankel matrix** is a matrix where, for each antidiagonal term, the element is the same.

For example, consider the following square Hankel matrix:

$$\begin{bmatrix} 17 & 16 & 15 & 24 \\ 16 & 15 & 24 & 33 \\ 15 & 24 & 33 & 72 \\ 24 & 33 & 72 & 41 \end{bmatrix}$$

Each antidiagonal has the same value. Now consider the elements of the antidiagonal running from the second row, first column and first row, second column. Both elements have the value 16. Consider another antidiagonal running from the fourth row, second column to the second row, fourth column. All of the elements have the value 33.

An example of a rectangular Hankel matrix would be

$$
\begin{bmatrix}
72 & 60 & 55 & 43 & 30 & 21 \\
60 & 55 & 43 & 30 & 21 & 10 \\
55 & 43 & 30 & 21 & 10 & 80
\end{bmatrix}
$$

Notice that a Hankel matrix is a symmetric matrix.[2]

Consider an infinite sequence of square $n \times n$ matrices:

$$
\mathbf{H}_0, \ \mathbf{H}_1, \ \cdots, \ \mathbf{H}_i, \cdots
$$

The infinite Hankel matrix H is the following matrix:

$$
\mathbf{H} =
\begin{bmatrix}
\mathbf{H}_0 & \mathbf{H}_1 & \mathbf{H}_2 & \cdots \\
\mathbf{H}_1 & \mathbf{H}_2 & \cdots & \cdots \\
\mathbf{H}_2 & \cdots & \cdots & \cdots \\
\cdots & & & \\
\cdots & & &
\end{bmatrix}
$$

The rank of a Hankel matrix can be defined in three different ways:

1. The **column rank** is the largest number of linearly independent sequence columns.
2. The **row rank** is the largest number of linearly independent sequence rows.
3. The **rank** is the superior of the ranks of all finite matrices of the type:

$$
\mathbf{H}_{N,N'} =
\begin{bmatrix}
\mathbf{H}_0 & \mathbf{H}_1 & \cdot & \mathbf{H}_{N'} \\
\mathbf{H}_1 & \mathbf{H}_2 & \cdot & \cdot \\
\cdot & \cdot & \cdot & \cdot \\
\mathbf{H}_N & \cdot & \cdot & \mathbf{H}_{N+N'}
\end{bmatrix}
$$

---

[2] A special case of a Hankel matrix is when the values for the elements in the first row of the matrix are repeated in each successive row such that its value appears one column to the left. For example, consider the following square Hankel matrix:

$$
\begin{bmatrix}
41 & 32 & 23 & 14 \\
32 & 23 & 14 & 41 \\
23 & 14 & 41 & 32 \\
14 & 41 & 32 & 23
\end{bmatrix}
$$

This type of Hankel matrix is called an **anticirculant matrix**.

As in the finite-dimensional case, the three definitions are equivalent in the sense that the three numbers are equal, if finite, or they are all three infinite.

VECTOR AND MATRIX OPERATIONS

Let's now introduce the most common operations performed on vectors and matrices. An **operation** is a mapping that operates on scalars, vectors, and matrices to produce new scalars, vectors, or matrices. The notion of operations performed on a set of objects to produce another object of the same set is the key concept of algebra. Let's start with vector operations.

Vector Operations

The following operations are usually defined on vectors: (1) transpose, (2) addition, and (3) multiplication.

Transpose The transpose operation transforms a row vector into a column vector and vice versa. Given the row vector $\mathbf{x} = [x_1 \ldots x_n]$ its transpose, denoted as $\mathbf{x}^T$ or $\mathbf{x}'$, is the column vector:

$$x^T = \begin{bmatrix} x_1 \\ \cdot \\ \cdot \\ x_n \end{bmatrix}$$

Clearly the transpose of the transpose is the original vector:

$$(\mathbf{x}^T)^T = \mathbf{x}$$

Addition Two row (or column) vectors $\mathbf{x} = [x_1 \ldots x_n]$, $\mathbf{y} = [y_1 \ldots y_n]$ with the same number n of components can be added. The **addition** of two vectors is a new vector whose components are the sums of the components:

$$\mathbf{x} + \mathbf{y} = [x_1 + y_1 \cdots x_n + y_n]$$

This definition can be generalized to any number N of summands:

$$\sum_{i=1}^{N} \mathbf{x}_i = \left[\sum_{i=1}^{N} x_{1i} \cdots \sum_{i=1}^{N} y_{ni} \right]$$

The summands must be both column or row vectors; it is not possible to add row vectors to column vectors.

It is clear from the definition of addition that addition is a commutative operation in the sense that the order of the summands does not matter: $\mathbf{x} + \mathbf{y} = \mathbf{y} + \mathbf{x}$. Addition is also an associative operation in the sense that $\mathbf{x} + (\mathbf{y} + \mathbf{z}) = (\mathbf{x} + \mathbf{y}) + \mathbf{z}$.

Multiplication We define two types of multiplication: (1) multiplication of a scalar and a vector and (2) scalar multiplication of two vectors (inner product).

The multiplication of a scalar λ and a row (or column) vector $\mathbf{x}$, denoted as $\lambda\mathbf{x}$, is defined as the multiplication of each component of the vector by the scalar:

$$\lambda\mathbf{x} = [\lambda x_1 \cdots \lambda x_n]$$

As an example of the multiplication of a vector by a scalar, consider the vector of portfolio weights $\mathbf{w} = [w_1 \ldots w_n]$. If the total portfolio value at a given moment is P, then the holding in each asset is the product of the value by the vector of weights:

$$P\mathbf{w} = [Pw_1 \cdots Pw_n]$$

A similar definition holds for column vectors. It is clear from this definition that

$$\|a\mathbf{x}\| = |a| \, \|\mathbf{x}\|$$

and that multiplication by a scalar is associative as

$$a(\mathbf{x} + \mathbf{y}) = a\mathbf{x} + a\mathbf{y}$$

The **scalar** (or **inner**) **product** of two vectors of the same dimensions $\mathbf{x}$, $\mathbf{y}$, denoted as $\mathbf{x} \cdot \mathbf{y}$, is defined between a row vector and a column vector. The scalar product between two vectors produces a scalar according to the following rule:

$$\mathbf{x} \cdot \mathbf{y} = \sum_{i=1}^{n} x_i y_i$$

For example, consider the column vector f of a particular attribute discussed earlier and the row vector $\mathbf{w}$ of portfolio weights. Then $\mathbf{w} \cdot f$ is a scalar that shows the exposure of the portfolio to the particular attribute. That is,

$$\mathbf{w} \cdot f = [w_1 \; w_2 \cdots \cdots w_N] \begin{bmatrix} f_1 \\ f_2 \\ \cdot \\ \cdot \\ f_N \end{bmatrix}$$

$$= \sum_{n=1}^{N} w_N f_n$$

As another example, a portfolio's excess return is found by taking vector of portfolio weights $\mathbf{w}$ and multiplying it by the transpose of the excess return vector, $\mathbf{r}$. That is,

$$\mathbf{w} \cdot \mathbf{r}^T = [w_1 \; w_2 \cdots \cdots w_N] \begin{bmatrix} r_1 \\ r_2 \\ \cdot \\ \cdot \\ r_N \end{bmatrix}$$

$$= \sum_{n=1}^{N} w_N r_n$$

Two vectors $\mathbf{x}, \mathbf{y}$ are said to be **orthogonal** if their scalar product is zero. The scalar product of two vectors can be interpreted geometrically as an orthogonal projection. In fact, the inner product of vectors $\mathbf{x}$ and $\mathbf{y}$, divided by the square norm of $\mathbf{y}$, can be interpreted as the orthogonal projection of $\mathbf{x}$ onto $\mathbf{y}$. The following two properties are an immediate consequence of the definitions:

$$\|\mathbf{x}\| = \sqrt{\mathbf{x} \cdot \mathbf{x}}$$

$$(a\mathbf{x}) \cdot (b\mathbf{y}) = ab\mathbf{x} \cdot \mathbf{y}$$

Matrix Operations

Let's define the following five operations on matrices: (1) transpose, (2) addition, (3) multiplication, (4) inverse, and (5) adjoint.

Transpose   The definition of the **transpose of a matrix** is an extension of the transpose of a vector. The transpose operation consists in exchanging rows with columns. Consider the $n \times m$ matrix

$$\mathbf{A} = \{a_{ij}\}_{nm}$$

The transpose of $\mathbf{A}$, denoted $\mathbf{A}^T$ or $\mathbf{A}'$, is the $m \times n$ matrix whose ith row is the ith column of $\mathbf{A}$:

$$\mathbf{A}^T = \{a_{ji}\}_{mn}$$

The following should be clear from this definition:

$$(\mathbf{A}^T)^T = \mathbf{A}$$

and that a matrix is symmetric if and only if

$$\mathbf{A}^T = \mathbf{A}$$

Addition   Consider two $n \times m$ matrices

$$\mathbf{A} = \{a_{ij}\}_{nm}$$

and

$$\mathbf{B} = \{b_{ij}\}_{nm}$$

The sum of the matrices $\mathbf{A}$ and $\mathbf{B}$ is defined as the $n \times m$ matrix obtained by adding the respective elements:

$$\mathbf{A} + \mathbf{B} = \{a_{ij} + b_{ij}\}_{nm}$$

Note that it is essential for the definition of addition that the two matrices have the same order $n \times m$.

The operation of addition can be extended to any number N of summands as follows:

$$\sum_{s=1}^{N} \mathbf{A}_i = \left\{ \sum_{s=1}^{N} a_{s_{ij}} \right\}_{nm}$$

where $a_{s_{ij}}$ is the generic i,j element of the sth summand.

The following properties of addition are immediate from the definition of addition:

$$A + B = B + A$$
$$A + (B + C) = (A + B) + C = A + B + C$$
$$\text{tr}(A + B) = \text{tr}\,A + \text{tr}\,B$$

The operation of addition of vectors defined above is clearly a special case of the more general operation of addition of matrices.

Multiplication Consider a scalar c and a matrix:

$$A = \{a_{ij}\}_{nm}$$

The **product** $cA = Ac$ is the $n \times m$ matrix obtained by multiplying each element of the matrix by c:

$$cA = Ac = \{ca_{ij}\}_{nm}$$

Multiplication of a matrix by a scalar is associative with respect to matrix addition:

$$c(A + B) = cA + cB$$

Let's now define the **product of two matrices**. Consider two matrices:

$$A = \{a_{it}\}_{np}$$

and

$$B = \{b_{sj}\}_{pm}$$

The product $C = AB$ is defined as follows:

$$C = AB = \{c_{ij}\} = \left\{ \sum_{t=1}^{p} a_{it} b_{tj} \right\}$$

The product $C = AB$ is therefore a matrix whose generic element $\{c_{ij}\}$ is the scalar product of the ith row of the matrix A and the jth column of the matrix B. This definition generalizes the definition of scalar product of vectors: The scalar product of two n-dimensional vectors is the product of an $n \times 1$ matrix (a row vector) for a $1 \times n$ matrix (the column vector).

Following the above definition, the matrix product operation is performed rows by columns. Therefore, two matrices can be multiplied only if the number of columns (i.e., the number of elements in each row) of the first matrix equals the number of rows (i.e., the number of elements in each column) of the second matrix.

Suppose we multiply a 3×3 matrix by a 3×2 matrix:

$$A = \begin{pmatrix} 1 & 2 & 3 \\ 4 & 5 & 6 \\ 7 & 8 & 9 \end{pmatrix}_{3 \times 3} \qquad B = \begin{pmatrix} x & y \\ a & b \\ \alpha & \beta \end{pmatrix}_{3 \times 2}$$

Using the inner product approach, we obtain

$$A_{3 \times 3} \cdot B_{3 \times 2} = \begin{pmatrix} 1x + 2a + 3\alpha & 1y + 2b + 3\beta \\ 4x + 5a + 6\alpha & 4y + 5b + 6\beta \\ 7x + 8a + 9\alpha & 7y + 8b + 9\beta \end{pmatrix}_{3 \times 2}$$

If we generalize, multiplying a $k \times m$ matrix by a $m \times n$ matrix yields a a $k \times n$ matrix.

The following two **distributive properties** hold:

$$\mathbf{C(A + B) = CA + CB}$$

$$\mathbf{(A + B)C = AC + BC}$$

The **associative property** also holds:

$$\mathbf{(AB)C = A(BC)}$$

However, the matrix product operation is not commutative. In fact, if $\mathbf{A}$ and $\mathbf{B}$ are two square matrices, in general $\mathbf{AB} \neq \mathbf{BA}$. Also $\mathbf{AB} = 0$ does not imply $\mathbf{A} = 0$ or $\mathbf{B} = 0$.

Inverse and Adjoint   Consider two square matrices of order n, $\mathbf{A}$ and $\mathbf{B}$. If $\mathbf{AB} = \mathbf{BA} = \mathbf{I}$, then the matrix $\mathbf{B}$ is called the **inverse** of $\mathbf{A}$ and is denoted as $\mathbf{A}^{-1}$. It can be demonstrated that the two following properties hold:

> *Property 1.* A square matrix $\mathbf{A}$ admits an inverse $\mathbf{A}^{-1}$ if and only if it is nonsingular, that is, if and only if its determinant is different from

zero. Otherwise stated, a matrix $\mathbf{A}$ admits an inverse if and only if it is of full rank.

Property 2. The inverse of a square matrix, if it exists, is unique. This property is a consequence of the property that, if $\mathbf{A}$ is nonsingular, then $\mathbf{AB} = \mathbf{AC}$ implies $\mathbf{B} = \mathbf{C}$.

Consider now a square matrix of order n $\mathbf{A} = \{a_{ij}\}$ and consider its cofactors α_{ij}. Recall that the cofactors α_{ij} are the signed minors $(-1)^{(i+j)}|M_{ij}|$ of the matrix $\mathbf{A}$. The **adjoint** of the matrix $\mathbf{A}$, denoted as $\text{Adj}(\mathbf{A})$, is the following matrix:

$$
\text{Adj}(\mathbf{A}) =
\begin{bmatrix}
\alpha_{1,1} & \cdot & \alpha_{1,j} & \cdot & \alpha_{1,n} \\
\cdot & \cdot & \cdot & \cdot & \cdot \\
\alpha_{i,1} & \cdot & \alpha_{i,j} & \cdot & \alpha_{i,n} \\
\cdot & \cdot & \cdot & \cdot & \cdot \\
\alpha_{n,1} & \cdot & \alpha_{n,j} & \cdot & \alpha_{n,n}
\end{bmatrix}^{T}
=
\begin{bmatrix}
\alpha_{1,1} & \cdot & \alpha_{2,1} & \cdot & \alpha_{n,1} \\
\cdot & \cdot & \cdot & \cdot & \cdot \\
\alpha_{1,i} & \cdot & \alpha_{2,i} & \cdot & \alpha_{n,i} \\
\cdot & \cdot & \cdot & \cdot & \cdot \\
\alpha_{1,n} & \cdot & \alpha_{2,n} & \cdot & \alpha_{n,n}
\end{bmatrix}
$$

The adjoint of a matrix $\mathbf{A}$ is therefore the transpose of the matrix obtained by replacing the elements of $\mathbf{A}$ with their cofactors.

If the matrix $\mathbf{A}$ is nonsingular, and therefore admits an inverse, it can be demonstrated that

$$
\mathbf{A}^{-1} = \frac{\text{Adj}(\mathbf{A})}{|\mathbf{A}|}
$$

A square matrix $\mathbf{A}$ of order n is said to be orthogonal if the following property holds:

$$
\mathbf{AA}' = \mathbf{A}'\mathbf{A} = \mathbf{I}_n
$$

Because in this case $\mathbf{A}$ must be of full rank, the transpose of an orthogonal matrix coincides with its inverse: $\mathbf{A}^{-1} = \mathbf{A}'$.

FINANCE APPLICATION

In financial economics, a **complete market** (or complete system of markets) is one in which the complete set of possible gambles on future states-of-the-world can be constructed with existing assets without friction. Every agent is able to exchange every good, directly or indirectly, with every other agent without transaction costs. Here goods are state-contingent; that is, a good includes the time and state of the world in which it is consumed. A state of the world is a complete specification of the values of all relevant variables over the relevant time horizon. A state-contingent claim is a contract whose future payoffs depend on future states of the world.

Consider the linear system of equations defined for a series of Q^i, indexed by the state of the world i:

$$\begin{pmatrix} S_{1,t_0} \\ \cdots \\ S_{n,t_0} \end{pmatrix} = \begin{pmatrix} z_1^1 & \cdots & z_1^n \\ & \cdots & \\ z_n^1 & \cdots & z_n^n \end{pmatrix} \cdot \begin{pmatrix} Q^1 \\ \cdots \\ Q^n \end{pmatrix}$$

The left-hand side shows that the vector of current asset prices observed at time t_0. The right-hand side has two components. The first is the matrix of possible values for these prices at time T, and the second is a vector of constants $\{Q^1, \ldots, Q^n\}$.

The fundamental theorem of asset pricing indicates that the time t_0 prices for the $\{S_{k,t_0}\}$ are arbitrage-free if and only if $\{Q^i\}$ exist and are positive. In fact, the theory works both ways. If $\{S_{k,t_0}\}$ are arbitrage-free, then $\{Q^i\}$ exist and are all positive. If $\{Q^i\}$ exist and are positive, then the $\{S_{k,t_0}\}$ are arbitrage-free.

As mentioned above, a complete set of financial assets on future states-of-the-world can be constructed with existing assets without financial market frictions.[3] We now present an example for this kind of replication. We will show how a set of elementary insurance contracts can be used in replicating another set of instruments with arbitrary payoffs. Consider an arbitrary financial asset, S_t, that is worth z_T^i in state of the world i at time T. Given n insurance contracts C_i, we can immediately form a replicating portfolio for this asset. We can consider buying the following portfolio:

$$\{z_T^1 \text{ units of } C_1, z_T^2 \text{ units of } C_2, \ldots, z_T^n \text{ units of } C_n\}$$

At time T, this portfolio should be worth exactly the same as the S_t, since whatever state occurs, the basket of insurance contracts will make the same time-T payoff as the original asset. This provides an immediate synthetic for the S_t. Accordingly, if there are no arbitrage opportunities, the value of the portfolio and the value of the S_t will be identical as of time t as well.

---

[3]Financial market frictions include transaction costs, taxes, and other factors that interfere with a trade.

As an example, consider four independent assets $S_{k,t}$, $k = 1, \ldots, 4$ with different payoffs z_k^i in the states $i = 1, \ldots, 4$. We can find one synthetic for each $S_{k,t}$ by purchasing the portfolios:

$$\{z_k^1 \text{ units of } C_1, z_k^2 \text{ units of } C_2, z_k^3 \text{ units of } C_3, z_k^4 \text{ units of } C_4\}$$

Putting these in matrix form, we see that arbitrage-free values, S_{k,t_0}, of these assets at time t_0 have to satisfy the matrix equation:

$$
\begin{bmatrix}
1 \\
S_{1,t_0} \\
S_{2,t_0} \\
S_{3,t_0} \\
S_{4,t_0}
\end{bmatrix}
=
\begin{bmatrix}
1 + r_{t_0} & 1 + r_{t_0} & 1 + r_{t_0} & 1 + r_{t_0} \\
z_1^1 & z_1^2 & z_1^3 & z_1^4 \\
z_2^1 & z_2^2 & z_2^3 & z_2^4 \\
z_3^1 & z_3^2 & z_3^3 & z_3^4 \\
z_4^1 & z_4^2 & z_4^3 & z_4^4
\end{bmatrix}
\cdot
\begin{bmatrix}
Q^1 \\
Q^2 \\
Q^3 \\
Q^4
\end{bmatrix}
$$

where the first asset above is a risk-free savings deposit account. If \$1 is deposited at time t_0, $(1 + r_{t_0})$ can be earned next period without any risk of default. The r_{t_0} is the rate that is observed as of time t_0. Given the prices of actively traded insurance contracts C_i, we can easily calculate the time-t cost of forming the portfolio:

$$\text{cost} = z_T^1 \cdot C_1 + z_T^2 \cdot C_2 + z_T^3 \cdot C_3 + z_T^4 \cdot C_4$$

Suppose the S_t has the following payoffs in the states of the world $i = 1, \ldots, 4$:

$$\{z_T^1 = 10, z_T^2 = 1, z_T^3 = 14, z_T^4 = 16\}$$

Suppose we observe the following prices for the insurance contracts:

$$\{C_1 = 0.3, C_2 = 0.2, C_3 = 0.4, C_4 = 0.07\}$$

Then, the total cost of the insurance contracts purchased will be:

$$\text{cost} = 10 \cdot (0.3) + 1 \cdot (0.2) + 14 \cdot (0.4) + 16 \cdot (0.07) = 9.92$$

Hence, the current price of S_t should be equal to 9.92 as well.

EIGENVALUES AND EIGENVECTORS

Consider a square matrix $\mathbf{A}$ of order n and the set of all n-dimensional vectors. The matrix $\mathbf{A}$ is a linear operator on the space of vectors. This means that $\mathbf{A}$ operates on each vector producing another vector and that the following property holds:

$$\mathbf{A}(a\mathbf{x} + b\mathbf{y}) = a\mathbf{A}\mathbf{x} + b\mathbf{A}\mathbf{y}$$

Consider now the set of vectors $\mathbf{x}$ such that the following property holds:

$$\mathbf{A}\mathbf{x} = \lambda\mathbf{x}$$

Any vector such that the above property holds is called an **eigenvector** of the matrix $\mathbf{A}$ and the corresponding value of λ is called an **eigenvalue**.

To determine the eigenvectors of a matrix and the relative eigenvalues, consider that the equation $\mathbf{A}\mathbf{x} = \lambda\mathbf{x}$ can be written as follows:

$$(\mathbf{A} - \lambda\mathbf{I})\mathbf{x} = 0$$

which can, in turn, be written as a system of linear equations:

$$(\mathbf{A} - \lambda\mathbf{I})\mathbf{x} = \begin{bmatrix} a_{1,1} - \lambda & \cdot & a_{1,j} & \cdot & a_{1,n} \\ & \cdot & \cdot & \cdot & \\ a_{i,1} & \cdot & a_{i,i} - \lambda & \cdot & a_{i,n} \\ & \cdot & \cdot & \cdot & \\ a_{n,1} & \cdot & a_{n,j} & \cdot & a_{n,n} - \lambda \end{bmatrix} \begin{bmatrix} x_1 \\ \cdot \\ x_i \\ \cdot \\ x_n \end{bmatrix} = 0$$

This system of equations has nontrivial solutions only if the matrix $\mathbf{A} - \lambda\mathbf{I}$ is singular. To determine the eigenvectors and the eigenvalues of the matrix $\mathbf{A}$ we must therefore solve the equation

$$|\mathbf{A} - \lambda\mathbf{I}| = \begin{bmatrix} a_{1,1} - \lambda & \cdot & a_{1,j} & \cdot & a_{1,n} \\ & \cdot & \cdot & \cdot & \\ a_{i,1} & \cdot & a_{i,i} - \lambda & \cdot & a_{i,n} \\ & \cdot & \cdot & \cdot & \\ a_{n,1} & \cdot & a_{n,j} & \cdot & a_{n,n} - \lambda \end{bmatrix} = 0$$

The expansion of this determinant yields a polynomial $\phi(\lambda)$ of degree n known as the **characteristic polynomial** of the matrix $\mathbf{A}$. The equation

$\phi(\lambda) = 0$ is known as the **characteristic equation** of the matrix $\mathbf{A}$. In general, this equation will have n roots λ_s which are the eigenvalues of the matrix $\mathbf{A}$. To each of these eigenvalues corresponds a solution of the system of linear equations as illustrated below:

$$
\begin{bmatrix}
a_{1,1} - \lambda_s & \cdot & a_{1,j} & \cdot & a_{1,n} \\
 & \cdot & \cdot & \cdot & \\
a_{i,1} & \cdot & a_{i,i} - \lambda_s & \cdot & a_{i,n} \\
 & \cdot & \cdot & \cdot & \\
a_{n,1} & \cdot & a_{n,j} & \cdot & a_{n,n} - \lambda_s
\end{bmatrix}
\begin{bmatrix}
x_{1_s} \\
\cdot \\
x_{i_s} \\
\cdot \\
x_{n_s}
\end{bmatrix}
= 0
$$

Each solution represents the eigenvector $\mathbf{x}_s$ corresponding to the eigenvector λ_s.

DIAGONALIZATION AND SIMILARITY

Diagonal matrices are much easier to handle than fully populated matrices. It is therefore important to create diagonal matrices equivalent (in a sense to be precisely defined) to a given matrix. Consider two square matrices $\mathbf{A}$ and $\mathbf{B}$. The matrices $\mathbf{A}$ and $\mathbf{B}$ are called **similar** if there exists a nonsingular matrix $\mathbf{R}$ such that

$$\mathbf{B} = \mathbf{R}^{-1}\mathbf{A}\mathbf{R}$$

The following two theorems can be demonstrated:

Theorem 1. Two similar matrices have the same eigenvalues.

Theorem 2. If $\mathbf{y}_i$ is an eigenvector of the matrix $\mathbf{B} = \mathbf{R}^{-1}\mathbf{A}\mathbf{R}$ corresponding to the eigenvalue λ_i, then the vector $\mathbf{x}_i = \mathbf{R}\mathbf{y}_i$ is an eigenvector of the matrix $\mathbf{A}$ corresponding to the same eigenvalue λ_i.

A diagonal matrix of order n always has n linearly independent eigenvectors. Consequently, a square matrix of order n has n linearly independent eigenvectors if and only if it is similar to a diagonal matrix.

Suppose the square matrix of order n has n linearly independent eigenvectors $\mathbf{x}_i$ and n distinct eigenvalues λ_i. This is true, for instance, if $\mathbf{A}$ is a real, symmetric matrix of order n. Arrange the eigenvectors, which are column vectors, in a square matrix: $\mathbf{P} = \{\mathbf{x}_i\}$. It can be demonstrated that $\mathbf{P}^{-1}\mathbf{AP}$ is a diagonal matrix where the diagonal is made up of the eigenvalues:

$$\mathbf{P}^{-1}\mathbf{AP} = \begin{bmatrix} \lambda_1 & 0 & 0 & 0 & 0 \\ 0 & \cdot & 0 & 0 & 0 \\ 0 & 0 & \lambda_i & 0 & 0 \\ 0 & 0 & 0 & \cdot & 0 \\ 0 & 0 & 0 & 0 & \lambda_n \end{bmatrix}$$

SINGULAR VALUE DECOMPOSITION

Suppose that the $n \times m$ matrix $\mathbf{A}$ with $m \geq n$ has rank$(\mathbf{A}) = r > 0$. It can be demonstrated that there exists three matrices $\mathbf{U}, \mathbf{W}, \mathbf{V}$ such that the following decomposition, called **singular value decomposition**, holds:

$$\mathbf{A} = \mathbf{UWV}'$$

and such that $\mathbf{U}$ is $n \times r$ with $\mathbf{U}'\,\mathbf{U} = \mathbf{I}_r$; $\mathbf{W}$ is diagonal, with nonnegative diagonal elements; and $\mathbf{V}$ is $m \times r$ with $\mathbf{V}'\mathbf{V} = \mathbf{I}_r$.

KEY POINTS

- In representing and modeling economic and financial phenomena it is useful to consider ordered arrays of numbers as a single mathematical object.
- Ordered arrays of numbers are called vectors and matrices; vectors are a particular type of matrix.
- It is possible to consistently define operations on vectors and matrices including the multiplication of matrices by scalars, sum of matrices, product of matrices, and inversion of matrices.
- Determinants are numbers associated with square matrices defined as the sum of signed products of elements chosen from different rows and columns.
- A matrix can be inverted only if its determinant is not zero.

- The eigenvectors of a square matrix are those vectors that do not change direction when multiplied by the matrix.
- The column rank of a matrix is the maximum number of linearly independent column vectors of the matrix.
- The row rank of a matrix is the maximum number of linearly independent row vectors of the matrix.
- A matrix that has a rank as large as possible is said to have full rank; otherwise, the matrix is rank deficient.

CHAPTER 5

Probability

Basic Concepts

S tandard finance theory generally rules out the conditions that investors have about uncertainty vis-à-vis the probability distribution of asset returns. However, Frank Knight in his book *Risk, Uncertainty and Profit*, published in 1921, draws a distinction between risk and true uncertainty and argues that uncertainty is more common in the decision-making process. He points out that risk occurs where the future is unknown, however, the probability of all possible outcomes is known. Uncertainty occurs where the probability distribution is itself unknown. Knight's distinction between risk and uncertainty implies that risk is related to the objective distribution of return or the subjective distribution of return commonly agreed on by all investors, whereas uncertainty is related to the probability distribution unique to an individual investor. Probability theory is useful to understand and investigate the changes in prices, riskiness, and uncertainty about financial instruments. Probability theory is also useful to understand and investigate the changes in state variables, such as financial factors and macroeconomic fundamentals, that affect consumption and investment opportunities for investors. Using probability theory:

- One can examine the empirical return distribution of assets such as stocks, bonds, currencies, and commodities.
- One can estimate expected return and risk of assets.
- One can determine how expected prices of assets change from one economic state to another (e.g., moving from economic recessions to expansions or vice versa).

- One can come up with a better option pricing model than the standard Black-Scholes model if it is detected that real market asset returns significantly depart from the commonly used assumption of returns being normally distributed.
- One can come up with more accurate predictions of future financial market downturns.
- One can focus on the tail events and estimate downside risk measures of a portfolio or a trading position more precisely.

What you will learn after reading this chapter:

- How to interpret probability and how to represent uncertainty with mathematics.
- How to define probability as a mathematical axiomatic theory.
- How to define probability with space, sigma-algebra, and probability measure.
- The meaning and statistical use of random variables and random vectors.
- How to define distribution and density functions of random variables.
- The meaning and statistical use of stochastic processes.
- Probabilistic representation of financial markets.

INTRODUCTION

Probability is the standard mathematical representation of risk and uncertainty in finance. In this chapter and the next, we provide the fundamentals of probability theory. Before we delve into the topic of probability theory, we provide a brief and helpful description of its role in one of the key tasks in asset management: generating superior returns by producing realistic and reasonable return expectations and forecasts. Probability, however, is only part of the analytical toolkit needed to accomplish this task. When we cover optimization techniques in Chapter 7, we describe the prevailing theory for the selection of assets to include in a portfolio (i.e., the theory that tells investors how to construct an optimal portfolio). This theory of portfolio selection is the Markowitz mean-variance framework. It says that an investor's objective is to construct a portfolio of securities that has the largest expected return for a given level of risk as measured by the portfolio's variance. Another key measure in the Markowitz mean-variance framework is the covariance. These three measures used in the Markowitz mean-variance framework—expected return, variance, and covariance—are measures that draw from probability theory, and we will explain each one in this chapter. Of course, since investors do not know the true values of the securities' expected returns, variances, and covariances, these must be estimated or forecasted. This is where the various statistical estimation models that draw from the field of financial econometrics come into play.

The concept of **forecastability** rests on how one can forecast the future given the current state of knowledge. In probability theory, the state of knowledge on a given date is referred to as the information set known at that date. Forecasting is the relationship between the information set today and future events. The merits of security return forecasting are the subject of an ongoing debate. Because most of our knowledge is uncertain, forecasts are also uncertain.

Probability theory provides the conceptual tools to represent and measure the level of uncertainty. Basically, probability theory assigns a number—which we refer to as the "probability"—to every possible event. How this number, the probability, might be interpreted is explained in this chapter. Because we must rely on probability to understand the concepts of predictability and unpredictability, we will need other concepts covered in the next chapter: conditional probability, conditional expectation, independent and identically distributed random variables, white noise, and martingale. Conditional probability and conditional expectation are fundamental in the probabilistic description of financial markets.

REPRESENTING UNCERTAINTY WITH MATHEMATICS

Because we cannot build purely deterministic models of financial markets we need a mathematical representation of uncertainty. **Probability theory** is the mathematical description of uncertainty that presently enjoys the broadest diffusion. It is the paradigm of choice for mainstream finance theory. However, it is by no means the only way to describe uncertainty. Other mathematical paradigms for uncertainty include, for example, fuzzy measures.

Though probability as a mathematical axiomatic theory is well known, its interpretation is still the subject of debate. There are three basic interpretations of probability:

- Probability as "intensity of belief"[1]
- Probability as "relative frequency"[2]
- Probability as an axiomatic system[3]

The idea of probability as intensity of belief was introduced by John Maynard Keynes in his *Treatise on Probability*. In science as in our daily lives, we have beliefs that we cannot strictly prove but to which we attribute various degrees of likelihood. We judge not only the likelihood of individual events but also the plausibility of explanations. If we espouse probability as intensity of belief, probability theory is then a set of rules for making consistent probability statements. The obvious difficulty here is that one can judge only the consistency of probability reasoning, not its truth. Bayesian probability theory (which we will discuss later in the chapter) is based on the interpretation of probability as intensity of belief.

Probability as relative frequency is the standard interpretation of probability in the physical sciences. Essentially, it equates probability statements with statements about the frequency of events in large samples; an unlikely event is an event that occurs only a small number of times. The difficulty with this interpretation is that relative frequencies are themselves uncertain. If we accept a probability interpretation of reality, there is no way to leap to certainty. In the physical sciences, we usually deal with very large numbers— so large that nobody expects probabilities to deviate from their relative frequency. Nevertheless, the conceptual difficulty exists. As the present state of affairs might be a very unlikely one, probability statements can never be proved empirically.

The two interpretations of probability—as intensity of belief and as relative frequency—are therefore complementary. We make probability statements such as statements of relative frequency that are, ultimately, based on an *a priori* evaluation of probability insofar as we rule out, in practice, highly unlikely events. This is evident in most procedures of statistical estimation.

---

[1] Keynes, *Treatise on Probability* (London: Macmillan, 1921).

[2] Mises, *Wahrscheinlichkeitsrechnung, Statistik unt Wahrheit* (Vienna: Julius Spring, 1928). (English edition published in 1939, *Probability, Statistics and Truth*.)

[3] Kolmogorov, *Grundbegriffe der Wahrscheinlichkeitsrechnung* (Berlin: Springer, 1933). (English edition published in 1950, *Foundations of the Theory of Probability*.)

A **statistical estimate** is a rule to choose the probability scheme in which one has the greatest faith. In performing statistical estimation, one chooses the probabilistic model that yields the highest probability based on the observed sample. This is strictly evident in maximum likelihood estimates but it is implicit in every statistical estimate. Bayesian statistics allow one to complement such estimates with additional *a priori* probabilistic judgment.

The axiomatic theory of probability avoids the above problems by interpreting probability as an abstract mathematical quantity. Developed primarily by the Russian mathematician Andrei Kolmogorov, the axiomatic theory of probability eliminated the logical ambiguities that had plagued probabilistic reasoning prior to his work. The application of the axiomatic theory is, however, a matter of interpretation.

In financial economic theory, probability might have two different meanings: (1) as a descriptive concept and (2) as a determinant of the agent decision-making process. As a descriptive concept, probability is used in the sense of relative frequency, similar to its use in the physical sciences: The probability of an event is assumed to be approximately equal to the relative frequency of its occurrence in a large number of experiments. There is one difficulty with this interpretation, which is peculiar to economics: empirical data (i.e., financial and economic time series) have only one realization. Every estimate is made on a single time-evolving series. If stationarity (or a well-defined time process) is not assumed, performing statistical estimation is impossible.

PROBABILITY IN A NUTSHELL

In making probability statements, we must distinguish between outcomes and events. **Outcomes** are the possible results of an experiment or an observation, such as the price of a security at a given moment. However, probability statements are not made on outcomes but on **events**, which are sets of possible outcomes. Consider, for example, the probability that the price of a security be in a given range, say from $10 to $12, in a given period.

In a discrete probability model (i.e., a model based on a finite or at most a countable number of individual events), the distinction between outcomes and events is not essential as the probability of an event is the sum of the probabilities of its outcomes. If, as happens in practice, prices can vary by only one-hundredth of a dollar, there are only a countable number of possible prices and the probability of each event will be the sum of the individual probabilities of each admissible price.

However, the distinction between outcomes and events is essential when dealing with continuous probability models. In a continuous probability model, the probability of each individual outcome is zero though the probability of an event might be a finite number. For example, if we represent prices as continuous functions, the probability that a price assumes any particular real number is strictly zero, though the probability that prices fall in a given interval might be other than zero.

Probability theory is a set of rules for inferring the probability of an event from the probability of other events. The basic rules are surprisingly simple. The entire theory is based on a few simple assumptions. First, the universe of possible outcomes or measurements must be fixed. This is a conceptually important point. If we are dealing with the prices of an asset, the universe is all possible prices; if we are dealing with n assets, the universe is the set of all possible n-tuples of prices. If we want to link n asset prices with k economic quantities, the universe is all possible $(n + k)$-tuples made up of asset prices and values of economic quantities.

Second, as our objective is to interpret probability as relative frequencies (i.e., percentages), the scale of probability is set to the interval $[0,1]$. The maximum possible probability is one, which is the probability that any of the possible outcomes occurs. The probability that none of the outcomes occurs is 0. In continuous probability models, the converse is not true as there are nonempty sets of measure zero. In other words, in continuous probability models, a probability of one is not equal to certainty.

Third, and last, the probability of the union of disjoint events is the sum of the probabilities of individual events.

All statements of probability theory are logical consequences of these basic rules. The simplicity of the logical structure of probability theory might be deceptive. In fact, the practical difficulty of probability theory consists in the description of events. For instance, derivative contracts link in possibly complex ways the events of the underlying with the events of the derivative contract. Though the probabilistic "dynamics" of the underlying phenomena can be simple, expressing the links between all possible contingencies renders the subject mathematically complex.

Probability theory is based on the possibility of assigning a precise uncertainty index to each event. This is a stringent requirement that might be too strong in many instances. In a number of cases we are simply uncertain without being able to quantify uncertainty. It might also happen that we can quantify uncertainty for some but not all events. There are representations of uncertainty that drop the strict requirement of a precise uncertainty index assigned to each event.[4]

---

[4]Examples include fuzzy measures and the Dempster-Schafer theory of uncertainty. The latter representations of uncertainty have been widely used in artificial intelligence (AI) and engineering applications, but their use in economics and finance has so far been limited.

Let's now examine probability as the key representation of uncertainty, starting with a more formal account of probability theory.

OUTCOMES AND EVENTS

The axiomatic theory of probability is based on three fundamental concepts: (1) outcomes, (2) events, and (3) measure. The outcomes are the set of all possible results of an experiment or an observation. The set of all possible outcomes is often written as the set Ω. For instance, in the dice game a possible outcome is a pair of numbers, one for each face, such as $6 + 6$ or $3 + 2$. The space Ω is the set of all 36 possible outcomes.

Events are sets of outcomes. Continuing with the example of the dice game, a possible event is the set of all outcomes such that the sum of the numbers is 10. Probabilities are defined on events, not on outcomes. To render definitions consistent, events must be a class $\mathfrak{I}$ of subsets of Ω with the following properties:

Property 1. $\mathfrak{I}$ is not empty.

Property 2. If $A \in \mathfrak{I}$ then $A^C \in \mathfrak{I}$; A^C is the complement of A with respect to Ω, made up of all those elements of Ω that do not belong to A.

Property 3. If $A_i \in \mathfrak{I}$ for $i = 1, 2, \ldots$ then $\bigcup_{i=1}^{\infty} A_i \in \mathfrak{I}$.

Every such class is called a σ-**algebra**. Any class for which Property 3 is valid only for a finite number of sets is called an **algebra**.

Given a set Ω and a σ-algebra $\mathfrak{G}$ of subsets of Ω, any set $A \in \mathfrak{G}$ is said to be **measurable** with respect to $\mathfrak{G}$. The pair $(\Omega, \mathfrak{G})$ is said to be a **measurable space** (not to be confused with a measure space, defined later in this chapter). Consider a class $\mathfrak{G}$ of subsets of Ω and consider the smallest σ-algebra that contains $\mathfrak{G}$, defined as the intersection of all the σ-algebras that contain $\mathfrak{G}$. That σ-algebra is denoted by $\sigma\{\mathfrak{G}\}$ and is said to be the σ-algebra generated by $\mathfrak{G}$.

A particularly important space in probability is the **Euclidean space**. Consider first the real axis R (i.e., the Euclidean space R^1 in one dimension). Consider the collection formed by all intervals open to the left and closed to the right, for example, $(a, b]$. The σ-algebra generated by this set is called the 1-dimensional Borel σ-algebra and is denoted by $\mathfrak{B}$. The sets that belong to $\mathfrak{B}$ are called **Borel sets**.

Now consider the n-dimensional Euclidean space R^n, formed by n-tuples of real numbers. Consider the collection of all generalized rectangles open to the left and closed to the right, for example, $((a_1, b_1] \times \cdots \times (a_n, b_n])$. The σ-algebra generated by this collection is called the n-dimensional Borel

σ-algebra and is denoted by $\mathfrak{B}^n$. The sets that belong to $\mathfrak{B}^n$ are called n-dimensional Borel sets.

The above construction is not the only possible one. The $\mathfrak{B}^n$, for any value of n, can also be generated by open or closed sets. As we will see later in this chapter, $\mathfrak{B}^n$ is fundamental to defining random variables. It defines a class of subsets of the Euclidean space on which it is reasonable to impose a probability structure: the class of every subset would be too big while the class of, say, generalized rectangles would be too small. The $\mathfrak{B}^n$ is a sufficiently rich class.

PROBABILITY

Intuitively speaking, probability is a set function that associates to every event a number between 0 and 1. Probability is formally defined by a triple $(\Omega, \mathfrak{I}, P)$ called a **probability space,** where Ω is the set of all possible outcomes, $\mathfrak{I}$ the event σ-algebra, and P a probability measure.

A probability measure P is a set function from $\mathfrak{I}$ to R (the set of real numbers) that satisfies three conditions:

Condition 1. $0 \leq P(A)$, for all $A \in \mathfrak{I}$.

Condition 2. $P(\Omega) = 1$.

Condition 3. $P(\cup A_i) = \Sigma P(A_i)$ for every finite or countable collection of disjoint events $\{A_i\}$ such that $A_i \in \mathfrak{I}$.

$\mathfrak{I}$ does not have to be a σ-algebra. The definition of a probability space can be limited to algebras of events. However it is possible to demonstrate that a probability defined over an algebra of events $\aleph$ can be extended in a unique way to the σ-algebra generated by $\aleph$.

Two events are said to be independent if:

$$P(A \cap B) = P(A)P(B)$$

The (conditional) probability of event A given event B, written as $P(A|B)$, is defined as follows:

$$P(A|B) = \frac{P(A \cap B)}{P(B)}$$

It is possible to deduct from simple properties of set theory and from the disjoint additivity of probability that

$$P(A \cup B) = P(A) + P(B) - P(A \cap B) \leq P(A) + P(B)$$
$$P(A) = 1 - P(A^C)$$

Bayes' theorem is a rule that links conditional probabilities. It can be stated in the following way:

$$P(A|B) = \frac{P(A \cap B)}{P(B)} = \frac{P(A \cap B)P(A)}{P(B)P(A)} = P(B|A)\frac{P(A)}{P(B)}$$

Bayes' theorem allows one to recover the probability of the event A given B from the probability of the individual events A, B, and the probability of B given A.

Discrete probabilities are a special instance of probabilities. Defined over a finite or countable set of outcomes, discrete probabilities are nonzero over each outcome. The probability of an event is the sum of the probabilities of its outcomes. In the finite case, discrete probabilities are the usual combinatorial probabilities.

MEASURE

A **measure** is a set function defined over an algebra or σ-algebra of sets, denumerably additive, and such that it takes value zero on the empty set but can otherwise assume any positive value including, conventionally, an infinite value. A probability is thus a measure of total mass 1 (i.e., it takes value 1 on the set Ω).

A measure can be formally defined as a function $M(A)$ from an algebra or a σ-algebra $\Im$ to R (the set of real numbers) that satisfies the following three properties:

Property 1. $0 \leq M(A)$, for every $A \in \Im$.

Property 2. $M(\varnothing) = 0$.

Property 3. $M(\cup A_i) = \Sigma M(A_i)$ for every finite or countable collection of disjoint events $\{A_i\}$ such that $A_i \in \Im$.

If M is a measure defined over a σ-algebra $\Im$, the triple $(\Omega, \Im, M)$ is called a **measure space** (this term is not used if $\Im$ is an algebra). Recall that the pair $(\Omega, \Im)$ is a **measurable space** if $\Im$ is a σ-algebra. Measures in general, and not only probabilities, can be uniquely extended from an algebra to the generated σ-algebra.

RANDOM VARIABLES

Probability is a set function defined over a space of events; **random variables** transfer probability from the original space Ω into the space of real numbers.

Given a probability space $(\Omega, \mathfrak{J}, P)$, a random variable X is a function $X(\omega)$ defined over the set Ω that takes values in the set R of real numbers such that

$$(\omega: X(\omega) \leq x) \in \mathfrak{J}$$

for every real number x. In other words, the inverse image of any interval $(-\infty, x]$ is an event. It can be demonstrated that the inverse image of any Borel set is also an event.

A real-valued set function defined over Ω is said to be measurable with respect to a σ-algebra $\mathfrak{J}$ if the inverse image of any Borel set belongs to $\mathfrak{J}$. Random variables are real-valued measurable functions. A random variable that is measurable with respect to a σ-algebra cannot discriminate between events that are not in that σ-algebra. This is the primary reason why the abstract and rather difficult concept of measurability is important in probability theory. By restricting the set of events that can be identified by a random variable, measurability defines the "coarse graining" of information relative to that variable. A random variable X is said to generate $\mathfrak{G}$ if $\mathfrak{G}$ is the smallest σ-algebra in which it is measurable.

INTEGRALS

In Chapter 3 where we discussed integral calculus we defined the integral of a real-valued function on the real line. However, the notion of the integral can be generalized to a general measure space. Though a bit technical, these definitions are important in the context of probability theory.

For each measure M, the **integral** is a number that is associated to every integrable function f. It is defined in the following two steps:

Step 1. Suppose that f is a measurable, nonnegative function and consider a finite decomposition of the space Ω, that is to say a finite collection of disjoint subsets $A_i \subset \Omega$ whose union is Ω:

$$A_i \subset \Omega \text{ such that } A_i \cap A_j = \emptyset \text{ for } i \neq j \text{ and } \cup A_i = \Omega$$

Consider the sum

$$\sum_i \inf(f(\omega) : \omega \in A_i) M(A_i)$$

The integral

$$\int_\Omega f dM$$

is defined as the supremum, if it exists, of all these sums over all possible decompositions of Ω. Suppose that f is bounded and non-negative and $M(\Omega) < \infty$. Let's call

$$S_- = \sup\left(\sum_i {}^{(\inf_{\omega \in A_i} f(\omega)M(A_i))}\right)$$

the lower integral and

$$S^+ = \inf\left(\sum_i {}^{(\sup_{\omega \in A_i} f(\omega)M(A_i))}\right)$$

the upper integral. It can be demonstrated that if the integral exists then $S^+ = S_-$. It is possible to define the integral as the common value $S = S^+ = S_-$. This approach is the Darboux-Young approach to integration.[5]

Step 2. Given a measurable function f not necessarily nonnegative, consider its decomposition in its positive and negative parts $f = f^+ - f^-$. The integral of f is defined as the difference, if a difference exists, between the integrals of its positive and negative parts.

The integral can be defined not only on Ω but on any measurable set G. In order to define the integral over a measurable set G, consider the indicator function I_G, which assumes value 1 on each point of the set G and 0 elsewhere. Consider now the function $f \cdot I_G$. The integral over the set G is defined as

$$\int_G fdM = \int_\Omega f \cdot I_G dM$$

The integral $\int_G fdM$ is called the indefinite integral of f.

Given a σ-algebra $\mathfrak{I}$, suppose that G and M are two measures and that a function f exists such that for $A \in \mathfrak{I}$

$$G(A) = \int_A fdM$$

---

[5]See Billingsley, *Probability and Measure*, 2nd ed. (New York: John Wiley & Sons, 1985).

In this case G is said to have density f with respect to M.

The integrals in the sense of Riemann and in the sense of Lebesgue-Stieltjes (see Chapter 3) are special instances of this more general definition of the integral. Note that the Lebesgue-Stieltjes integral was defined in Chapter 3 in one dimension. Its definition can be extended to n-dimensional spaces. In particular, it is always possible to define the Lebesgue-Stieltjes integral with respect to a n-dimensional distribution function. We omit the definitions which are rather technical.[6]

Given a probability space $(\Omega, \Im, P)$ and a random variable X, the expected value of X is its integral with respect to the probability measure P

$$E[X] = \int_{\Omega} X \, dP$$

where integration is extended to the entire space.

DISTRIBUTIONS AND DISTRIBUTION FUNCTIONS

Given a probability space $(\Omega, \Im, P)$ and a random variable X, consider a set $A \in \mathcal{B}^1$. Recall that a random variable is a real-valued measurable function defined over the set of outcomes. Therefore, the inverse image of A, $X^{-1}(A)$ belongs to $\Im$ and has a well-defined probability $P(X^{-1}(A))$.

The measure P thus induces another measure on the real axis called **distribution** or **distribution law** of the random variable X given by $\mu_X(A) = P(X^{-1}(A))$. It is easy to see that this measure is a probability measure on the Borel sets. A random variable therefore transfers the probability originally defined over the space Ω to the set of real numbers.

The function F defined by $F(x) = P(X \leq x)$ for $x \in R$ is the **cumulative distribution function** (c.d.f.), or simply **distribution function** (d.f.), of the random variable X. Suppose that there is a function f such that

$$F(x) = \int_{-\infty}^{x} f \, dy$$

or $F'(x) = f(x)$, then the function f is called the **probability density function** of the random variable X.

---

[6] For details, see Chow and Teicher, *Probability Theory*, 2nd ed. (New York: Springer, 1988).

RANDOM VECTORS

After considering a single random variable, the next step is to consider not only one but a set of random variables referred to as **random vectors**. Random vectors are formed by n-tuples of random variables. Consider a probability space $(\Omega, \mathfrak{I}, P)$. A random variable is a measurable function from Ω to R^1; a random vector is a measurable function from Ω to R^n.

We can therefore write a random vector $\mathbf{X}$ as a vector-valued function

$$f(\omega) = [\, f_1(\omega)\, f_2(\omega) \cdots f_n(\omega)]$$

Measurability is defined with respect to the Borel σ-algebra $\mathfrak{B}^n$. It can be demonstrated that the function f is measurable $\mathfrak{I}$ if and only if each component function $\phi_i(\omega)$ is measurable $\mathfrak{I}$.

Conceptually, the key issue is to define joint probabilities (i.e., the probabilities that the n variables are in a given set). For example, consider the joint probability that the inflation rate is in a given interval *and* the economic growth rate in another given interval.

Consider the Borel σ-algebra $\mathfrak{B}^n$ on the real n-dimensional space R^n. It can be demonstrated that a random vector formed by n random variables X_i, $i = 1, 2, \ldots, n$ induces a probability measure over $\mathfrak{B}^n$. In fact, the set $(\omega \in \Omega : (X_1(\omega), X_2(\omega), \cdots, X_n(\omega)) \in H;\ H \in \mathfrak{B}^n) \in \mathfrak{I}$ (i.e., the inverse image of every set of the σ-algebra $\mathfrak{B}^n$ belongs to the σ-algebra $\mathfrak{I}$). It is therefore possible to induce over every set H that belongs to $\mathfrak{B}^n$ a probability measure, which is the joint probability of the n random variables X_i. The function

$$F(x_1, \cdots, x_n) = P(X_1 \leq x_1, \cdots, X_n \leq x_n)$$

where $x_i \in R$ is called the **n-dimensional cumulative distribution function** or simply **n-dimensional distribution function** (**c.d.f.** or **d.f.**). Suppose there exists a function $f(x_1, \ldots, x_n)$ for which the following relationship holds:

$$F(x_1, \cdots, x_n) = \int\limits_{-\infty}^{x_1} \cdots \int\limits_{-\infty}^{x_n} f(u_1, \cdots, u_n) du_1 \cdots du_n$$

The function $f(x_1, \ldots, x_n)$ is called the **n-dimensional probability density function** (**p.d.f.**) of the random vector X. Given a n-dimensional probability density function $f(x_1, \ldots, x_n)$, if we integrate with respect to all variables except the jth variable, we obtain the **marginal density** of that variable:

$$f_{X_j}(y) = \int\limits_{-\infty}^{\infty} \cdots \int\limits_{-\infty}^{\infty} f(u_1, \ldots, u_n) du_1 \cdot du_{j-1} du_{j+1} \cdot du_n$$

Given an n-dimensional d.f., we define the **marginal distribution function** with respect to the jth variable, $F_{xj}(y) = P(X_j \le y)$ as follows:

$$F_{xj}(y) = \lim_{\substack{x_i \to \infty \\ i \ne j}} F(x_1, \ldots, x_{j-1}, y, x_{j+1}, \ldots, x_n)$$

If the distribution admits a density we can also write

$$F_{X_j}(y) = \int\limits_{-\infty}^{y} f_{X_j}(u) du$$

These definitions can be extended to any number of variables. Given an n-dimensional p.d.f., if we integrate with respect to k variables $(x_{i_1}, \ldots, x_{i_k})$ over R^k, we obtain the marginal density functions with respect to the remaining variables. Marginal distribution functions with respect to any subset of variables can be defined taking the infinite limit with respect to all other variables.

Any d.f. $F_{X_j}(y)$ defines a Lebesgue-Stieltjes measure and a Lebesgue-Stieltjes integral. For example, as we have seen in Chapter 3 in the 1-dimensional case, the measure is defined by the differences $F_{X_j}(x_i) - F_{X_j}(x_{i-1})$. We can now write expectations in two different, and more useful, ways. In an earlier section in this chapter, given a probability space $(\Omega, \Im, P)$, we defined the expectation of a random variable X as the following integral

$$E[X] = \int\limits_{\Omega} X dP$$

Suppose now that the random variable X has a d.f. $F_X(u)$. It can be demonstrated that the following relationship holds:

$$E[X] = \int\limits_{\Omega} X dP = \int\limits_{-\infty}^{\infty} u dF_X(u)$$

where the last integral is intended in the sense of Riemann-Stieltjes. If, in addition, the d.f. $F_{X_j}(u)$ has a density $f_X(u) = F'_X(u)$, then we can write the expectation as follows:

$$E[X] = \int_{\Omega} X\,dP = \int_{-\infty}^{\infty} u\,dF_X(u) = \int_{-\infty}^{\infty} u f(u)\,du$$

where the last integral is intended in the sense of Riemann. More in general, given a measurable function g the following relationship holds:

$$E[g(X)] = \int_{-\infty}^{\infty} g(u)\,dF_X(u) = \int_{-\infty}^{\infty} g(u) f(u)\,du$$

This latter expression of expectation is the most widely used in practice.

In general, however, knowledge of the distributions and of distribution functions of each random variable is not sufficient to determine the joint probability distribution function. The joint distribution is determined by the marginal distributions plus a statistical concept known as a copula function.

Two random variables X, Y are said to be independent if

$$P(X \in A, \ Y \in B) = P(X \in A)P(Y \in B)$$

for all $A \in \mathcal{B}$, $B \in \mathcal{B}$. This definition generalizes in obvious ways to any number of variables and therefore to the components of a random vector. It can be shown that if the components of a random vector are independent, the joint probability distribution is the product of distributions. Therefore, if the variables $(X_1, \ldots, X_n)$ are all mutually independent, we can write the joint d.f. as a product of marginal distribution functions:

$$F(x_1, \cdots, x_n) = \prod_{j=1}^{n} F_{X_j}(x_j)$$

It can also be demonstrated that if a d.f. admits a joint p.d.f., the joint p.d.f. factorizes as follows:

$$f(x_1, \cdots, x_n) = \prod_{j=1}^{n} f_{X_j}(x_j)$$

Given the marginal p.d.f.'s, the joint d.f. can be recovered as follows:

$$
\begin{aligned}
F(x_1, \cdots, x_n) &= \int_{-\infty}^{x_1} \cdots \int_{-\infty}^{x_n} f(u_1, \cdots, u_n) du_1 \cdots du_n \\
&= \int_{-\infty}^{x_1} \cdots \int_{-\infty}^{x_n} \left[\prod_{j=1}^{n} f_{X_j}(u_j) \right] du_1 \cdots du_n \\
&= \prod_{j=1}^{n} \int_{-\infty}^{x_j} f_{X_j}(u_j) du_j \\
&= \prod_{j=1}^{n} F_{X_j}(x_j)
\end{aligned}
$$

STOCHASTIC PROCESSES

Given a probability space $(\Omega, \mathfrak{I}, P)$, a stochastic process is a parameterized collection of random variables $\{X_t\}$, $t \in [0, T]$ that are measurable with respect to $\mathfrak{I}$. The parameter t is often interpreted as time. The interval in which a stochastic process is defined might extend to infinity in both directions.

When it is necessary to emphasize the dependence of the random variable from both time t and the element ω, a stochastic process is explicitly written as a function of two variables: $X = X(t, \omega)$. Given ω, the function $X = X_t(\omega)$ is a function of time that is referred to as the **path** of the stochastic process.

The variable X might be a single random variable or a multidimensional random vector. A stochastic process is therefore a function $X = X(t, \omega)$ from the product space $[0, T] \times \Omega$ into the n-dimensional real space R^n. Because to each ω corresponds a time path of the process—in general formed by a set of functions $X = X_t(\omega)$—it is possible to identify the space Ω with a subset of the real functions defined over an interval $[0, T]$.

Let's now discuss how to represent a stochastic process $X = X(t, \omega)$ and the conditions of identity of two stochastic processes. As a stochastic process is a function of two variables, we can define equality as pointwise identity for each couple (t,ω). However, as processes are defined over probability spaces, pointwise identity is seldom used. It is more fruitful to define equality modulo sets of measure zero or equality with respect to probability distributions. In general, two random variables X,Y will be considered equal if the equality $X(\omega) = Y(\omega)$ holds for every ω with the exception of a set of probability zero. In this case, it is said that the equality holds almost everywhere (denoted *a.e.*).

A rather general (but not complete) representation is given by the finite dimensional probability distributions. Given any set of indices $t_1, \ldots, t_m$, consider the distributions

$$\mu_{t_1,\ldots,t_m}(H) = P\left[\left(X_{t1}, \ldots, X_{t_m}\right) \in H, \ H \in \mathcal{B}^n\right]$$

These probability measures are, for any choice of the t_i, the finite-dimensional joint probabilities of the process. They determine many, but not all, properties of a stochastic process. For example, the finite dimensional distributions of a Brownian motion do not determine whether or not the process paths are continuous.

In general, the various concepts of equality between stochastic processes can be described as follows:

Property 1. Two stochastic processes are weakly equivalent if they have the same finite-dimensional distributions. This is the weakest form of equality.

Property 2. The process $X = X(t,\omega)$ is said to be equivalent or to be a modification of the process $Y = Y(t,\omega)$ if, for all t,

$$P(X_t = Y_t) = 1$$

Property 3. The process $X = X(t,\omega)$ is said to be strongly equivalent to or indistinguishable from the process $Y = Y(t,\omega)$ if

$$P(X_t = Y_t, \text{ for all } t) = 1$$

Property 3 implies Property 2, which in turn implies Property 1. Implications do not hold in the opposite direction. Two processes having the same finite distributions might have completely different paths. However, it is possible to demonstrate that if one assumes that paths are continuous functions of time, Properties 2 and 3 become equivalent.

PROBABILISTIC REPRESENTATION OF FINANCIAL MARKETS

We are now in the position to summarize the probabilistic representation of financial markets. From a financial point of view, an **asset** is a contract which gives the right to receive a distribution of future cash flows. In the case of common stock, the stream of cash flows will be uncertain. It includes the common stock dividends and the proceeds of the eventual liquidation of the firm. A **debt instrument** is a contract that gives its owner the right to receive periodic interest payments and the repayment of the principal by the maturity date. Except in the case of debt instruments of governments whose risk of default is perceived as extremely low, payments are uncertain as the issuing entity might default.

Suppose that all payments are made at the trading dates and that no transactions take place between trading dates. Let's assume that all assets are traded (i.e., exchanged in the market) at either discrete fixed dates, variable dates or continuously. At each trading date there is a market price for each asset. Each asset is therefore modeled with two time series, a series of market prices and a series of cash flows. As both series are subject to uncertainty, cash flows and prices are time-dependent random variables (i.e., they are stochastic processes). The time dependence of random variables in this probabilistic setting is a delicate question and will be examined shortly.

Following Kenneth Arrow[7] and using a framework now standard, the economy and the financial markets in a situation of uncertainty are described with the following basic concepts:

- It is assumed that the economy is in one of the states of a probability space $(\Omega, \Im, P)$.
- Every security is described by two stochastic processes formed by two time-dependent random variables $S_t(\omega)$ and $d_t(\omega)$ representing prices and cash flows of the asset.

---

[7]Arrow, "The Role of Securities in the Optimal Allocation of Risk Bearing," *Review of Economic Studies* 32, no. 2 (1964): 91–96.

This representation is completely general and is not linked to the assumption that the space of states is finite.

INFORMATION STRUCTURES

Let's now turn our attention to the question of time. The previous discussion considered a space formed by states in an abstract sense. We must now introduce an appropriate representation of time as well as rules that describe the evolution of information, that is, **information propagation**, over time. The concepts of information and information propagation are fundamental in economics and finance theory.

The concept of information in finance is different from both the intuitive notion of information and that of information theory in which information is a quantitative measure related to the *a priori* probability of messages.[8] In our context, information means the (progressive) revelation of the set of events to which the current state of the economy belongs. Though somewhat technical, this concept of information sheds light on the probabilistic structure of finance theory. The point is the following. Assets are represented by stochastic processes, that is, time-dependent random variables. However, the probabilistic states on which these random variables are defined represent entire histories of the economy. To embed time into the probabilistic structure of states in a coherent way calls for information structures and filtrations (a concept we explain in the next section).

Recall that it is assumed that the economy is in one of many possible states and that there is uncertainty on the state that has been realized. Consider a time period of the economy. At the beginning of the period, there is complete uncertainty on the state of the economy (i.e., there is complete uncertainty on what path the economy will take). Different events have different probabilities, but there is no certainty. As time passes, uncertainty is reduced as the number of states to which the economy can belong is progressively reduced. Intuitively, revelation of information means the progressive reduction of the number of possible states; at the end of the period, the realized state is fully revealed. In continuous time and continuous states, the number of events is infinite at each instant. Thus its cardinality remains the same. We cannot properly say that the number of events shrinks. A more formal definition is required.

---

[8] There is indeed a deep link between information theory and econometrics embodied in concepts such as the Fisher Information Matrix.

The progressive reduction of the set of possible states is formally expressed in the concepts of information structure and filtration. Let's start with **information structures**. Information structures apply only to discrete probabilities defined over a discrete set of states. At the initial instant T_0, there is complete uncertainty on the state of the economy; the actual state is known only to belong to the largest possible event (that is, the entire space Ω). At the following instant T_1, assuming that instants are discrete, the states are separated into a **partition**, a partition being a denumerable class of disjoint sets whose union is the space itself. The actual state belongs to one of the sets of the partitions. The revelation of information consists in ruling out all sets but one. For all the states of each partition, and only for these, random variables assume the same values.

Suppose, to exemplify, that only two assets exist in the economy and that each can assume only two possible prices and pay only two possible cash flows. At every moment there are 16 possible price-cash flow combinations. We can thus see that at the moment T_1 all the states are partitioned into 16 sets, each containing only one state. Each partition includes all the states that have a given set of prices and cash distributions at the moment T_1. The same reasoning can be applied to each instant. The evolution of information can thus be represented by a tree structure in which every path represents a state and every point a partition. Obviously the tree structure does not have to develop as symmetrically as in the above example; the tree might have a very generic structure of branches.

FILTRATION

The concept of information structure based on partitions provides a rather intuitive representation of the propagation of information through a tree of progressively finer partitions. However, this structure is not sufficient to describe the propagation of information in a general probabilistic context. In fact, the set of possible events is much richer than the set of partitions. It is therefore necessary to identify not only partitions but also a structure of events. The structure of events used to define the propagation of information is called a **filtration**. In the discrete case, however, the two concepts—information structure and filtration—are equivalent.

The concept of filtration is based on identifying all events that are known at any given instant. It is assumed that it is possible to associate to each trading moment t a σ-algebra of events $\Im_t \subset \Im$ formed by all events that are known prior to or at time t. It is assumed that events are never "forgotten," that is, that $\Im_t \subset \Im_s$, if $t < s$. An ordering of time is thus created. This ordering is formed by an increasing sequence of σ-algebras, each associated to the time at which all its events are known. This sequence is a filtration. Indicated as $\{\mathfrak{I}_t\}$, a filtration is therefore an increasing sequence of all σ-algebras $\mathfrak{I}_t$, each associated to an instant t.

In the finite case, it is possible to create a mutual correspondence between filtrations and information structures. In fact, given an information structure, it is possible to associate to each partition the algebra generated by the same partition. Observe that a tree information structure is formed by partitions that create increasing refinement: By going from one instant to the next, every set of the partition is decomposed. One can then conclude that the algebras generated by an information structure form a filtration.

On the other hand, given a filtration $\{\mathfrak{I}_t\}$, it is possible to associate a partition to each $\mathfrak{I}_t$. In fact, given any element that belongs to Ω, consider any other element that belongs to Ω such that, for each set of $\mathfrak{I}_t$, both either belong to or are outside this set. It is easy to see that classes of equivalence are thus formed, that these create a partition, and that the algebra generated by each such partition is precisely the $\mathfrak{I}_t$ that has generated the partition.

A stochastic process is said to be adapted to the filtration $\{\mathfrak{I}_t\}$ if the variable X_t is measurable with respect to the σ-algebra $\mathfrak{I}_t$. It is assumed that the price and cash distribution processes $S_t(\omega)$ and $d_t(\omega)$ of every asset are adapted to $\{\mathfrak{I}_t\}$. This means that, for each t, no measurement of any price or cash distribution variable can identify events not included in the respective algebra or σ-algebra. Every random variable is a partial image of the set of states seen from a given point of view and at a given moment.

The concepts of filtration and of processes adapted to a filtration are fundamental. They ensure that information is revealed without anticipation. Consider the economy and associate at every instant a partition and an algebra generated by the partition. Every random variable defined at that moment assumes a value constant on each set of the partition. The knowledge of the realized values of the random variables does not allow identifying sets of events finer than partitions.

One might well ask: Why introduce the complex structure of σ-algebras as opposed to simply defining random variables? The point is that, from a logical point of view, the primitive concept is that of states and events. The evolution of time has to be defined on the primitive structure—it cannot simply be imposed on random variables. In practice, filtrations become an important concept when dealing with conditional probabilities in a continuous environment. As the probability that a continuous random variable assumes a specific value is zero, the definition of conditional probabilities requires the machinery of filtration.

KEY POINTS

- Probability is a set function defined over a class of events where events are sets of possible outcomes of an experiment.
- A probability space is a triple formed by a set of outcomes, a σ-algebra of events, and a probability measure.
- A random variable is a real-valued function defined over the set of outcomes such that the inverse image of any interval is an event.
- n-dimensional random vectors are functions from the set of outcomes into the n-dimensional Euclidean space with the property that the inverse image of n-dimensional generalized rectangles is an event.
- Stochastic processes are time-dependent random variables.
- An information structure is a collection of partitions of events associated to each instant of time that become progressively finer with the evolution of time.
- A filtration is an increasing collection of σ-algebras associated to each instant of time.
- The states of the economy, intended as full histories of the economy, are represented as a probability space.
- The revelation of information with time is represented by information structures or filtrations.
- Prices and other financial quantities are represented by adapted stochastic processes.

CHAPTER 6

Probability

Random Variables and Expectations

The rapid globalization of financial and product markets, innovations in the design of derivative instruments, and the spectacular investor losses associated with derivatives over the past two decades have made financial institutions recognize the growing importance of risk management. A primary tool for financial risk assessment is the value-at-risk (VaR) measure, which is defined as the potential loss in value a portfolio of risky assets over a certain holding period at a given confidence level (probability). The use of VaR and its variants in risk management has exploded over the past decade because of its endorsement by bank regulators. Financial institutions now routinely use VaR techniques in managing their trading risk. Many implementations of VaR assume that asset returns are normally distributed. This assumption simplifies the computation of VaR considerably. However, it is inconsistent with the empirical evidence of asset returns, which finds that the distribution of asset returns is skewed and fat tailed. This implies that extreme events are much more likely to occur in practice than would be predicted by the symmetric thinner-tailed normal distribution. This also suggests that the normality assumption can produce VaR numbers that are inappropriate measures of the true risk faced by financial institutions. In addition to departures from normality, there is substantial evidence for time-varying probability distributions suggesting dynamic modeling of conditional mean, volatility, and higher-order moments. Under these conditions, an alternative approach that approximates the tail areas asymptotically is more appropriate than imposing an explicit functional form like the normal or lognormal on the distribution. The traditional VaR models estimate the potential loss of an institution under normal market conditions. Therefore, the standard VaR measures cannot be used during highly volatile periods corresponding to financial crises. The concepts of random variables and expectations discussed in this chapter can be used as follows:

- One can introduce conditional time-varying measures of downside risk that provide good predictions of catastrophic market risks during extraordinary periods.
- One can estimate time-varying conditional expected returns and volatilities of assets such as stocks, bonds, currencies, and commodities.
- One can introduce a new asset allocation framework in the conditional mean—a conditional VaR framework that produces optimal portfolio weights leading to higher risk-adjusted portfolio returns during economic downturns.
- One can compare the relative performance of static versus dynamic asset allocation models that take into account time-series variation in the probability distribution of asset returns.
- One can come up with future forecasts of the time-varying mean, variance, and correlation measures.
- One can introduce a more accurate option pricing model since the discrete-time stochastic processes of underlying assets can be modeled more accurately with the time-varying skewed fat-tailed probability distributions.

What you will learn after reading this chapter:

- What is a conditional probability.
- How to describe financial markets with conditional probabilities and conditional expectations.
- The meaning and statistical use of distributional moments and correlations.
- What is meant by an independent and identically distributed sequence.

- The problems with the correlation measure.
- How the copula function provides an alternative to the correlation.
- What is meant by convergence in probability theory.
- How to approximate the tails of a probability distribution using the Cornish-Fisher expansion and Hermite polynomials.
- What the normal or Gaussian distribution is.
- What a regression function is.
- What is meant by the tail of a distribution
- What is meant by fat-tailed and light-tailed distributions.
- What are the classes of fat-tailed distributions.
- What are the subexpontial, Pareto, and stable distributions.

INTRODUCTION

In the previous chapter, we provided an introduction to probability theory, setting forth the conceptual tools to represent and measure the level of uncertainty. In this chapter, we cover the topics of conditional probability, conditional expectation, independent and identically distributed random variables, white noise, and martingale. Conditional probability and conditional expectation are fundamental in the probabilistic description of financial markets. A conditional probability of some random variable X is the probability for X given a particular value for another random variable Y is known. Similarly, a conditional probability distribution can be determined. For the conditional probability distribution, an expected value can be computed and is referred to as a conditional expected value or conditional mean or, more commonly, a conditional expectation. The statistical concept of independent and identically distributed variables means two conditions about probability distributions for random variables. First consider "independent." This means if we have a time series for some random variable, then at each time the random variable has a probability distribution. By "independently distributed," it is meant that the probability distributions remain the same regardless of the history of past values for the random variable. "Identically" distributed means that all returns have the same distribution in every time period. These two conditions entail that, over time, the mean and the variance do not change from period to period. In the parlance of the statistician, we have a stationary time-series process.

CONDITIONAL PROBABILITY AND CONDITIONAL EXPECTATION

Conditional probabilities and conditional averages are fundamental in the stochastic description of financial markets. For instance, one is generally interested in the probability distribution of the price of an asset at some date given its price at an earlier date. The widely used regression models are an example of conditional expectation models.

The **conditional probability** of event A given event B was defined in the previous chapter as

$$P(A|B) = \frac{P(A \cap B)}{P(B)}$$

This simple definition cannot be used in the context of continuous random variables because the conditioning event (i.e., one variable assuming a given value) has probability zero. To avoid this problem, we condition on σ-algebras and not on single zero-probability events. In general, as each instant is characterized by a σ-algebra $\mathfrak{J}_t$, the conditioning elements are the $\mathfrak{J}_t$.

The general definition of conditional expectation is the following. Consider a probability space $(\Omega, \mathfrak{J}, P)$ and a σ-algebra $\mathfrak{G}$ contained in $\mathfrak{J}$ and suppose that X is an integrable random variable on $(\Omega, \mathfrak{J}, P)$. We define the conditional expectation of X with respect to $\mathfrak{G}$, written as $E[X \mid \mathfrak{G}]$, as a random variable measurable with respect to $\mathfrak{G}$ such that

$$\int_G E[X|\mathfrak{G}]dP = \int_G XdP$$

for every set $G \in \mathfrak{G}$. In other words, the **conditional expectation** is a random variable whose average on every event that belongs to $\mathfrak{G}$ is equal to the average of X over those same events, but it is $\mathfrak{G}$-measurable while X is not. It is possible to demonstrate that such variables exist and are unique up to a set of measure zero.

Econometric models usually condition a random variable given another variable. In the previous framework, conditioning one random variable X with respect to another random variable Y means conditioning X given $\sigma\{Y\}$ (i.e., given the σ-algebra generated by Y). Thus $E[X \mid Y]$ means $E[X \mid \sigma\{Y\}]$.

This notion might seem to be abstract and to miss a key aspect of conditioning: intuitively, conditional expectation is a function of the conditioning variable. For example, given a stochastic price process, X_t, one would like to visualize conditional expectation $E[X_t \mid X_s], s < t$ as a **function** of X_s that yields the expected price at a future date given the present price. This intuition is not wrong insofar as the conditional expectation $E[X \mid Y]$ of X given Y is a random variable function of Y. For example, a regression function is a function that yields the conditional expectation.

However, we need to specify how conditional expectations are formed, given that the usual conditional probabilities cannot be applied as the conditioning event has probability zero. Here is where the above definition comes into play. The conditional expectation of a variable X given a variable Y is defined in full generality as a variable that is measurable with respect to the σ-algebra $\sigma(Y)$ generated by the conditioning variable Y and has the same expected value of Y on each set of $\sigma(Y)$. Later in this section we will see how conditional expectations can be expressed in terms of the joint p.d.f. of the conditioning and conditioned variables.

One can define conditional probabilities starting from the concept of conditional expectations. Consider a probability space $(\Omega, \Im, P)$, a sub-σ-algebra $\mathfrak{G}$ of $\Im$, and two events $A \in \Im$, $B \in \Im$. If I_A, I_B are the indicator functions of the sets A, B (the indicator function of a set assumes value 1 on the set, 0 elsewhere), we can define conditional probabilities of the event A, respectively, given $\mathfrak{G}$ or given the event B as

$$P(A|\mathfrak{G}) = E[I_A|\mathfrak{G}] \quad P(A|B) = E[I_A|I_B]$$

Using these definitions, it is possible to demonstrate that given two random variables X and Y with joint density $f(x,y)$, the conditional density of X given Y is

$$f(x|y) = \frac{f(x, y)}{f_Y(y)}$$

where the marginal density, defined as

$$f_Y(y) = \int\limits_{-\infty}^{\infty} f(x, y)dx$$

is assumed to be strictly positive.

In the discrete case, the conditional expectation is a random variable that takes a constant value over the sets of the finite partition associated to $\Im_t$. Its value for each element of Ω is defined by the classical concept of conditional probability. Conditional expectation is simply the average over a partition assuming the classical conditional probabilities.

An important econometric concept related to conditional expectations is that of a **martingale**. Given a probability space $(\Omega,\Im,P)$ and a filtration $\{\Im_t\}$, a sequence of $\Im_i$-measurable random variables X_i is called a martingale if the following condition holds:

$$E[X_{i+1}|\Im_i] = X_i$$

A martingale translates the idea of a "fair game" as the expected value of the variable at the next period is equal to the present value of the same variable.

MOMENTS AND CORRELATION

If X is a random variable on a probability space $(\Omega,\Im,P)$, the quantity $E[|X|^p]$, $p > 0$ is called the **pth absolute moment** of X. If k is any positive integer, $E[X^k]$, if it exists, is called the **kth moment**. In the general case of a probability measure P we can therefore write:

- $E[|X|^p] = \int_\Omega |X|^p \, dP, p > 0$, is the pth absolute moment.

- $E[X^k] = \int_\Omega X^k \, dP$, if it exists for k positive integer, is the kth moment.

In the case of discrete probabilities p_i, $\Sigma p_i = 1$, the above expressions become

$$E[|X|^p] = \sum |x_i|^p p_i$$

and

$$E[X^k] = \sum x_i^k p_i$$

respectively. If the variable X is continuous and has a density $p(x)$ such that

$$\int_{-\infty}^{\infty} p(x)dx = 1$$

we can write

$$E[|X|^p] = \int_{-\infty}^{\infty} |x|^p p(x)dx$$

and

$$E[X^k] = \int_{-\infty}^{\infty} x^k p(x)dx$$

respectively.

The centered moments are the moments of the fluctuations of the variables around its mean. For example, the **variance** of a variable X is defined as the centered moment of second order:

$$\text{var}(X) = \sigma_x^2 = \sigma^2(X) = E[(X - \bar{X})^2]$$
$$= \int_{-\infty}^{\infty} (x - \bar{X})^2 p(x)dx = \int_{-\infty}^{\infty} x^2 p(x)dx - \left[\int_{-\infty}^{\infty} xp(x)dx \right]^2$$

where $\bar{X} = E[X]$.

The positive square root of the variance, σ_x is called the **standard deviation** of the variable.

We can now define the covariance and the correlation coefficient of a variable. **Correlation** is a quantitative measure of the strength of the dependence between two variables. Intuitively, two variables are dependent if they move together. If they move together, they will be above or below their respective means in the same state. Therefore, in this case, the product of their respective deviations from the means will have a positive mean. We call this mean the **covariance** of the two variables.

The covariance divided by the product of the standard deviations is a dimensionless number called the **correlation coefficient**.

Given two random variables X, Y with finite expected values and finite variances, we can write the following definitions:

- $\text{cov}(X, Y) = \sigma_{X,Y} = E[(X - \bar{X})(Y - \bar{Y})]$ is the covariance of X, Y.
- $\rho_{X,Y} = \frac{\sigma_{X,Y}}{\sigma_X \sigma_Y}$ is the correlation coefficient of X, Y.

The correlation coefficient can assume values in the interval $[-1, 1]$. If two variables X, Y are independent, their correlation coefficient vanishes.

However, uncorrelated variables, that is, variables whose correlation coefficient is zero, are not necessarily independent.

It can be demonstrated that the following property of variances holds:

$$\text{var}\left(\sum_i X_i\right) = \sum_i \text{var}(X_i) + \sum_{i \neq j} \text{cov}(X_i, X_j)$$

Further, it can be demonstrated that the following properties hold:

$$\sigma_{X,Y} = E[XY] - E[X]E[Y]$$

$$\sigma_{X,Y} = \sigma_{Y,X}$$

$$\sigma_{aX,bY} = ab\sigma_{Y,X}$$

$$\sigma_{X+Y,Z} = \sigma_{X,Z} + \sigma_{Y,Z}$$

$$\text{cov}\left(\sum_i a_i X_i, \sum_i b_j Y_j\right) = \sum_i \sum_j a_i b_j \, \text{cov}(X_i, Y_j)$$

COPULA FUNCTIONS

Understanding dependences or functional links between variables is a key theme of financial econometrics. In general terms, functional dependences are represented by dynamic models. Many important models are linear models whose coefficients are correlation coefficients. In many instances, in particular in risk management, it is important to arrive at a quantitative measure of the strength of dependencies.

The correlation coefficient provides such a measure. In many instances, however, the correlation coefficient might be misleading. In particular, there are cases of nonlinear dependencies that result in a zero correlation coefficient. Moreover, the correlation cannot explain joint extreme events, since it can deal only with linear dependencies. From the point of view of risk management this situation is particularly dangerous as it leads to substantially underestimated risk.

Different measures of dependence have been proposed, in particular **copula functions**. We will give only a brief introduction to copula functions.[1] Copula functions[2] are based on Sklar's Theorem. Sklar demonstrated[3] that any joint probability distribution can be written as a functional link, i.e., a copula function, between its marginal distributions. Let's suppose that $F(x_1, x_2, \ldots, x_n)$ is a joint multivariate distribution function with marginal distribution functions $F_1(x_1), F_2(x_2), \ldots, F_n(x_n)$. Then there is a copula function C such that the following relationship holds:

$$F(x_1, x_2, \ldots, x_n) = C[F_1(x_1), F_2(x_2), \ldots, F_n(x_n)]$$

The joint probability distribution contains all the information related to the co-movement of the variables. The copula function allows one to capture this information in a synthetic way as a link between marginal distributions. The concept of copula functions is used in risk modeling. There are many types of bivariate copula function based on the assumption about the distribution of the two variables. Probably the one most commonly used is the Gaussian copula model where both variables are assumed to follow a normal distribution. However, the global financial crisis that began in the summer of 2007 highlighted the failure of this copula model in measuring dependencies for structured products known as collateralized debt obligations.[4] The realization was that a copula model that accounted for extreme values or fat tails (discussed later in this chapter) would be more suitable in financial modeling. In practice, the alternative to the normal copula model that is used is the Student t-copula model. When the copula approach is applied to

---

[1]The interested reader might consult the following reference: P. Embrechts, F. Lindskog, and A. McNeil, "Modelling Dependence with Copulas and Applications to Risk Management," Chapter 8 in S.T. Rachev (ed.), *Handbook of Heavy Tailed Distributions in Finance* (Amsterdam: North Holland, 2003). Patton [37] reviews the use of copulas in econometric modeling.

[2]According to Cassell's *Latin Dictionary*, in Latin, "copula" is a noun that means a link, a tie, or a bond.

[3]A. Sklar, "Random Variables, Joint Distribution Functions and Copulas," *Kybernetika* 9 (1973), pp. 449–460.

[4]In fact, in one article, the author writes that the "Gaussian copula formula will go down in history as instrumental in causing the unfathomable losses that brought the world financial system to its knees." See F. Salmon, "Recipe for Disaster: The Formula That Killed Wall Street," Wired Magazine, February 23, 2009. (http://www.wired.com/techbiz/it/magazine/17-03/wp_quant?currentPage=all) The use of the normal copula function for the risk assessment of collateralized debt obligations was in D. Li, "On Default Correlation: A Copula Function Approach," Journal of Fixed Income 9 (2001), pp. 43–54.

the more than two variables (i.e., the multivariate copula), there have been several models suggested for dealing with tail risk behavior.[5] Despite the criticism regarding the misapplication of the normal copula function in finance, the advantages of the copula approach it that it can (1) capture non-linear dependence, (2) quantify dependence for fat-tail distributions, and (3) be used to investigate asymptotic properties of dependence structures. In practice for financial modeling, the copula approach involves the following two steps: identifying the marginal distributions and then determining the most suitable copula function to represent the dependence structure.

SEQUENCES OF RANDOM VARIABLES

Consider a probability space $(\Omega, \Im, P)$. A sequence of random variables is an infinite family of random variables X_i on $(\Omega, \Im, P)$ indexed by integer numbers: $i = 0, 1, 2, \ldots, n \ldots$ If the sequence extends to infinity in both directions, it is indexed by positive and negative integers: $i = \ldots, -n, \ldots, 0, 1, 2, \ldots, n \ldots$.

A sequence of random variables can **converge** to a **limit random variable**. Several different notions of the limit of a sequence of random variables can be defined. The simplest definition of convergence is that of pointwise convergence. A sequence of random variables X_i, $i \geq 1$ on $(\Omega, \Im, P)$, is said to **converge almost surely to a random variable** X, denoted

$$X_i \overset{a.s.}{\to} X$$

if the following relationship holds:

$$P\{\omega : \lim_{i \to \infty} X_i(\omega) = X(\omega)\} = 1$$

In other words, a sequence of random variables converges almost surely to a random variable X if the sequence of real numbers $X_i(\omega)$ converges to $X(\omega)$ for all ω except a set of measure zero.

A sequence of random variables X_i, $i \geq 1$ on $(\Omega, \Im, P)$, is said to **converge in mean of order p to a random variable** X if

$$\lim_{i \to \infty} E[|X_i(\omega) - X(\omega)|^p] = 0$$

---

[5] See H. Joe, Multivariate Models and Dependence Concepts (London: Chapman and Hall, 1997).

provided that all expectations exist. Convergence in mean of order one and two are called convergence in mean and convergence in mean square, respectively.

A weaker concept of convergence is that of convergence in probability. A sequence of random variables X_i, $i \geq 1$ on $(\Omega, \mathfrak{J}, P)$, is said to **converge in probability to a random variable** X, denoted

$$X_i \xrightarrow{P} X$$

if the following relationship holds:

$$\lim_{i \to \infty} P\{\omega : |X_i(\omega) - X(\omega)| \leq \varepsilon\} = 1, \ \forall \varepsilon > 0$$

It can be demonstrated that if a sequence converges almost surely then it also convergences in probability while the converse is not generally true. It can also be demonstrated that if a sequence converges in mean of order $p > 0$, then it also convergences in probability while the converse is not generally true.

A sequence of random variables X_i, $i \geq 1$ on $(\Omega, \mathfrak{J}, P)$ with distribution functions F_{X_i} is said to **converge in distribution to a random variable** X with distribution function F_X, denoted

$$X_i \xrightarrow{d} X$$

if

$$\lim_{i \to \infty} F_{X_i}(x) = F_X(x), \ x \in C$$

where C is the set of points where all the functions F_{X_i} and F_X are continuous.

It can be demonstrated that if a sequence converges almost surely (and thus converges in probability) it also converges in distribution while the converse is not true in general.

INDEPENDENT AND IDENTICALLY DISTRIBUTED SEQUENCES

Consider a probability space $(\Omega, \mathfrak{J}, P)$. A sequence of random variables X_i on $(\Omega, \mathfrak{J}, P)$ is called a sequence of **independent and identically distributed** (IID) **sequence** if the variables X_i have all the same distribution and are all mutually independent. An IID sequence is the strongest form of white noise: it embodies the notion of a completely random sequence of variables. Note that in many applications white noise is defined as a sequence of uncorrelated variables. This is a weaker definition as an uncorrelated sequence might be forecastable.

An IID sequence is completely unforecastable in the sense that the past does not influence the present or the future in any possible sense. In an IID sequence all conditional distributions are identical to unconditional distributions. Note, however, that an IID sequence presents a simple form of reversion to the mean. In fact, suppose that a sequence X_i assumes at a given time t a value larger than the common mean of all variables: $X_t > E[X]$. By definition of mean it is more likely that X_t be followed by a smaller value: $P(X_{t+1} < X_t) > P(X_{t+1} > X_t)$.

Note that this type of mean reversion does not imply forecastability as the probability distribution of asset returns at time $t + 1$ is independent from the distribution at time t.

SUM OF VARIABLES

Given two random variables $X(\omega)$, $Y(\omega)$ on the same probability space $(\Omega, \Im, P)$, the **sum of variables** $Z(\omega) = X(\omega) + Y(\omega)$ is another random variable. The sum associates to each state ω a value $Z(\omega)$ equal to the sum of the values taken by the two variables X, Y. Let's suppose that the two variables $X(\omega)$, $Y(\omega)$ have a joint density $p(x,y)$ and marginal densities $p_X(x)$ and $p_Y(x)$, respectively. Let's call H the cumulative distribution of the variable Z. The following relationship holds:

$$H(u) = P[Z(\omega) \leq u] = \int\int_A p(x, y)dxdy$$

$$A = \{y \leq -x + u\}$$

In other words, the probability that the sum $X + Y$ be less than or equal to a real number u is given by the integral of the joint probability distribution function in the region A. The region A can be described as the region of the x,y plane below the straight line $y = -x + u$.

If we assume that the two variables are independent, then the distribution of the sum admits a simple representation. In fact, under the assumption of independence, the joint density is the product of the marginal densities: $p(x,y) = p_X(x)p_Y(x)$. Therefore, we can write

$$H(u) = P[Z(\omega) \le u] = \int\int_A p(x, y)dxdy = \int_{-\infty}^{\infty} \left\{ \int_{-\infty}^{u-y} p_X(x)dx \right\} p_Y(y)dy$$

We can now use a property of integral called the **Leibnitz rule**, which allows one to write the following relationship:

$$\frac{dH}{du} = p_Z(u) = \int_{-\infty}^{\infty} p_X(u-y)p_Y(y)dy$$

Recall from Chapter 3 that the above formula is a convolution of the two marginal distributions. This formula can be reiterated for any number of summands: the density of the sum of n random variables is the convolution of their densities.

Computing directly the convolution of a number of functions might be very difficult or impossible. However, if we take the Fourier transforms of the densities, $P_Z(\omega)$, $P_X(\omega)$, $P_Y(\omega)$ computations are substantially simplified as the transform of the convolution is the product of the transforms:

$$p_Z(u) = \int_{-\infty}^{\infty} p_X(u-y)p_Y(y)dy \Rightarrow P_Z(\omega) = P_X(\omega) \times P_Y(s)$$

This relationship can be extended to any number of variables.

In probability theory, given a random variable X, the following expectation is called the **characteristic function (c.f.) of the variable X**

$$\varphi_X(t) = E[e^{itX}] = E[\cos tX] + i E[\sin tX]$$

If the variable X admits a d.f. $F_X(y)$, it can be demonstrated that the following relationship holds:

$$\varphi_X(t) = E[e^{itX}] = \int_{-\infty}^{\infty} e^{itX}dF_X(x) = \int_{-\infty}^{\infty} \cos tx \ dF_X(x) + \int_{-\infty}^{\infty} \sin tx \ dF_X(x)$$

In this case, the characteristic function therefore coincides with the Fourier-Stieltjes transform. It can be demonstrated that there is a one-to-one correspondence between c.d.s and d.f.s. In fact, it is well known that the Fourier-Stieltjes transform can be uniquely inverted.

In probability theory convolution is defined, in a more general way, as follows. Given two d.f.s $F_X(y)$ and $F_Y(y)$, their convolution is defined as

$$F^*(u) = (F_X * F_Y)(u) = \int\limits_{-\infty}^{\infty} F_X(u - y)dF_Y(y)$$

It can be demonstrated that the d.f. of the sum of two variables X, Y with d.f.s $F_X(y)$ and $F_Y(y)$ is the convolution of their respective d.f.s:

$$P(X + Y \leq u) = F_{X+Y}(u) = F^*(u) = (F_X * F_Y)(u) = \int\limits_{-\infty}^{\infty} F_X(u - y)dF_Y(y)$$

If the d.f.s admit p.d.f.s, then the inversion formulas are those established earlier. Inversion formulas also exist in the case that the d.f.s do not admit densities but these are more complex and will not be given here.[6]

We can therefore establish the following property: the characteristic function of the sum of n independent random variables is the product of the characteristic functions of each of the summands.

GAUSSIAN VARIABLES

Gaussian random variables are extremely important in probability theory and statistics. Their importance stems from the fact that any phenomenon made up of a large number of independent or weakly dependent variables has a **Gaussian distribution**. Gaussian distributions are also known as **normal distributions**.

Let's start with the univariate case. A **normal variable** is a variable whose probability distribution function has the following form:

$$f(x|\mu, \sigma^2) = \frac{1}{\sigma\sqrt{2\pi}} \exp\left[-\frac{(x - \mu)^2}{2\sigma^2}\right]$$

---

[6] Y.-S. Chow and H. Teicher, *Probability Theory*, 2nd ed. (New York: Springer, 1988).

The **univariate normal distribution** is a distribution characterized by only two parameters, (μ, σ^2), which represent, respectively, the mean and the variance of the distribution. We write $X \sim N(\mu, \sigma^2)$ to indicate that the variable X has a normal distribution with parameters (μ, σ^2). We define the **standard normal distribution** as the normal distribution with zero mean and unit variance. It can be demonstrated by direct calculation that if $X \sim N(\mu, \sigma^2)$ then the variable

$$Z = \frac{X - \mu}{\sigma}$$

is standard normal. The variable Z is called the **score** or **Z-score**. The cumulative distribution of a normal variable is generally indicated as

$$F(x) = \Phi\left(\frac{x - \mu}{\sigma}\right)$$

where $\Phi(x)$ is the cumulative distribution of the standard normal.

It can be demonstrated that the sum of n independent normal distributions is another normal distribution whose expected value is the sum of the expected values of the summands and whose variance is the sum of the variances of the summands.

The normal distribution has a typical bell-shaped graph symmetrical around the mean. Figure 6.1 shows the graph of a normal distribution.

Multivariate normal distributions are characterized by the same exponential functional form. However, a multivariate normal distribution in n variables is identified by n means, one for each axis, and by a $n \times n$ symmetrical variance-covariance matrix. For instance, a bivariate normal distribution is characterized by two expected values, two variances and one covariance. We can write the general expression of a bivariate normal distribution as follows:

$$f(x, y) = \frac{\exp\left\{-\frac{1}{2}Q\right\}}{2\pi\sigma_X\sigma_Y\sqrt{1 - \rho^2}}$$

$$Q = \frac{1}{1 - \rho^2}\left\{\left(\frac{x - \mu_X}{\sigma_X}\right)^2 - 2\rho\left(\frac{x - \mu_X}{\sigma_X}\right)\left(\frac{y - \mu_Y}{\sigma_Y}\right) + \left(\frac{y - \mu_Y}{\sigma_Y}\right)^2\right\}$$

where ρ is the correlation coefficient.

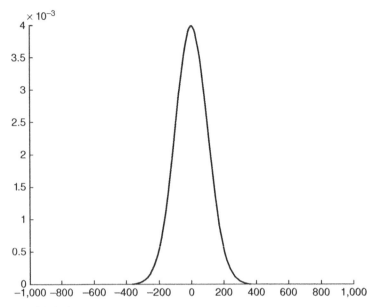

FIGURE 6.1 Graph of a Normal Variable with Zero Mean and $\sigma = 100$

This expression generalizes to the case of n random variables. Using matrix notation, the joint normal probability distributions of the random n vector $\mathbf{V} = \{X_i\}$, $i = 1, 2, \ldots, n$ has the following expression:

$$\mathbf{V} = \{X_i\} \sim N_n(\boldsymbol{\mu}, \boldsymbol{\Sigma})$$

where

$$\mu_i = E[X_i]$$

and $\boldsymbol{\Sigma}$ is the variance-covariance matrix of the $\{X_i\}$,

$$\boldsymbol{\Sigma} = E[(\mathbf{V} - \boldsymbol{\mu})(\mathbf{V} - \boldsymbol{\mu})^T]$$

$$f(\mathbf{v}) = [(2\pi)^n |\boldsymbol{\Sigma}|]^{-1/2} \exp[(-1/2)(\mathbf{v} - \boldsymbol{\mu})^T \boldsymbol{\Sigma}^{-1}(\mathbf{v} - \boldsymbol{\mu})]$$

where $|\boldsymbol{\Sigma}| = \det\boldsymbol{\Sigma}$, the determinant of $\boldsymbol{\Sigma}$.

For $n = 2$ we find the previous expression for the bivariate normal, taking into account that variances and correlation coefficients have the following relationships:

$$\sigma_{ij} = \rho_{ij}\sigma_i\sigma_j$$

It can be demonstrated that a linear combination

$$W = \sum_{i=1}^{n} \alpha_i X_i$$

of n jointly normal random variables $X_i \sim N(\mu_i, \sigma_i^2)$ with $\text{cov}(X_i, X_j) = \sigma_{ij}$ is a normal random variable $W \sim N(\mu_W, \sigma_W^2)$ where

$$\mu_W = \sum_{i=1}^{n} \alpha_i \mu_i$$

$$\sigma_W^2 = \sum_{i=1}^{n}\sum_{j=1}^{n} \alpha_i \alpha_j \sigma_{ij}$$

APPPROXIMATING THE TAILS OF A PROBABILITY DISTRIBUTION: CORNISH-FISHER EXPANSION AND HERMITE POLYNOMIALS

Two methods for approximating the tails of a probability distribution are the Cornish-Fisher expansion and Hermite polynomials.

Cornish-Fisher Expansion

The Cornish-Fisher expansion is a formula for approximating quantiles of a random variable based only on its first few cumulants.[7] In finance, it is often used in the calculation of a popular risk measure, value-at-risk (VaR). Defined as a confidence interval, VaR is the maximum loss that can be incurred with a given probability.[8] Suppose we choose a confidence level of 95%. We

---

[7]E. A. Cornish and R. A. Fisher, "Moments and Cumulants in the Specification of Distributions," *Extrait de la Revue de l'Institute International de Statistique* 4 (1937): 1–14.

[8]When JP Morgan released its RiskMetrics model in 1994, VaR was the risk measure it proposed. As a measure of risk, VaR has many drawbacks. It does not specify the

say, for example, that a financial position has a given VaR, say $1 million, if there is a 95% probability that losses above $1 million will not be incurred. This does not mean that the given the financial position cannot lose more than $1 million, it means only that losses above $1 million will happen with a probability of 5%.

The cumulants of a random variable X are conceptually similar to its moments. They are defined as those values κ_r such that the identity

$$\exp\left(\sum_{r=1}^{\infty} \frac{\kappa_r t^r}{r!}\right) = \sum_{r=1}^{\infty} \frac{E(X^r)t^r}{r!}$$

holds for all t where r is a moment index (i.e., $r = 1$ refers to the first moment, $r = 2$ refers to the second moment, and so on). Cumulants of a random variable X can be expressed in terms of its mean $\mu = E(X)$ and central moments $\mu_r = E[(X - r)^r]$.[9] Expressions for the first five cumulants are

$$\kappa_1 = \mu_1$$
$$\kappa_2 = \mu_2$$
$$\kappa_3 = \mu_3$$
$$\kappa_4 = \mu_4 - 3\mu_2^2$$
$$\kappa_5 = \mu_5 - 10\mu_3\mu_2$$

Suppose X has a mean of 0 and a standard deviation one of 1. Cornish and Fisher provide an expansion for approximating the q-quantile, $\Phi_x^{-1}(q)$, of X based upon its cumulants. Using the first five cumulants, the expansion is

$$\Phi_x^{-1}(q) \approx \Phi_z^{-1}(q) + \frac{\Phi_z^{-1}(q)^2 - 1}{6}\kappa_3 + \frac{\Phi_z^{-1}(q)^3 - 3\Phi_z^{-1}(q)}{24}\kappa_4$$
$$- \frac{2\Phi_z^{-1}(q)^3 - 5\Phi_z^{-1}(q)}{36}\kappa_3^2 + \frac{\Phi_z^{-1}(q)^4 - 6\Phi_z^{-1}(q)^2 + 3}{120}\kappa_5$$
$$- \frac{\Phi_z^{-1}(q)^4 - 5\Phi_z^{-1}(q)^2 + 2}{24}\kappa_3\kappa_4 + \frac{12\Phi_z^{-1}(q)^4 - 53\Phi_z^{-1}(q)^2 + 17}{324}\kappa_3^3$$

---

amount of losses exceeding VaR. Different distributions might have the same VaR but totally different distributions of extreme values. Perhaps the most serious drawback of VaR is the fact that is that the VaR of aggregated financial portfolios might be larger than the sum of individual VaRs. This is unreasonable as one expects risk to decrease in aggregate due to diversification.

[9] A. Stuart and K. Ord, *Kendall's Advanced Theory of Statistics, Distribution Theory,* vol. 1 (Hoboken, NJ: John Wiley & Sons, 2010).

where $\Phi_z^{-1}(q)$ is the q-quantile of a standard normal random variable Z. Although the previous equation applies only if X has a mean of 0 and a standard deviation of 1, one can still use it to approximate quantiles if X has some other mean μ and standard deviation σ. Simply use the Z-score defined in the previous section

$$Z = \frac{X - \mu}{\sigma}$$

which has a mean of 0 and a standard deviation of 1. Central moments $\tilde{\mu}_r$ of Z can be calculated from central moments of X with

$$\tilde{\mu}_r = \frac{\mu_r}{\sigma_r}$$

Apply the Cornish-Fisher expansion to obtain the q-quantile $\tilde{x}$ of $\tilde{X}$. The corresponding q-quantile x of X is then $x = \tilde{x} \cdot \sigma + \mu$.

Hermite Polynomials

The Hermite polynomials $H_n(x)$ are a set of orthogonal polynomials over the domain $(-\infty, \infty)$ with weighting function e^{-x^2}.[10] The Hermite polynomial $H_n(x)$ can be defined by the contour integral

$$H_n(z) = \frac{n!}{2\pi i} \oint e^{-t^2 + 2tz} t^{-n-1} dt$$

where the contour encloses the origin and is traversed in a counterclockwise direction. The first few Hermite polynomials are as follows:

$H_0(x) = 1$
$H_1(x) = 2x$
$H_2(x) = 4x^2 - 2$
$H_3(x) = 8x^3 - 12x$
$H_4(x) = 16x^4 - 48x^2 + 12$
$H_5(x) = 32x^5 - 160x^3 + 120x$
$H_6(x) = 64x^6 - 480x^4 + 720x^2 - 120$
$H_7(x) = 128x^7 - 1344x^5 + 3360x^3 - 1680x$
$H_8(x) = 256x^8 - 3584x^6 + 13440x^4 - 13440x^2 + 1680$
$H_9(x) = 512x^9 - 9216x^7 + 48384x^5 - 80640x^3 + 30240x$
$H_{10}(x) = 1024x^{10} - 23040x^8 + 161280x^6 - 403200x^4 + 302400x^2 - 30240$

---

[10]C. Hermite, "Sur un nouveau développement en série de fonctions [On a New Development in Series for Functions]," *Compt. Rend. Acad. Sci. Paris* 58 (1864): 93–100; 266–273.

The values $H_n(0)$ are called **Hermite numbers**:

$$H_0 = 1$$
$$H_1 = 0$$
$$H_2 = -2$$
$$H_3 = 0$$
$$H_4 = +12$$
$$H_5 = 0$$
$$H_6 = -120$$
$$H_7 = 0$$
$$H_8 = +1680$$
$$H_9 = 0$$
$$H_{10} = -30240$$

The Hermite polynomials are a **Sheffer sequence** with

$$g(t) = e^{t^2/4}$$
$$f(t) = \frac{1}{2}t$$

giving the exponential generating function

$$\exp\left(2xt - t^2\right) = \sum_{n=0}^{\infty} \frac{H_n(x)t^n}{n!}$$

Using a Taylor series shows that

$$H_n(x) = (-1)^n e^{x^2} \frac{d^n}{dx^n} e^{-x^2}$$

$$H_n(x) = e^{x^2/2} \left(x - \frac{d}{dx}\right)^n e^{-x^2/2}$$

Two interesting identities involving $H_n(x + y)$ are given by

$$\sum_{k=0}^{n} \binom{n}{k} H_k(x) H_{n-k}(y) = 2^{n/2} H_n\left(2^{-1/2}(x + y)\right)$$

and

$$\sum_{k=0}^{n} \binom{n}{k} H_k(x)(2y)^{n-k} = H_n(x+y)$$

Another identity is

$$H_n(x+y) = (H+2y)^n$$

where $H^k = H_k(x)$. They also obey the sum

$$\sum_{k=0}^{n} (-1)^{n-k} \binom{n}{k} H_n(k) = 2^n n!$$

A class of generalized Hermite polynomials $\gamma_n^m(x)$ satisfies the following condition:

$$e^{mxt-t^m} = \sum_{n=0}^{\infty} \gamma_n^m(x)t^n$$

A class of related polynomials is defined as

$$b_{n,m} = \gamma_n^m\left(\frac{2x}{m}\right)$$

with generating function

$$e^{2xt-t^m} = \sum_{n=0}^{\infty} b_{n,m}(x)t^n$$

that satisfies the following condition:

$$H_n(x) = n!b_{n,2}(x)$$

A modified version of the Hermite polynomial is sometimes defined as

$$He_n(x) = 2^{-n/2} H_n\left(\frac{x}{\sqrt{2}}\right)$$

The first few of these polynomials are given by

$$He_1(x) = x$$
$$He_2(x) = x^2 - 1$$
$$He_3(x) = x^3 - 3x$$
$$He_4(x) = x^4 - 6x^2 + 3$$
$$He_5(x) = x^5 - 10x^3 + 15x$$

Cornish-Fisher Expansion with Hermite Polynomials

We now define the Cornish-Fisher expansion using Hermite polynomials.

$$y \approx m + \sigma w$$

where

$$w = x + [\gamma_1 h_1(x)] + [\gamma_2 h_2(x) + \gamma_1^2 h_{11}(x)] + [\gamma_3 h_3(x) + \gamma_1 \gamma_2 h_{12}(x) + \gamma_1^3 h_{111}(x)]$$
$$= [\gamma_4 h_4(x) + \gamma_2^2 h_{22}(x) + \gamma_1 \gamma_3 h_{13}(x) + \gamma_1^2 \gamma_2 h_{112}(x) + \gamma_1^4 h_{1111}(x)]$$

where $x = \Phi_z^{-1}(q)$ is the q-quantile of a standard normal random variable, γ_i was defined earlier, and the combinations of Hermite polynomials are

$$h_1(x) = \frac{1}{6} He_2(x)$$

$$h_2(x) = \frac{1}{24} He_3(x)$$

$$h_{11}(x) = -\frac{1}{36} [2 He_3(x) + He_1(x)]$$

$$h_3(x) = \frac{1}{120} He_4(x)$$

$$h_{12}(x) = -\frac{1}{24} [He_4(x) + He_2(x)]$$

$$h_{111}(x) = \frac{1}{324} [12 He_4(x) + 19 He_2(x)]$$

$$h_4(x) = \frac{1}{720} He_5(x)$$

$$h_{22}(x) = -\frac{1}{384} [3 He_5(x) + 6 He_3(x) + 2 He_1(x)]$$

$$h_{13}(x) = -\frac{1}{180} [2 He_5(x) + 3 He_3(x)]$$

$$h_{112}(x) = \frac{1}{288}[14He_5(x) + 37He_3(x) + 8He_1(x)]$$

$$h_{1111}(x) = -\frac{1}{7776}[252He_5(x) + 832He_3(x) + 227He_1(x)]$$

THE REGRESSION FUNCTION

Given a probability space $(\Omega, \Im, P)$, consider a set of $p + 1$ random variables. Let's suppose that the random vector $\{X\ Z_1\ \ldots\ Z_p\} \equiv \{X\ Z\}$, $Z = \{Z_1 \ldots Z_p\}$ has the joint multivariate probability density function:

$$f(xz_1 \ldots z_p) = f(x, z), z = \{z_1 \ldots z_p\}$$

Let's consider the conditional density

$$f(x|z_1, \ldots, z_p) = f(x, |z)$$

and the marginal density of Z,

$$f_z(z) = \int_{-\infty}^{\infty} (x, z)dx$$

Recall from an earlier section that the joint multivariate density $f(x,z)$ factorizes as

$$f(x, z) = f(x|z)\,f_z(z)$$

Let's consider now the conditional expectation of the variable X given $Z = z = \{z_1 \ldots z_p\}$:

$$g(z) = E[X|Z = z] = \int_{-\infty}^{\infty} vf(v|z)dv$$

The function g, that is, the function which gives the conditional expectation of X given the variables Z, is called the **regression function**. Otherwise stated, the regression function is a real function of real variables which is the locus of the expectation of the random variable X given that the variables Z assume the values z.

Linear Regression

In general, the regression function depends on the joint distribution of $[X\ Z_1 \ldots Z_p]$. In financial econometrics it is important to determine what joint distributions produce a linear regression function. It can be demonstrated that joint normal distributions produce a linear regression function. Consider the joint normal distribution

$$f(\mathbf{v}) = [(2\pi)^n |\boldsymbol{\Sigma}|]^{-\frac{1}{2}} \exp\left[-\frac{1}{2}(\mathbf{v} - \boldsymbol{\mu})^T \boldsymbol{\Sigma}^{-1}(\mathbf{v} - \boldsymbol{\mu})\right]$$

where parameters are those defined in an earlier section in this chapter. Let's partition the parameters as follows:

$$v = \begin{pmatrix} x \\ z \end{pmatrix}, \quad \mu = \begin{pmatrix} \mu_x \\ \mu_z \end{pmatrix}, \quad \Sigma = \begin{pmatrix} \sigma_{x,x} & \sigma_{z,x} \\ \sigma_{x,z} & \Sigma_z \end{pmatrix}$$

where μ_x, μ_z are respectively a scalar and a p-vector of expected values, $\sigma_{x,x}$, $\sigma_{x,z}$, $\sigma_{z,x}$, and Σ_z are respectively a scalar, p-vectors and a $p \times p$ matrix of variances and covariances and $\sigma_{x,x} = \sigma_x^2$, $\sigma_{z_i,z_i} = \sigma_{z_i}^2$. It can be demonstrated that the variable $(X|Z = z)$ is normally distributed with the following parameters:

$$(X|\mathbf{Z} = \mathbf{z}) \sim N\left[\mu_x - (\Sigma_z^{-1}\sigma_{z,x})'\ (\mu_z - \mathbf{z}),\ \sigma_{x,x} - \sigma_{x,z}\Sigma_z^{-1}\sigma_{z,x}+\right]$$

From the above expression we can conclude that the conditional expectation is linear in the conditioning variables. Let's call

$$\alpha = \mu_x - (\Sigma_z^{-1}\sigma_{z,x})'\ \mu_z \text{ and } \beta = \Sigma_z^{-1}\sigma_{z,x}$$

We can therefore write

$$g(\mathbf{z}) = E[X|\mathbf{Z} = \mathbf{z}] = \alpha + \beta'\,\mathbf{z}$$

If the matrix Σ is diagonal, the random variables $(X, Z_1, \ldots, Zp)$ are independent, such that $\sigma_{z,x} = 0$ and $\beta = \Sigma_z^{-1}\sigma_{z,x} = 0$ and therefore the regression function is a constant that does not depend on the conditioning variables. If the matrix Σ_z is diagonal but $\sigma_{x,z}$, $\sigma_{z,x}$ do not vanish, then the linear regression takes the following form

$$g(\mathbf{z}) = E[X|\mathbf{Z} = \mathbf{z}] = \mu_x - \sum_{i=1}^{p} \frac{\sigma_{x,z_i}}{\sigma_{z_i}^2}\mu_{z_i} + \sum_{i=1}^{p} \frac{\sigma_{x,z_i}}{\sigma_{z_i}^2} z_i$$

In particular, a bivariate normal distribution factorizes in a linear regression as follows:

$$(X|Z=z) \sim N\left[\mu_x - \frac{\sigma_{x.z}}{\sigma_z^2}(\mu_z - z),\ \sigma_x^2 - \frac{(\sigma_{x.z})^2}{\sigma_z^2}\right]$$

$$g(z) = E[X|Z=z] = \mu_x - \frac{\sigma_{x.z}}{\sigma_z^2}\,\mu_z + \frac{\sigma_{x.z}}{\sigma_z^2}z$$

FAT TAILS AND STABLE LAWS

Most models of stochastic processes and time series examined thus far in this chapter assume that distributions have finite mean and finite variance. Now we describe fat-tailed distributions with infinite variance. Fat-tailed distributions have been found in many financial economic variables ranging from forecasting returns on financial assets to modeling recovery distributions in bankruptcies.[11]

The failure of financial models has been identified by some market observers as a major contributor—indeed some have argued that is it the single most important contributor—for the latest global financial crisis. The allegation is that financial models used by risk managers, portfolio managers, and even regulators simply did not reflect the realities of real-world financial markets. More specifically, the underlying assumption regarding asset returns and prices failed to reflect real-world movements of these quantities. Pinpointing the criticism more precisely, it is argued that the underlying assumption made in most financial models is that distributions of prices and returns are normally distributed, popularly referred to as the "normal model."

In this section, we review the different but related concepts and properties of fat tails and stable laws. These two concepts appear frequently in the financial economic literature, applied to both random variables and stochastic processes.

---

[11] See S. T. Rachev and S. Mittnik, *Stable Paretian Models in Finance* (New York: John Wiley & Sons, 2000); S. T. Rachev (ed.), *Handbook of Heavy-Tailed Distributions in Finance* (Amsterdam: Elsevier/North-Holland, 2003); and S.T. Rachev, C. Menn, and F. J. Fabozzi, *Fat Tails and Skewed Asset Returns Distributions* (Hoboken, NJ: John Wiley & Sons, 2005).

Fat Tails

Consider a random variable X. By definition, X is a real-valued function from the set Ω of the possible outcomes to the set R of real numbers, such that the set $(X \leq x)$ is an event. Recall from Chapter 5 that if $P(X \leq x)$ is the probability of the event $(X \leq x)$, the function $F(x) = P(X \leq x)$ is a well-defined function for every real number x. The function $F(x)$ is the cumulative distribution function, or simply the distribution function, of the random variable X. Note that X denotes a function $\Omega \rightarrow R$, x is a real variable, and $F(x)$ is an ordinary real-valued function that assumes values in the interval $[0,1]$. If the function $F(x)$ admits a derivative

$$f(x) = \frac{dF(x)}{dx}$$

As explained in the previous chapter, the function $f(x)$ is the probability density of the random variable X. The function $\bar{F}(x) = 1 - F(x)$ is the tail of the distribution $F(x)$. The function $\bar{F}(x)$ is called the **survival function**.

Fat tails are somewhat arbitrarily defined. Intuitively, a fat-tailed distribution is a distribution that has more weight in the tails than some reference distribution. The exponential decay of the tail is generally assumed as the borderline separating fat-tailed from light-tailed distributions. In the literature, distributions with a power-law decay of the tails are referred to as **heavy-tailed distributions**. It is sometimes assumed that the reference distribution is the Gaussian distribution (i.e., normal distribution), but this is unsatisfactory; it implies, for instance, that exponential distributions are fat tailed because Gaussian tails decay as the *square* of an exponential and thus faster than an exponential.

These characterizations of fat tailedness (or heavy tailedness) are not convenient from a mathematical and statistical point of view. It would be preferable to define fat tailedness in terms of a function of some essential property that can be associated to it. Several proposals have been advanced. Widely used definitions focus on the moments of the distribution. Definitions of fat tailedness based on a single moment focus either on the second moment, the variance, or the kurtosis, defined as the fourth moment divided by the square of the variance. In fact, a distribution is often considered fat tailed if its variance is infinite or if it is leptokurtic (i.e., its kurtosis is greater than 3). However, as remarked by Bryson[12] definitions of this type are too crude and should be replaced by more complete descriptions of tail behavior.

---

[12]M.C. Bryson, "Heavy-Tailed Distributions," in *Encyclopedia of Statistical Sciences*, vol. 3, ed. N. L. Kotz and S. Read (New York: John Wiley & Sons, 1982), 598–601.

Others consider a distribution fat tailed if all its exponential moments are infinite, $E[e^{sX}] = \infty$ for every $s \geq 0$. This condition implies that the moment-generating function does not exist. Some suggest weakening this condition, defining fat-tailed distributions as those distributions that do not have a finite exponential moment of first order. Exponential moments are particularly important in finance and economics when the logarithm of variables, for instance the logarithm of stock prices, are the primary quantity to be modeled.[13]

Fat tailedness has a consequence of practical importance: the probability of **extremal events** (i.e., the probability that the random variable assumes large values) is much higher than in the case of normal distributions. A fat-tailed distribution assigns higher probabilities to extremal events than would a normal distribution. For instance, a "six-sigma event" (i.e., a realized value of a random variable whose difference from the mean is six times the size of the standard deviation) has a near zero probability in a Gaussian distribution but might have a nonnegligible probability in fat-tailed distributions.

The notion of fat tailedness can be made quantitative as different distributions have different degrees of fat tailedness. The degree of fat tailedness dictates the weight of the tails and thus the probability of extremal events. The field of extreme value theory attempts to estimate the entire tail region, and therefore the degree of fat tailedness, from a finite sample. A number of indicators for evaluating the size of extremal events have been proposed.

The Class $\mathfrak{L}$ of Fat-Tailed Distributions

Many important classes of fat-tailed distributions have been defined; each is characterized by special statistical properties that are important in given application domains. We will introduce a number of such classes in order of inclusion, starting from the class with the broadest membership: the class $\mathfrak{L}$, which is defined as follows. Suppose that F is a distribution function defined in the domain $(0, \infty)$ with $F < 1$ in the entire domain (i.e., F is the distribution function of a positive random variable with a tail that never decays to zero). It is said that $F \in \mathfrak{L}$ if, for any $y > 0$, the following property holds:

$$\lim_{x \to \infty} \frac{\bar{F}(x - y)}{\bar{F}(x)} = 1, \ \forall y > 0$$

---

[13] See G. Bamberg and D. Dorfleitner, "Fat Tails and Traditional Capital Market Theory," Working Paper, University of Augsburg, August 2001.

We can rewrite the above property in an equivalent (and perhaps more intuitive from the probabilistic point of view) way. Under the same assumptions as above, it is said that, given a positive random variable X, its distribution function $F \in \mathfrak{L}$ if the following property holds for any $y > 0$:

$$\lim_{x \to \infty} P(X > x + y | X > x) = \lim_{x \to \infty} \frac{\bar{F}(x + y)}{\bar{F}(x)} = 1, \ \forall y > 0$$

Intuitively, this second property means that if it is known that a random variable exceeds a given value, then it will exceed any bigger value. Some authors define a distribution as being heavy-tailed if it satisfies this property.[14]

It can be demonstrated that if a distribution $F(x) \in \mathfrak{L}$, then it has the following properties:

- Infinite exponential moments of every order: $E[e^{sX}] = \infty$ for every $s \geq 0$
- $\lim_{x \to \infty} \bar{F}(x)e^{\lambda x} = \infty, \ \forall \lambda > 0$

As distributions in class $\mathfrak{L}$ have infinite exponential moments of every order, they satisfy one of the previous definitions of fat tailedness. However they might have finite or infinite mean and variance.

The class $\mathfrak{L}$ is in fact quite broad. It includes, in particular, the two classes of subexponential distributions and distributions with regularly varying tails that are discussed in the following sections.

Subexponential Distributions   A class of fat-tailed distributions, widely used in insurance and telecommunications, is the class S of **subexponential distributions**.

Subexponential distributions can be characterized by two equivalent properties: (1) the convolution closure property of the tails and (2) the property of the sums.[15]

The **convolution closure property** of the tails prescribes that the shape of the tail is preserved after the summation of independent and identically

[14]See, for example, K. Sigman, "A Primer on Heavy-Tailed Distributions," *Queueing Systems*, 1999.
[15]See, for example, C. M. Goldie and C. Kluppelberg, "Subexponential Distributions," in *A Practical Guide to Heavy Tails: Statistical Techniques and Applications*, ed. R. J. Adler, R. E. Feldman, and M. S. Taqqu (Boston: Birkhauser, 1998), 435–459; and P. Embrechts, C. Kluppelberg, and T. Mikosch, *Modelling Extremal Events for Insurance and Finance* (Berlin: Springer, 1999).

distributed variables. This property asserts that, for $x \to \infty$, the tail of a sum of independent and identically distributed variables has the same shape as the tail of the variable itself. As the distribution of a sum of n independent variables is the n-convolution of their distributions, the convolution closure property can be written as

$$\lim_{x \to \infty} \frac{\bar{F}^{n*}(x)}{\bar{F}(x)} = n$$

Note that Gaussian distributions do not have this property although the sum of independent Gaussian distributions is again a Gaussian distribution. Subexponential distributions can be characterized by another important (and perhaps more intuitive) property, which is equivalent to the convolution closure property: In a sum of n variables, the largest value will be of the same order of magnitude as the sum itself. For any n, define

$$S_n(x) = \sum_{i=1}^{n} X_i$$

as a sum of independent and identically distributed variables X_i and call M_n their maxima. In the limit of large x, the probability that the tail of the sum exceeds x equals the probability that the largest summand exceeds x:

$$\lim_{x \to \infty} \frac{P(S_n > x)}{P(M_n > x)} = 1$$

The class S of subexponential distributions is a proper subset of the class $\mathcal{L}$. Every subexponential distribution belongs to the class $\mathcal{L}$ while it can be demonstrated (but this is not trivial) that there are distributions that belong to the class $\mathcal{L}$ but not to the class S. Distributions that have both properties are subexponential as it can be demonstrated that, as all distributions in $\mathcal{L}$, they satisfy the property

$$\lim_{x \to \infty} \bar{F}(x)e^{\lambda x} = \infty, \ \forall \lambda > 0$$

Note, however, that the class of distributions that satisfies the latter property is broader than the class of subexponential distributions; this is because the former includes, for instance, the class $\mathcal{L}$.[16]

---

[16]See Sigman, "A Primer on Heavy-Tailed Distributions."

Subexponential distributions do not have finite exponential moments of any order, that is, $E[e^{sX}] = \infty$ for every $s \geq 0$. They may or may not have a finite mean and/or a finite variance. Consider, in fact, that the class of subexponential distributions includes both Pareto and Weibull distributions. The former have infinite variance but might have finite or infinite mean depending on the index; the latter have finite moments of every order (see below).

The key indicators of subexponentiality are (1) the equivalence in the distribution of the tail between a variable and a sum of independent and identically distributed variables and (2) the fact that a sum is dominated by its largest term.

The class of subexponential distributions is quite large. It includes not only Pareto and stable distributions but also log-gamma, lognormal, Benkander, Burr, and Weibull distributions.[17] Pareto distributions and stable distributions are a particularly important subclass of subexponential distributions; these will be described in some detail below.

Power-Law Distributions   Power-law distributions are a particularly important subset of subexponential distributions. Their tails follow approximately an inverse power law, decaying as $x^{-\alpha}$. The exponent α is called the **tail index** of the distribution. To express formally the notion of approximate power-law decay, we need to introduce the class $\Re(\alpha)$, equivalently written as $\Re_\alpha$ of regularly varying functions.

A positive function f is said to be regularly varying with index α or $f \in \Re(\alpha)$ if the following condition holds:

$$\lim_{x \to \infty} \frac{f(tx)}{f(x)} = t^\alpha$$

A function $f \in \Re(0)$ is called **slowly varying**. It can be demonstrated that a regularly varying function $f(x)$ of index α admits the representation $f(x) = x^\alpha l(x)$ where $l(x)$ is a slowly varying function.

A distribution F is said to have a **regularly varying tail** if the following property holds:

$$\bar{F} = x^{-\alpha} l(x)$$

---

[17]These distributions are discussed in most statistics textbooks.

where l is a slowly varying function. An example of a distribution with a regularly varying tail is Pareto's law. The latter can be written in various ways, including the following:

$$\bar{F}(x) = P(X > x) = \frac{c}{c + x^\alpha} \text{ for } x \geq 0$$

Power-law distributions are thus distributions with regularly varying tails. It can be demonstrated that they satisfy the convolution closure property of the tail. The distribution of the sum of n independent variables of tail index α is a power-law distribution of the same index α. Note that this property holds in the limit for $x \to \infty$. Distributions with regularly varying tails are therefore a proper subset of subexponential distributions.

Being subexponential, power laws have all the general properties of fat-tailed distributions and some additional ones. One particularly important property of distributions with regularly varying tails, valid for every tail index, is the **rank-size order property**. Suppose that samples from a power law of tail index α are ordered by size, and call S_r the size of the rth sample. One then finds that the law

$$S_r = ar^{-\frac{1}{\alpha}}$$

is approximately verified. The well-known **Zipf's law** is an example of this rank-size ordering. Zipf's law states that the size of an observation is inversely proportional to its rank. For example, the frequency of words in an English text is inversely proportional to their rank. The same is approximately valid for the size of U.S. cities.

Many properties of power-law distributions are distinctly different in the three following ranges of α: $0 < \alpha \leq 1$, $1 < \alpha \leq 2$, $\alpha > 2$. The threshold $\alpha = 2$ for the tail index is important as it marks the separation between the applicability of the Central Limit Theorem that we discuss next. The threshold $\alpha = 1$ is important as it separates variables with a finite mean from those with infinite mean. Let's take a closer look at the Law of Large Numbers and the Central Limit Theorem.

The Law of Large Numbers and the Central Limit Theorem

There are four basic versions of the Law of Large Numbers (LLN), two Weak Laws of Large Numbers (WLLN), and two Strong Laws of Large Numbers (SLLN).

The two versions of the WLLN are formulated as follows:

1. Suppose that the variables X_i are IID with finite mean $E[X_i] = E[X] = \mu$. Under this condition it can be demonstrated that the empirical average tends to the mean in probability:

$$\bar{X}_n = \frac{\sum\limits_{i=1}^{n} X_i}{n} \xrightarrow[n \to \infty]{P} E[X] = \mu$$

2. If the variables are only independently distributed (ID) but have finite means and variances (μ_i, σ_i), then the following relationship holds:

$$\bar{X}_n = \frac{\sum\limits_{i=1}^{n} X_i}{n} \xrightarrow[n \to \infty]{P} \frac{\sum\limits_{i=1}^{n} \bar{X}_i}{n} = \frac{\sum\limits_{i=1}^{n} \mu_i}{n}$$

In other words, the empirical average of a sequence of finite-mean finite-variance variables tends to the average of the means.

The two versions of the SLLN are formulated as follows:

1. The empirical average of a sequence of IID variables X_i tends almost surely to a constant a if and only if the expected value of the variables is finite. In addition, the constant a is equal to μ. Therefore, if and only if $|E[X_i]| = |E[X]| = |\mu| < \infty$ the following relationship holds:

$$\bar{X}_n = \frac{\sum\limits_{i=1}^{n} X_i}{n} \xrightarrow[n \to \infty]{A.S.} E[X] = \mu$$

where convergence is in the sense of almost sure convergence.

2. If the variables X_i are only independently distributed (ID) but have finite means and variances (μ_i, σ_i) and

$$\lim_{n \to \infty} \frac{1}{n^2} \sum_{i=1}^{n} \sigma_i^2 < \infty$$

then the following relationship holds:

$$\bar{X}_n = \frac{\sum\limits_{i=1}^{n} X_i}{n} \xrightarrow[n \to \infty]{A.S.} \frac{\sum\limits_{i=1}^{n} \bar{X}_i}{n} = \frac{\sum\limits_{i=1}^{n} \mu_i}{n}$$

Suppose the variables are IID. If the scaling factor n is replaced with $\sqrt{n}$, then the limit relation no longer holds as the normalized sum

$$\frac{\sum_{i=1}^{n} X_i}{\sqrt{n}}$$

diverges. However, if the variables have finite second-order moments, the classical version of the Central Limit Theorem (CLT) can be demonstrated. In fact, under the assumption that both first- and second-order moments are finite, it can be shown that

$$\frac{S_n - n\mu}{\sigma\sqrt{n}} \xrightarrow{D} \Phi$$

$$S_n = \sum_{i=1}^{n} X_i$$

where μ, σ are respectively the expected value and standard deviation of X, and Φ the standard normal distribution.

If the tail index $\alpha > 1$, variables have finite expected value and the SLLN holds. If the tail index $\alpha > 2$, variables have finite variance and the CLT in the previous form holds. If the tail index $\alpha \leq 2$, then variables have infinite variance: The CLT in the previous form does not hold. In fact, variables with $\alpha \leq 2$ belong to the domain of attraction of a stable law of index α as explained in the next section. This means that a sequence of properly normalized and centered sums tends to a stable distribution with infinite variance. In this case, the CLT takes the form

$$\frac{S_n - n\mu}{n^{\frac{1}{\alpha}}} \xrightarrow{D} G_\alpha, \text{ if } 1 < \alpha \leq 2$$

$$\frac{S_n}{n^{\frac{1}{\alpha}}} \xrightarrow{D} G_\alpha, \text{ if } 0 < \alpha \leq 1$$

where G are stable distributions as defined below. Note that the case $\alpha = 2$ is somewhat special: variables with this tail index have infinite variance but fall nevertheless in the domain of attraction of a normal variable, that is, G_2. Below the threshold 1, distributions have neither finite variance nor finite mean. There is a sharp change in the normalization behavior at this tail-index threshold.

Stable Distributions

Stable distributions are *not*, in their generality, a subset of fat-tailed distributions as they include the normal distribution. There are different, equivalent ways to define stable distributions. Let's begin with a key property: the equality in distribution between a random variable and the (normalized) independent sum of any number of identical replicas of the same variable. This is a different property than the closure property of the tail insofar as (1) it involves not only the tail but the entire distribution and (2) equality in distribution means that distributions have the same functional form but, possibly, with different parameters. Normal distributions have this property: The sum of two or more normally distributed variables is again a normally distributed variable. But this property holds for a more general class of distributions called **stable distributions** or **Levy-stable distributions**. Normal distributions are thus a special type of stable distributions.

The above can be formalized as follows: Stable distributions can be defined as those distributions for which the following identity in distribution holds for any number $n \geq 2$:

$$\sum_{i=1}^{n} X_i \stackrel{D}{=} C_n X + D_n$$

where X_i are identical independent copies of X and the C_n, D_n are constants. Alternatively, the same property can be expressed stating that stable distributions are distributions for which the following identity in distribution holds:

$$AX_1 + BX_2 \stackrel{D}{=} CX + D$$

Stable distributions are also characterized by another property that might be used in defining them: a stable distribution has a **domain of attraction** (i.e., it is the limit in distribution of a normalized and centered sum of identical and independent variables). Stable distributions coincide with all variables that have a domain of attraction.

Except in the special cases of Gaussian ($\alpha = 2$), symmetric Cauchy ($\alpha = 1$, $\beta = 0$), and stable inverse Gaussian ($\alpha = \frac{1}{2}$, $\beta = 0$) distributions, stable distributions cannot be written as simple formulas; formulas have been discovered but are not simple. However, stable distributions can be characterized in a simple way through their characteristic function, the Fourier transform of the distribution function. In fact, this function can be written as

$$\Phi_X(t) = \exp\{i\gamma t - c|t|^\alpha \, [1 - i\beta \, \text{sign}\,(t)z(t, \, \alpha)]\}$$

where $t \in R$, $\gamma \in R$, $c > 0$, $\alpha \in (0,2)$, $\beta \in [-1,1]$, and

$$z(t, \, \alpha) = \tan \frac{\pi\alpha}{2} \text{ if } \alpha \neq 1$$

$$z(t, \, \alpha) = -2\log|t| \text{ if } \alpha = 1$$

It can be shown that only distributions with this characteristic function are stable distributions (i.e., they are the only distributions closed under summation). A stable law is characterized by four parameters: α, β, c, and γ. Normal distributions correspond to the parameters: $\alpha = 2$, $\beta = 0$, $\gamma = 0$.

Even if stable distributions cannot be written as simple formulas, the asymptotic shape of their tails can be written in a simple way. In fact, with the exception of Gaussian distributions, the tails of stable laws obey an inverse power law with exponent α (between 0 and 2). Normal distributions are stable but are an exception as their tails decay exponentially.

For stable distributions, the CLT holds in the same form as for inverse power-law distributions. In addition, the functions in the domain of attraction of a stable law of index $\alpha < 2$ are characterized by the same tail index. This means that a distribution G belongs to the domain of attraction of a stable law of parameter $\alpha < 2$ if and only if its tail decays as α. In particular, Pareto's law belongs to the domain of attraction of stable laws of the same tail index.

Normal vs. Stable Distribution and Its Extensions The normal distribution has found many applications in the natural sciences and social sciences. However, there are those who have long warned about the misuse of the normal distribution, particularly in the social sciences.[18] In finance, where the normal distribution was the underlying assumption in describing asset returns in major financial theories such as the capital asset pricing theory

---

[18] See T. Goertzel and J. Fashing, "The Myth of the Normal Curve: A Theoretical Critique and Examination of its Role in Teaching and Research," *Humanity and Society* 5 (1981): 18–23; and R. Herrnstein and C. Murray, *The Bell Curve: Intelligence and Class Structure in American Life* (New York: Free Press, 1994).

and option pricing theory, the attack came in the early 1960s from Benoit Mandelbrot, a mathematician at IBM's Thomas J. Watson Research Center. Although primarily known for his work in fractal geometry, the finance profession was introduced to his study of returns on commodity prices and interest rate movements that strongly rejected the assumption that asset returns are normally distributed.

The mainstream financial models at the time relied on the work of Louis Bachelier, a French mathematician who at the beginning of the twentieth century was the first to formulate random walk models for stock prices. Bachelier's work assumed that relative price changes followed a normal distribution. Mandelbrot, however, was not the first to attack the use of the normal distribution in finance. As he notes, Wesley Clair Mitchell, an American economist who taught at Columbia University and founded the National Bureau of Economics Research, was the first to do so in 1914. The bottom line is that, in the findings of Mandelbrot, empirical distributions do not follow a normal distribution. This led a leading financial economist, Paul Cootner of MIT, to warn the academic community that Mandelbrot's finding may mean that "past econometric work is meaningless." However, the overwhelming empirical evidence of asset returns in real-world financial market since the publication of Mandelbrot's work is that they are not normally distributed. In Mandelbrot's attack on the normal distribution, he suggested that asset returns are more appropriately described by a nonnormal stable distribution referred to as a stable **Paretian distribution** or **alpha-stable distribution**, so named because the tails of this distribution have Pareto power-type decay. The reason for describing this distribution as "nonnormal stable" is that, as noted earlier, the normal distribution is a special case of the stable distribution. Because of the work by Paul Lévy, a French mathematician, who introduced and characterized the nonnormal stable distribution, this distribution is also referred to as the **Lévy stable distribution** and the **Pareto-Lévy stable distribution**.

Despite the empirical evidence rejecting the normal distribution and in support of the stable distribution, there have been several barriers to the application of stable distribution models, both conceptual and technical. The major problem is that the variance of the stable nonnormal distributions is infinite as noted earlier. As a result, it is difficult to use this distribution within the Markowitz mean-variance framework. A second criticism of the stable distribution concerns the fact that without a general expression for stable probability densities—except the four cases (the normal distribution and three other distributions—one cannot directly implement estimation methodologies for fitting these densities. However, today because of advances in computational finance, there are methodologies for fitting densities for stable distributions.

Although the empirical evidence of observed market returns is inconsistent with the normal distribution and better explained by the stable distribution, the empirical suggests that there may be better models than the traditional stable distribution for describing return distributions. More specifically, the empirical evidence suggests that the tails of the distribution for asset returns are heavier than the normal distribution but thinner than the stable distribution.[19] To overcome the drawbacks of the stable distribution, the tails can be appropriately tempered or truncated in order to obtain a proper distribution that can be utilized to better price financial derivatives. Several alternatives to the stable distribution have been proposed in the literature. One alternative is the classical tempered stable distribution—introduced under the names truncated Lévy flight distribution,[20] KoBoL distribution,[21] and CGMY distribution[22]—and its extension, the KR distribution.[23] The modified tempered stable (MTS) distribution is another alternative.[24] These distributions, sometimes called the **tempered stable distributions**,[25] have not only heavier tails than the normal distribution and thinner than the stable distribution, but also have finite moments for all orders and exponential moments of some order.

---

[19]M. Grabchak and G. Samorodnitsky, "Do Financial Returns Have Finite or Infinite Variance? A Paradox and An Explanation," Technical Report, ORIE, Cornell University, 2008.

[20]I. Koponen, "Analytic Approach to the Problem of Convergence of Truncated Lévy Flights Towards the Gaussian Stochastic Process," *Physical Review* E 52 (1995): 1197–1199.

[21]S.I. Boyarchenko, S.Z. Levendorskii, "Option Pricing For Truncated Lévy Processes," *International Journal of Theoretical and Applied Finance* 3 (2000): 549–553.

[22]P. Carr, H. Geman, D. Madan, and M. Yor, "The Fine Structure of Asset Returns: An Empirical Investigation," *Journal of Business* 75 (2002): 305–332.

[23]Y. Kim, S. T. Rachev, M. Bianchi, and F. J. Fabozzi, "A New Tempered Stable Distribution and Its Application to Finance," in *Risk Assessment: Decisions in Banking and Finance*, ed. G. Bol, S. T. Rachev, and R. Wurth (Berlin: Physika Verlag/Springer, 2008), 51–84.

[24]Y. Kim, S.T. Rachev, D. Chung, and M. Bianchi, "The Modified Tempered Stable Distribution, GARCH Models and Option Pricing," *Probability and Mathematical Statistics* 29 (2009): 91–117.

[25]Rosinski extended the CTS distribution under the name of the tempered stable distribution. (See J. Rosinski, "Tempering Stable Processes," *Stochastic Processes and Their Applications* 117 (2007): 677–707.) Note that the KR distribution is included in this extension, but MTS distribution is not. (See M. L. Bianchi, S. T. Rachev, Y. S. Kim, and F.J. Fabozzi, "Tempered Infinitely Divisible Distributions and Processes," *Theory of Probability and Its Applications* 55 (2010): 59–86.)

KEY POINTS

- Conditioning means the change in probabilities due to the acquisition of some information. In general terms, conditioning means conditioning with respect to a filtration or an information structure.
- It is possible to condition with respect to an event if the event has nonzero probability.
- A martingale is a stochastic process such that the conditional expected value is always equal to its present value. It embodies the idea of a fair game where today's asset price is the best forecast of the asset's future price.
- The correlation coefficient between two variables is a number that measures how the two variables move together. It is zero for independent variables, plus/minus one for linearly dependent deterministic variables.
- There are applications in finance where the correlation coefficient might be misleading. In particular, there are cases of nonlinear dependencies that result in a zero correlation coefficient. Different measures of dependence have been proposed. One such measure is the copula function which allows one to capture nonlinearities in a synthetic way as a link between marginal distributions.
- Three advantages of the copula approach for dealing with dependencies over the correlation measure are that it can (1) capture non-linear dependence, (2) quantify dependence for fat-tailed distributions, and (3) be used to investigate asymptotic properties of dependence structures.
- A sequence of random variables is referred to as a sequence of independent and identically distributed sequence if the variables have all the same distribution and are all mutually independent.
- An infinite sequence of random variables might converge to a limit random variable.
- Different types of convergence can be defined: pointwise convergence, convergence in probability, or convergence in distribution.
- Random variables can be added to produce another random variable.
- The characteristic function of the sum of two random variables is the product of the characteristic functions of each random variable.
- The Gaussian distribution, also referred to as the normal distribution, is an extremely important probability distribution in probability theory because of the fact that any phenomenon made up of a large number of independent or weakly dependent random variables has this distribution. There are criticisms of the misuse of this distribution in financial market applications.
- The Cornish-Fisher expansion and Hermite polynomials can be used to approximate the tails of a probability distribution.

- Given a multivariate distribution, the regression function of one random variable with respect to the others is the conditional expectation of that random variable given the values of the others.
- Joint normal distributions admits a linear regression function.
- Although somewhat arbitrarily defined, a fat-tailed distribution is a distribution that has more weight in the tails than some reference distribution such as the normal distribution.
- Fat tailedness has a consequence of practical importance: the probability of external events (i.e., the probability that the random variable assumes large values) is much higher than in the case of normal distributions.
- Fat-tailed laws have been found in many variables studies in finance such as asset returns.
- There exist many important classes of fat-tailed distributions, with each characterized by special statistical properties that are important in given application domains.
- Power-law distributions are thus distributions with regularly varying tails.
- The nonnormal distribution often proposed for modeling extreme events is the stable Paretian distribution. The normal distribution is a special case of the general stable distribution. In only three cases does the density function of a stable distribution have a closed-form expression. In the general case, stable distributions are described by their characteristic function.

CHAPTER 7

Optimization

In mathematics and statistics, optimization means the selection of a best element (with regard to some criteria) from some set of available alternatives. In the simplest case, an optimization problem consists of maximizing or minimizing a function by choosing input values from within an allowed set and computing the value of the function. The generalization of optimization theory and techniques to other formulations comprises a large area of applied mathematics. In finance, optimization is widely used in asset allocation, bond portfolio management, and derivative pricing. Using optimization:

- One can determine the mean-variance efficient frontier by maximizing expected return of a portfolio subject to a risk constraint. Alternatively, one can minimize the portfolio's risk subject to an expected return constraint.
- One can find the optimal portfolio weights by maximizing expected utility of a risk-averse investor defined as the expected return of a portfolio minus the product of the risk aversion parameter and the portfolio's variance.
- One can construct an immunized portfolio, which means a portfolio created so as to have an assured return for a specific time horizon irrespective of interest rate changes, one can deal with cash flow matching, also referred to as a dedicated portfolio strategy or the problem of matching a predetermined set of liabilities with an investment portfolio that produces a deterministic stream of cash flows.
- One can compute the optimal profit of a company given the sources of earnings and cost structure.
- One can rebalance a portfolio so as to minimize transaction costs.

What you will learn after reading this chapter:

- The general concept of optimization and mathematical programming.
- How to use a Hessian matrix and Hessian determinants to find the maxima and minima.
- How to use Lagrange multipliers to find a local optimum.
- What linear, quadratic, and stochastic programming techniques are.
- What are calculus of variations and optimal control theory.
- How to deal with bond portfolio management and portfolio immunization.
- How to determine optimal portfolio weights in portfolio construction.

INTRODUCTION

The concept of optimization is intrinsic to finance theory. The seminal work of Harry Markowitz demonstrated that financial decision making is essentially a question of an optimal trade-off between risk and return. In modern terminology, an optimization problem is called a **mathematical programming problem**.

From an analytical perspective, a static mathematical program attempts to identify the maxima or minima of a function $f(x_1, \ldots, x_n)$ of n real-valued variables, called the **objective function**, in a domain identified by a set of constraints. The latter might take the general form of inequalities $g_i(x_1, \ldots, x_n) \geq b_i$. **Linear programming** is the specialization of mathematical programming to instances where both f and the constraints are linear. **Quadratic programming** is the specialization of mathematical programming to instances where f is a quadratic function. The Markowitz mean-variance approach leads to a quadratic programming problem.

A different, and more difficult, problem is the optimization of a dynamic process. In this case, the objective function depends on the entire realization of a process, which is often not deterministic but stochastic. Decisions might be taken at intermediate steps on the basis of information revealed up to that point. This is the concept of **recourse**, that is, revision of past decisions. This area of optimization is called **stochastic programming**.

From an application perspective, mathematical programming is an optimization tool that allows the rationalization of many business or technological decisions. The computational tractability of the resulting analytical models is a key issue in mathematical programming. The simplex algorithm, developed in 1947 by George Dantzig, was one of the first tractable mathematical programming algorithms to be developed for linear programming. Its subsequent successful implementation contributed to the acceptance of optimization as a scientific approach to decision making and initiated the field known as operations research.

Optimization is a highly technical subject, which we will not fully develop in this chapter. Instead, our objective is to give the reader a general understanding of the technology. We begin with an explanation of maxima or minima of a multivariate function subject to constraints. We then discuss the basic tools for static optimization: linear programming and quadratic programming. After introducing the idea of optimizing a process and defining the concepts of the **calculus of variations** and **control theory**, we briefly cover the techniques of stochastic programming.

MAXIMA AND MINIMA

Consider a multivariate function $f(x_1, \ldots, x_n)$ of n real-valued variables. Suppose that f is twice differentiable. Define the gradient of f, grad$f$ also written ∇f, as the vector whose components are the first-order partial derivatives of f

$$\text{grad}[f(x_1, \ldots, x_n)] = \nabla f = \left(\frac{\partial f}{\partial x_1}, \ldots, \frac{\partial f}{\partial x_n} \right)$$

Given a multivariate function $f(x_1, \ldots, x_n)$, consider the matrix formed by the second-order partial derivatives. This matrix is called the **Hessian matrix** and its determinant, denoted by H, is called the **Hessian determinant** (see Chapter 4 for definition of a matrix and determinants):

$$H = \begin{vmatrix} \dfrac{\partial^2 f}{\partial x_1^2} & \cdots & \dfrac{\partial^2 f}{\partial x_1 \partial x_n} \\ \vdots & \ddots & \vdots \\ \dfrac{\partial^2 f}{\partial x_1 \partial x_n} & \cdots & \dfrac{\partial^2 f}{\partial x_n^2} \end{vmatrix}$$

A point $(a_1, \ldots, a_n)$ is called a **relative local maxima** or a **relative local minima** of the function f if the relationship

$$f(a_1 + h_1, \ldots, x_n + h_n) \leq f(a_1, \ldots, a_n), |h| \leq d > 0$$

or, respectively,

$$f(a_1 + h_1, \ldots, x_n + h_n) \geq f(a_1, \ldots, a_n), |h| \leq d > 0$$

holds for some real positive number $d > 0$.

A necessary, but not sufficient, condition for a point $(x_1, \ldots, x_n)$ to be a relative maximum or minimum is that all first-order partial derivatives evaluated at that point vanish, that is, that the following relationship holds:

$$\text{grad}[\, f(x_1, \ldots, x_n)] = \left(\frac{\partial f}{\partial x_1} \cdots \frac{\partial f}{\partial x_n} \right) = (0, \ldots, 0)$$

A point where the gradient vanishes is called a **critical point**.

A critical point can be a maximum, a minimum, or a **saddle point**. For functions of one variable, the following sufficient conditions hold:

- ▨ If the first derivative evaluated at a point a vanishes and the second derivative evaluated at a is positive, then the point a is a (relative) minimum.
- ▨ If the first derivative evaluated at a point a vanishes and the second derivative evaluated at a is negative, then the point a is a (relative) maximum.
- ▨ If the first derivative evaluated at a point a vanishes and the second derivative evaluated at a also vanishes, then the point a is a saddle point.

In the case of a function $f(x,y)$ of two variables x,y, the following conditions hold:

- ▨ If $\nabla f = 0$ at a given point a and if the Hessian determinant evaluated at a is positive, then the function f has a relative maximum in a if $f_{xx} < 0$ or $f_{yy} < 0$ and a relative minimum if $f_{xx} > 0$ or $f_{yy} > 0$. Note that if the Hessian is positive the two second derivatives f_{xx} and f_{yy} must have the same sign.
- ▨ If $\nabla f = 0$ at a given point a and if the Hessian determinant evaluated at a is negative, then the function f has a saddle point in a.
- ▨ If $\nabla f = 0$ at a given point a and if the Hessian determinant evaluated at a vanishes, then the point a is degenerate and no conclusion can be drawn in this case.

The above conditions can be expressed in a more compact way if we consider the eigenvalues (see Chapter 4) of the Hessian matrix. If both eigenvalues are positive at a critical point a, the function has a local minimum at a; if both are negative the function has a local maximum; if they have opposite signs, the function has a saddle point; and if at least one of them is 0, the critical point is degenerate. Recall that the product of the eigenvalues is equal to the Hessian determinant.

This analysis can be carried over to the three-dimensional case. In this case, there will be three eigenvalues, all of which are positive at a local minimum and negative at a local maximum. A critical point of a function of three variables is degenerate if at least one of the eigenvalues of the Hessian determinant is 0 and has a saddle point if at least one eigenvalue is positive, at least one is negative, and none is 0.

In higher dimensions, the situation is more complex and goes beyond the scope of our introduction to optimization.

LAGRANGE MULTIPLIERS

Consider a multivariate function $f(x_1, \ldots, x_n)$ of n real-valued variables. In the previous section we saw that, if the n variables are unconstrained, a local optimum of f can be found by solving the n equations:

$$\nabla f = \left(\frac{\partial f}{\partial x_1}, \ldots, \frac{\partial f}{\partial x_n} \right) = (0, \ldots, 0)$$

Let's now discuss how to find maxima and minima when the optimization problem has equality constraints. Suppose that the n variables $(x_1, \ldots, x_n)$ are not independent, but satisfy $m < n$ constraint equations

$$g_1(x_1, \ldots, x_n) = 0$$
$$\vdots$$
$$g_m(x_1, \ldots, x_n) = 0$$

These equations define, in general, an $(n\text{-}m)$-dimensional surface. For instance, in the case of two variables, a constraint $g_1(x,y) = 0$ defines a line. In the case of three variables, one constraint $g_1(x,y,z) = 0$ defines a two-dimensional surface while two constraints $g_1(x,y,z) = 0$, $g_2(x,y,z) = 0$ define a line in the three-dimensional space, and so on.

Our objective is to find the maxima or minima of the function f for the set of points that also satisfy the constraints. It can be demonstrated that, under this restriction, the gradient ∇f of f need not vanish at the maxima or minima, but need only be orthogonal to the $(n\text{-}m)$-dimensional surface described by the constraint equations. That is, the following relationships must hold

$$\nabla f = \lambda^T \nabla g, \text{ for some } \lambda = (\lambda_1, \ldots, \lambda_m)$$

or, in the usual notation,

$$\frac{\partial f}{\partial x_i} = \sum_{j=1}^{m} \lambda_j \frac{\partial g_j}{\partial x_i}, \; i = 1, \ldots, n$$

The coefficients $(\lambda_1, \ldots, \lambda_m)$ are called **Lagrange multipliers**.

If we define the function

$$F(x_1, \ldots, x_n, \lambda_1, \ldots, \lambda_m) = f(x_1, \ldots, x_n) - \sum_{j=1}^{m} \lambda_j g_j$$

the above equations together may be written as

$$\nabla F = 0$$

or

$$\frac{\partial F}{\partial x_1} = \cdots = \frac{\partial F}{\partial x_n} = \frac{\partial F}{\partial \lambda_1} = \cdots = \frac{\partial F}{\partial \lambda_m} = 0$$

In other words, the method of Lagrange multipliers transforms a constrained optimization problem into an unconstrained optimization problem. The method consists in replacing the original objective function f to be optimized subject to the constraints g with another objective function

$$F = f - \sum_{j=1}^{m} \lambda_j g_j$$

to be optimized without constraints in the variables $(x_1, \ldots, x_n, \lambda_1, \ldots, \lambda_m)$. The Lagrange multipliers are not only a mathematical device. In many applications they have a useful physical or economic interpretation:

Example 1. Suppose we wish to maximize $f(x, y) = x + y$ subject to a constraint $x^2 + y^2 = 1$. Using the method of Lagrange multipliers, we have $g(x, y) - c = x^2 + y^2 - 1$. Hence, the constrained optimization can be written as:

$$\Lambda(x, y, \lambda) = f(x, y) + \lambda(g(x, y) - c) = x + y + \lambda(x^2 + y^2 - 1)$$

Maximizing $\Lambda(x, y, \lambda)$ with respect to x, y, and λ yields the system of equations:

$$\frac{\partial \Lambda}{\partial x} = 1 + 2\lambda x = 0$$

$$\frac{\partial \Lambda}{\partial y} = 1 + 2\lambda y = 0$$

$$\frac{\partial \Lambda}{\partial \lambda} = x^2 + y^2 - 1 = 0$$

where the last equation is the original constraint.

The first two equations yield $x = -1/2\lambda$ and $y = -1/2\lambda$, where $\lambda \neq 0$. Substituting into the last equation yields $1/(4\lambda^2) + 1/(4\lambda^2) = 1$, so $\lambda = \mp\sqrt{2}/2$, which implies that the optimal solutions are $(\sqrt{2}/2, \sqrt{2}/2)$ and $(-\sqrt{2}/2, -\sqrt{2}/2)$. Evaluating the objective function f at these points yields

$$f\left(\sqrt{2}/2, \sqrt{2}/2\right) = \sqrt{2}$$

and

$$f\left(-\sqrt{2}/2, -\sqrt{2}/2\right) = -\sqrt{2}$$

thus the maximum is $\sqrt{2}$, which is attained at $(\sqrt{2}/2, \sqrt{2}/2)$, and the minimum is $-\sqrt{2}$, which is attained at $(-\sqrt{2}/2, -\sqrt{2}/2)$.

Example 2. A firm uses two inputs, denoted by x and y, to produce one output. Its production function is

$$f(x, y) = x^a y^b$$

The price of output is p, and the prices of the inputs are w_x and w_y. Suppose the firm is constrained by a law that says it must use exactly the same number of units of both inputs. Thus the firm's optimization problem is to maximize profit:

$$\left[px^a y^b - w_x x - w_y y \right]$$

subject to $y - x = 0$.

The Lagrangian is

$$\Lambda(x, y, \lambda) = px^a y^b - w_x x - w_y y - \lambda(y - x)$$

so the first-order conditions are

$$apx^{a-1} y^b - w_x + \lambda = 0$$
$$bpx^a y^{b-1} - w_y + \lambda = 0$$
$$y - x = 0$$

These equations have a single solution, with

$$x = y = \frac{w_x + w_y}{(p(a+b))^{1/(a+b-1)}}$$

$$\lambda = \frac{bw_x - aw_y}{a + b}$$

Given the values of a and b in the production function, the prices of inputs (w_x and w_y), and the price of output (p), we can find the optimal values of inputs (x, y) that maximize profit.

Example 3. Consider the following utility maximization problem:

$$\max_{c_1, c_2} c_1 c_2^{0.6}$$

subject to $y_1 = \$1,000$, $y_2 = \$648$, and $r = .08$, so that

$$w_1 = y_1 + \frac{y_2}{1+r} + r = \$1,000 + \frac{648}{1.08} = \$1,600$$

Here we have assumed a specific form of the utility function and specific values for incomes and the interest rate, so that we can obtain a numerical answer to the consumption-investment problem. The function $c_1 c_2^{0.6}$ is the utility function; $c_1 c_2^{0.6}$ = constant represents the equation of an indifference curve.

The consumer's problem is to maximize utility by finding the optimal consumption pattern (c_1^*, c_2^*) with a present value of $1,600. That is, the solution to the problem must satisfy[1]

$$c_1 + \frac{c_2}{1.08} = \$1,600$$

We can rewrite the last condition as

$$c_2 = (\$1,600 - c_1)(1.08)$$

Then, substitution into the original maximization problem gives

$$\max_{c_1} \; c_1[(\$1,600 - c_1)(1.08)]^{0.6}$$

A solution to the last problem can be found by setting the derivative taken with respect to c_1 equal to zero. Taking the derivative gives

$$(\$1,600 - c_1)^{0.6} - c_1(0.6)(\$1,600 - c_1)^{-0.4} = 0$$

We then have

$$(\$1,600 - c_1)^{0.6} = 0.6c_1(\$1,600 - c_1)^{-0.4}$$

or

$$(\$1,600 - c_1) = 0.6c_1$$

so that

$$1.6c_1 = \$1,600$$

and hence the solution for time 1 consumption is

$$c_1^* = \$1,000$$

---

[1]Actually, it cannot exceed $1,600. But since spending more money on consumption is assumed to give greater satisfaction, the consumer will always spend all available funds. Incidentally, some of this spending can be interpreted as a bequest, so the consumer, while a materialist, need not be lacking in altruism.

Moreover, since

$$c_1^* + \frac{c_2^*}{1.08} = \$1,600, \quad \frac{c_2^*}{1.08} = \$600$$

so that

$$c_2^* = \$600(1.08) = \$648$$

This consumer is atypical in neither borrowing nor lending; that is, the optimal consumption pattern is exactly the same as the income stream. Formally,

$$c_1^* = y_1$$

and

$$c_2^* = y_2$$

NUMERICAL ALGORITHMS

The method of Lagrange multiplers works with equality constraints, that is, when the solution is constrained to stay on the surface defined by the constraints. Optimization problems become more difficult if inequality constraints are allowed. This means that the admissible solutions must stay within the boundary defined by the constraints. In this case, approximate numerical methods are often needed. Numerical algorithms or "solvers" to many standard optimization problems are available in many computer packages.

Linear Programming

The general form for a linear programming (LP) problem is as follows. Minimize a **linear objective function**

$$f(x_1, \ldots, x_n) = c_1 x_1 + \cdots + c_n x_n$$

or, in vector notation,

$$f(x_1, \ldots, x_n) = \mathbf{c}^T \mathbf{x}, \quad \mathbf{c} = (c_1, \ldots, c_n), \mathbf{x} = (x_1, \ldots, x_n)$$

subject to the constraints

$$a_{i,1}x_1 + \cdots + a_{i,n}x_n \begin{pmatrix} \leq \\ = \\ \geq \end{pmatrix} b_i, \quad i = 1, 2, \ldots, m$$

or, in matrix notation,

$$\mathbf{A}\mathbf{x} \begin{pmatrix} \leq \\ = \\ \geq \end{pmatrix} \mathbf{b}$$

with additional **sign restrictions** such as $x_i \leq 0$, $x_i \geq 0$, or x_i unrestricted in sign.

The largest or smallest value of the objective function is called the **optimal value**, and a vector $[x_1 \ldots x_n]$ that gives the optimal value constitutes an **optimal solution**. The variables $x_1, \ldots, x_n$ are called the **decision variables**. The **feasible region** determined by a collection of linear inequalities is the collection of points that satisfy all of the inequalities. The optimal solution belongs to the feasible region.

The above formulation has the general structure of a mathematical programming problem as outlined in the introduction to the chapter, but is characterized, in addition, by the fact that the objective function and the constraints are *linear*.

LP problems can be transformed into **standard form**. An LP is said to be in *standard form* if (1) all *constraints* are *equality* constraints and (2) all the variables have a *nonnegativity sign restriction*. An LP problem in standard form can therefore be written as follows

$$\min \ \mathbf{c}^T \mathbf{x}$$

subject to constraints

$$\left. \begin{array}{l} \mathbf{A}\mathbf{x} = \mathbf{b} \\ \mathbf{x} \geq 0 \end{array} \right\}$$

where $\mathbf{A}$ is an $m \times n$ matrix and $\mathbf{b}$ is an m-vector.

Every LP can be brought into standard form through the following transformations:

1. An inequality constraint

$$a_{i,1} x_1 + \cdots + a_{i,n} x_n \begin{pmatrix} \leq \\ = \\ \geq \end{pmatrix} b_i$$

can be converted into an equality constraint through the introduction of a **slack variable**, denoted by S, or an **excess variable**, denoted by E, such that

$$a_{i,1} x_1 + \cdots + a_{i,n} x_n + S = b_i$$

or

$$a_{i,1} x_1 + \cdots + a_{i,n} x_n - E = b_i$$

2. A variable with negative sign restriction $x_i \leq 0$ can be substituted by $x_i = -x_i', x_i' \geq 0$ while an unrestricted variable can be substituted by $x_i = x_i' - x_i'', x_i', x_i'' \geq 0$.

Quadratic Programming

The general quadratic programming (QP) problem is a mathematical programming problem where the objective function is quadratic and constraints are linear as follows:

$$\text{minimize } f(x_1, \ldots, x_n) = \mathbf{c}^T \mathbf{x} + \frac{1}{2} \mathbf{x}^T \mathbf{D} \mathbf{x}$$

where $\mathbf{c} = (c_1, \ldots, c_n)$, $\mathbf{x} = (x_1, \ldots, x_n)$ are n-vectors, and $\mathbf{D}$ is a $n \times n$ matrix, subject to

$$\mathbf{a}_i \mathbf{x} \leq b_i, i \in I$$
$$\mathbf{a}_i \mathbf{x} = b_i, i \in E$$
$$\mathbf{x} \geq 0$$

where $\mathbf{b}$ is an m-vector $\mathbf{b} = (b_1, \ldots, b_m)$, $\mathbf{A} = [\mathbf{a}_i]$ is an $m \times n$ matrix, and I and E specify the nonequality and equality constraints respectively.

The major classification criteria for these problems come from the characteristics of the matrix **D** as follows:

- If the matrix **D** is positive semidefinite or positive definite, then the QP problem is a convex quadratic problem. For convex quadratic problems, every local maximum is a global maximum. The Markowitz mean-variance optimization problem is of this type.
- If the matrix **D** is negative semidefinite, that is, its eigenvalues are all nonpositive, then the QP problem is a concave quadratic problem. All solutions lie at some vertex of the feasible regions. There are efficient algorithms for solving this problem.
- If the matrix **D** is such that the problem is bilinear, that is, the variables **x** can be split into two subvectors such that the problem is linear when one of the two subvectors is fixed, then the QP problem is bilinear. There are efficient algorithms for solving this problem.
- If the matrix **D** is indefinite, that is, it has both positive and negative eigenvalues, then the QP problem is very difficult to solve. Depending on the matrix **D**, the complexity of the problem might grow exponentially with the number of variables.

Many modern software optimization packages have solvers for several of these problems.

The Markowitz mean-variance optimization provides a maximum expected return of a portfolio subject to a risk constraint or provides a minimum portfolio risk subject to an expected return constraint. To illustrate we assume a two-asset portfolio with a short-sale constraint.[2]

Suppose that expected returns on assets A and B are given by $E(R_A)$ and $E(R_B)$, respectively. The standard deviations are σ_A and σ_B, and the correlation between assets A and B is denoted by ρ. Then, investors maximize expected return of a portfolio:

$$\max_{\{w_A, w_B\}} E(R_p) = w_A E(R_A) + w_B E(R_B)$$

subject to a risk constraint

$$\sigma_p \leq \bar{\sigma}_p$$

[2] H. M. Markowitz, "Portfolio Selection," *Journal of Finance* 7 1 (1952): 77–91.

where w_A and w_B are the portfolio weights or proportion of wealth invested on assets A and B, respectively. The risk of the portfolio is measured by the standard deviation:

$$\sigma_p = \sqrt{w_A^2 \sigma_A^2 + w_B^2 \sigma_B^2 + 2 w_A w_B \rho \sigma_A \sigma_B}$$

Alternatively, investors may choose to minimize risk of the portfolio

$$\min_{\{w_A, w_B\}} \sigma_p = \sqrt{w_A^2 \sigma_A^2 + w_B^2 \sigma_B^2 + 2 w_A w_B \rho \sigma_A \sigma_B}$$

subject to an expected return constraint

$$E(R_p) \geq \bar{R}_p$$

Since we impose a short-sale constraint as well, the Markowitz optimization is formulated as

$$\max_{\{w_A, w_B\}} E(R_p) = w_A E(R_A) + w_B E(R_B)$$

s.t.,

$$\sigma_p \leq \bar{\sigma}_p, w_A \geq 0, w_B \geq 0$$

and

$$w_A + w_B = 1$$

For example, if $E(R_A) = 10\%$, $E(R_B) = 20\%$, $\sigma_A = 25\%$, $\sigma_B = 35\%$, $\rho = -0.5$, and $\bar{\sigma}_p = 15\%$, the constraint optimization yields the portfolio weights $w_A = 53.77\%$ and $w_B = 46.23\%$.

Similarly, if we minimize the portfolio risk:

$$\min_{\{w_A, w_B\}} \sigma_p = \sqrt{w_A^2 \sigma_A^2 + w_B^2 \sigma_B^2 + 2 w_A w_B \rho \sigma_A \sigma_B}$$

s.t.,

$$E(R_p) \geq \bar{R}_p, w_A \geq 0, w_B \geq 0$$

and

$$w_A + w_B = 1$$

For example, if $E(R_A) = 10\%$, $E(R_B) = 20\%$, $\sigma_A = 25\%$, $\sigma_B = 35\%$, $\rho = -0.5$, and $\bar{R}_p = 12\%$, the constraint optimization gives the portfolio weights $w_A = 61.01\%$ and $w_B = 38.99\%$.

CALCULUS OF VARIATIONS AND OPTIMAL CONTROL THEORY

We have thus far discussed the problem of finding the maxima or minima of a function of n real variables. The solution to these problems is typically one point in a domain. This formulation is sufficient for problems such as finding the optimal composition of a portfolio for a single period of a finite horizon: An investment is made at the initial time and a payoff is received at the end of the period. However, many other important optimization problems in finance require finding an optimal function or path throughout time and over multiple periods.

The mathematical foundation for problems whose solution requires finding an optimal function or path of this kind is the **calculus of variations**. The basic setting of the calculus of variations is the following. An infinite set of admissible functions $y = f(x)$, $x_0 \leq x \leq x_1$ is given. The end points might vary from curve to curve. Let's assume all curves are differentiable in the given interval $[x_0, x_1]$. A function of three variables $F(x, y, z)$ is given such that the integral

$$J_y = \int_{x_0}^{x_1} F(x, y, y') dx$$

is well defined where $y' = dy/dx$. The value of J depends on the curve y. The basic problem of the calculus of variations is to find the curve $y = f(x)$ that minimizes J. This problem could be easily reformulated in many variables.

One strategy for solving this problem is the following. Any solution $y = f(x)$ has the property that, if we slightly displace the curve y, the integral assumes higher values. Therefore if we parameterize parallel displacements with a variable ε (denoting by $\{y_\varepsilon\}$ the collection of all such displacements from the optimal y such that $y_\varepsilon |_{\varepsilon=0} = y$), the derivative of J with respect to ε must vanish for $\varepsilon = 0$.

If we compute this derivative, we arrive at the following differential equation that must be satisfied by the optimal solution y:

$$\frac{\partial F(x, y, y')}{\partial y} - \frac{d}{dx} \frac{\partial F(x, y, y')}{\partial y'} = 0$$

First established by Leonard Euler in 1744, this differential equation is known as the **Euler equation** or the **Euler-Lagrange equation**.

Though fundamental in the physical sciences, this formulation of variational principles is rarely encountered in finance theory. In finance theory, as in engineering, one is primarily interested in controlling the evolution of a process. For instance, in investment management, one is interested in controlling the composition of a portfolio in order to attain some objective. This is the realm of control theory. Let's now define control theory in a deterministic setting. The following section will discuss stochastic programming—a computational implementation of control theory in a stochastic setting.

Consider a dynamic process which starts at a given initial time t_0 and ends at a given terminal time t_1. Let's suppose that the state of the system is described by only one variable $x(t)$ called the **state variable**. The state of the system is influenced by a set of control variables that we represent as a vector $\mathbf{u}(t) = [u_1(t), \ldots, u_n(t)]$. The control vector must lie inside a given subset of a Euclidean r-dimensional space, U which is assumed to be closed and time-invariant. An entire path of the control vector is called a control. A control is admissible if it stays in U and satisfies some regularity conditions.

The dynamics of the state variables are specified through the differential equation

$$\frac{dx}{dt} = f_1[x(t), \mathbf{u}(t)]$$

where f_1 is assumed to be continuously differentiable with respect to both arguments. Suppose that the initial state is given but the terminal state is unrestricted.

The problem to be solved is that of maximizing the objective functional:

$$J_y = \int_{t_0}^{t_1} f_0[t, x(t), \mathbf{u}(t)]dt + S[t_1, x(t_1)]$$

A **functional** is a mapping from a set of functions into the set of real numbers; it associates a number to each function. The definite integral is an example of a functional.

To solve the above optimal control problem, a useful strategy is to find a set of differential equations that must be satisfied by the control. Two major approaches for solving this problem are available: **Bellman's Dynamic Programming**[3] and **Pontryagin's Maximum Principle**.[4] The former approach is based on the fact that the value of the state variable at time t captures all the necessary information for the decision-making from time t and onward: The paths of the control vector and the state variable up to time t do not make any difference as long as the state variable at time t is the same. Bellmann showed how to derive from this observation a partial differential equation that uniquely determines the control. Pontryagin's Maximum Principle introduces additional auxiliary variables and derives differential equations via the calculus of variations that might be simpler to solve than those of Bellmann's dynamic programming.

STOCHASTIC PROGRAMMING

The model formulations discussed thus far assume that the data for the given problem are known precisely. However, in financial economics, data are stochastic and cannot be known with certainty. Stochastic programming can be used to make optimal decisions under uncertainty. The fundamental idea behind stochastic programming is the concept of stages and recourse. **Recourse** is the ability to take corrective action at a future time, that is, a decision stage, after a random event has taken place.

To formulate problems of dynamic decision making under uncertainty as a stochastic program, we must first characterize the uncertainty in the model. The most common method is to formulate scenarios and to assign to each scenario a probability. A **scenario** is a complete path of data. To illustrate the problem of stochastic programming, let's consider a two-stage program that seeks to minimize the cost of the first-period decision plus the expected cost of the second-period recourse decision. In the next section, we provide an example related to bond portfolio management.

To cast the stochastic programming problem in the framework of LP, we need to create a deterministic equivalent of the stochastic problem. This is obtained introducing a new set of variables at each stage and taking expectations. The first-period direct cost is $c^T x$ while the recourse cost at the

---

[3]R. Bellman, *Dynamic Programming* (Princeton, NJ: Princeton University Press, 1957).
[4]For a discussion of Pontryagin's Maximum Principle see, for instance: E. B. Lee and L. Marcus, *Foundations of Optimal Control Theory* (New York: John Wiley & Sons, 1967).

second stage is $d_i^T y_i$ where $i = 1, \ldots, S$ represents the different states. The first-period constraints are represented as $\mathbf{Ax} = \mathbf{b}$. At each stage, recourse is subject to some recourse function $\mathbf{Tx} + \mathbf{Wy} = \mathbf{h}$. This constraint can be, for example, self-financing conditions in portfolio management. It should be noted that in stochastic programs the first-period decision is independent of which second-period scenario actually occurs. This is called the **nonanticipativity property**.

A two-stage problem can be formulated as follows:

$$\text{minimize } \mathbf{c}^T\mathbf{x} + \sum_{i=1}^{s} p_i \mathbf{d}_i^T \mathbf{y}i$$

subject to

$$\mathbf{Ax} = \mathbf{b}$$
$$\mathbf{T}_i\mathbf{x} + \mathbf{W}_i\mathbf{y}_i = \mathbf{h}_i, \quad i = 1, \ldots, S$$
$$\mathbf{x} \geq 0$$
$$\mathbf{y}_i \geq 0$$

where S is the number of states and p_i is the probability of each state such that

$$\sum_{i=1}^{S} p_i = 1$$

Notice that the nonanticipativity constraint is met. There is only one first-period decision whereas there are S second-period decisions, one for each scenario. In this formulation, the stochastic programming problem has been reduced to an LP problem. This formulation can be extended to any number of intermediate stages.

APPLICATION TO BOND PORTFOLIO: LIABILITY-FUNDING STRATEGIES

In bond portfolio management, **liability-funding strategies** are strategies whose objective is to match a given set of liabilities due at future times. These strategies provide the cash flows needed at given dates at a minimum cost and with zero or minimal interest rate risk. However, depending on the universe of bonds that are permitted to be included in the portfolio, there may be credit risk and/or call risk. Liability-funding strategies are used by (1) sponsors of defined benefit pension plans (i.e., there is a contractual liability to make payments to beneficiaries); (2) insurance companies for single premium deferred annuities (i.e., a policy in which the issuer agrees for a single premium to make payments to policyholders over time), guaranteed investment contracts (i.e., a policy in which the issuer agrees for a single premium to make a single payment to a policyholder at a specified date with a guaranteed interest rate); and (3) municipal governments for prefunding municipal bond issues (i.e., creating a portfolio that replicates the payments that must be made for an outstanding municipal government bond issue), and, for states, payments that must be made to lottery winners who have agreed to accept payments over time rather than a lump sum.

There are two types of solutions to the problem of liability funding currently used by practitioners: (1) numerical/analytical solutions based on the concept of duration and convexity and (2) numerical solutions based on optimization methodologies. Ultimately, all methodologies can be cast in the framework of optimization, but duration and convexity play an important role from the practical as well as conceptual point of view. We will begin by discussing the cash-flow matching approach in a deterministic context and then successively discuss strategies based on duration and convexity (see Chapter 2) and lastly a full stochastic programming approach.

Cash Flow Matching

Cash flow matching (CFM), also referred to as a **dedicated portfolio strategy,** in a deterministic environment is the problem of matching a predetermined set of liabilities with an investment portfolio that produces a deterministic stream of cash flows.[5] In this context, fluctuations of interest rates, credit risk, and other sources of uncertainty are ignored. There are, however, conditions where financial decisions have to be made. Among them we will consider:

- Reinvestment of excess cash
- Borrowing against future cash flows to match liabilities
- Trading constraints such as odd lots

---

[5]For an illustration of cash flow matching applied to pension fund liabilities, see F. J. Fabozzi and P. F. Christensen, "Dedicated Bond Portfolios," Chapter 45 in *The Handbook of Fixed Income Securities*, ed. F. J. Fabozzi (New York: McGraw-Hill, 2000).

To formulate the model, consider a set of m dates $\{t_0, t_1, \ldots, t_m\}$ and a universe U of investable assets $U = \{1, 2, \ldots, n\}$. Call $\{K_{i,0}, \ldots, K_{i,m}\}$ the stream of cash flows related to the ith asset. We will consider only bonds but most considerations that will be developed apply to broader classes of assets with positive and negative cash flows. In the case of a bond with unit price P_i per unit par value 1, with coupon $c_{i,t}$, and with maturity k, the cash flows are

$$\{-P_i, c_{i,1}, \ldots, c_{i,k-1}, c_{i,k} + 1, 0, \ldots, 0\}$$

Let's call L_t the liability at time t. Liabilities must be met with a portfolio

$$\sum_{i \in U} \alpha_i P_i$$

where α_i is the amount of bond i in the portfolio. The CFM problem can be written, in its simplest form, in the following way:

$$\text{Minimize } \sum_{i \in U} \alpha_i P_i, \text{ subject to the constraints,}$$

$$\sum_{i \in U} \alpha_i K_{i,t} \geq L_t$$

$$\alpha_i \geq 0$$

The last constraint specifies that short selling is not permitted.

The above formulation of the CFM as an optimization problem is too crude as it takes into account only the fact that it is practically impossible to create exactly the required cash flows. In fact, in this formulation at each date there will be an excess of cash not used to satisfy the liability due at that date. If borrowing and reinvesting are allowed, as is normally the case, excess cash can be reinvested and used at the next date while small cash shortcomings can be covered with borrowing.

Suppose, therefore, that it is possible to borrow in each period an amount b_t at the rate β_t and reinvest an amount r_t at the rate ρ_t. Suppose that these rates are the same for all periods. At each period we will require that the positive cash flow exactly matches liabilities. Therefore, coupon payments of that period plus the amount reinvested in the previous period augmented by the interest earned on this amount plus the reinvestment of that period will be equal to the liabilities of the same period, plus the repayment of borrowing in the previous period plus the eventual new borrowing of the period. The optimization problem can be formulated as follows:

$$\text{Minimize} \sum_{i \in U} \alpha_i P_i, \text{ subject to the constraints,}$$

$$\sum_{i \in U} \alpha_i K_{i,t} + (1 + \rho_t)r_{t-1} + b_t = L_t + (1 + \beta_t)b_{t-1} + r_t$$

$$b_m = 0$$

$$\alpha_i \geq 0; \ i \in U$$

The CFM problem formulated in this way is a LP problem discussed earlier in this chapter. Problems of this type can be routinely solved on desktop computers using standard off-the-shelf software.

The next step is to consider trading constraints, such as the need to purchase "even" lots of assets. Under these constraints, assets can be purchased only in multiples of some minimal quantity, the even lots. For a large organization, purchasing smaller amounts, "odd" lots, might be suboptimal and might result in substantial costs and illiquidity.

The optimization problem that results from the purchase of assets in multiples of a minimal quantity is much more difficult. It is no longer a relatively simple LP problem but it becomes a much harder mixed-integer programming (MIP) problem. An MIP problem is conceptually more difficult and computationally much more expensive to solve than an LP problem.

The next step involves allowing for transaction costs. The objective of including transaction costs is to avoid portfolios made up of many assets held in small quantities. Including transaction costs, which must be divided between fixed and variable costs, will again result in an MIP problem which will, in general, be quite difficult to solve.

In the formulation of the CFM problem discussed thus far, it was implicitly assumed that the dates of positive cash flows and liabilities are the same. This might not be the case. There might be a small misalignment due to the practical availability of funds or positive cash flows might be missing when liabilities are due. To cope with these problems, one could simply generate a bigger model with more dates so that all the dates corresponding to inflows and outflows are properly considered. In a number of cases, this will be the only possible solution. A simpler solution, when feasible, consists in adjusting the dates so that they match, considering the positive interest earnings or negative costs incurred to match dates.

In the above formulation of the CFM problem, the initial investment cost is the only variable to optimize: The eventual residual cash at the end of the last period is considered lost. However, it is possible to design a different model under the following scenario. One might try to maximize the final cash position, subject to the constraint of meeting all the liabilities and within the constraint of an investment budget. In other words, one starts with an investment budget which should be at least sufficient to cover all the liabilities. The optimization problem is to maximize the final cash position.

We have just described the CFM problem in a deterministic setting. This is more than an academic exercise as many practical dedication problems can be approximately cast into this framework. Generally speaking, however, a dedication problem would require a stochastic formulation, which in turn requires multistage stochastic optimization.[6] Later we discuss dedication in a multistage stochastic formulation, as well as other bond portfolio optimization problems. Let's now discuss portfolio immunization, which is the numerical/analytical solution of a special dedication problem under a stochastic framework.

Portfolio Immunization

The actuary generally credited with pioneering the immunization strategy is Reddington, who defined immunization in 1952 as "the investment of the assets in such a way that the existing business is immune to a general change in the rate of interest."[7] The mathematical formulation of the immunization problem was proposed by Fisher and Weil in 1971.[8] The framework is the following in the single liability case (which we refer to as **single-period immunization**): Given a predetermined liability at a fixed time horizon, create a portfolio able to satisfy the given liability even if interest rates change.

The problem would be simple to solve if investors were happy to invest in U.S. Treasury zero-coupon bonds (i.e., U.S. Treasury strips) maturing at

---

[6]For a discussion of the stochastic case, see H. Dahl, A. Meeraus, and S.A. Zenios, "Some Financial Optimization Models," in *Financial Optimization*, ed. S. A. Zenios (Cambridge: Cambridge University Press, 1993).

[7]F. M. Reddington, "Review of the Principle of Life-Office Valuations," *Journal of the Institute of Actuaries* 78, no. 3 (1952): 286–340.

[8]L. Fisher and R. L. Weil, "Coping with the Risk of Interest-Rate Fluctuations: Returns to Bondholders from Naive and Optimal Strategies," *Journal of Business* 44, no. 4 (1971): 408–431.

exactly the given date of the liability. However, investors seek to earn a return greater than the risk-free rate. For example, the typical product where a portfolio immunization strategy is used is a guaranteed investment contract (GIC) offered by a life insurance company. This product is typically offered to a pension plan. The insurer receives a single premium from the pension sponsor and in turn guarantees an interest rate that will be earned such that the payment to the policyholder at a specified date is equal to the premium plus the guaranteed interest. The interest rate offered on the policy is greater than that on existing risk-free securities, otherwise a potential policy buyer can do the immunization without the need for the insurance company's service. The objective of the insurance company is to earn a higher rate than that offered on the policy (i.e., the guaranteed interest rate).[9]

The solution of the problem is based on the fact that a rise in interest rates produces a drop in bond prices but an increase in the reinvestment income on newly invested sums, while a fall of interest rates increases bond prices but decreases the reinvestment income on newly invested sums. One can therefore choose an investment strategy such that the change in a portfolio's value is offset by changes in the returns earned by the reinvestment of the cash obtained through coupon payments or the repayment of the principal of bonds maturing prior to the liability date.

The principle applies in the case of multiple liabilities. To see how **multiple-period immunization** works, let's first demonstrate that—given a stream of cash flows at fixed dates—there is one instant at which the value of the stream is insensitive to small parallel shifts in interest rates. Consider a case where a sum V_0 is initially invested in a portfolio of risk-free bonds (i.e., bonds with no default risk) that produces a stream of N deterministic cash flows K_i at fixed dates t_i. At each time t_i the sum K_i is reinvested at the risk-free rate. Suppose that there is only one interest rate r common to all periods. The following relationship holds:

$$V_0 = \sum_{i=1}^{N} K_i e^{-rt_i}$$

where we have used the formula for the present value in continuous time.

---

[9]For a discussion of the implementation issues associated with immunization, see F. J. Fabozzi and P. F. Christensen, "Bond Immunization: An Asset/Liability Optimization Strategy," Chapter 44 in *The Handbook of Fixed Income Securities*, 6th ed.

As each intermediate payment is reinvested, the value of the portfolio at any instant t is given by the following expression:

$$V_t = \sum_{i=1}^{N} K_i e^{-r(t-t_i)} = e^{rt} V_0$$

Our objective is to determine a time t such that the value V_t at time t of the portfolio is insensitive to parallel shifts in the interest rate. The quantity V_t is a function of the interest rate r. The derivative of V_t with respect to r must be zero so that V_t is insensitive to interest rate changes. Let's compute the derivative:

$$\frac{dV_t}{dr} = \sum_{i=1}^{N} K_i (t - t_i) e^{r(t-t_i)}$$

$$= tV_t - V_t \frac{\sum_{i=1}^{N} K_i t_i e^{-rt_i}}{V_0}$$

$$= V \left[t - \sum_{i=1}^{N} t_i \left(\frac{K_i e^{-rt_i}}{V_0} \right) \right]$$

From this expression it is clear that the derivative

$$\frac{dV_t}{dr}$$

is zero at a time horizon equal to the portfolio duration. In fact, the quantity

$$\sum_{i=1}^{N} t_i \left(\frac{K_i e^{-rt_i}}{V_0} \right)$$

is the portfolio's duration expressed in continuous time.

Therefore, if the term structure of interest rates is flat, we can match a given liability with a portfolio whose duration is equal to the time of the liability and whose present value is equal to the present value of the liability. This portfolio will be insensitive to small parallel shifts of the term structure of interest rates.

We can now extend and generalize this reasoning. Consider a stream of liabilities L_t. Our objective is to match this stream of liabilities with a stream of cash flows from some initial investment insensitive to changes in interest rates. First we want to prove that the present value of liabilities and of cash flows must match. Consider the framework of CFM with reinvestment but no borrowing:

$$\sum_{i \in U} \alpha_i K_{i,t} + (1 + \rho_t) r_{t-1} = L_t + r_t$$

$$\sum_{i \in U} \alpha_i K_{i,t} - L_t \geq 0$$

$$a_i \geq 0; i \in U$$

We can recursively write the following relationships:

$$\sum_{i \in U} \alpha_i K_{i,1} - L_t = r_1$$

$$\sum_{i \in U} \alpha_i K_{i,2} + (1 + \rho_2) \sum_{i \in U} \alpha_i K_{i,1} = (1 + \rho_2) L_1 + L_2 + r_2$$

$$\dots$$

$$\sum_{i=1}^{n} \left[\alpha_i K_{i,1} \prod_{t=2}^{m} (1 + \rho_t) + \cdots + \alpha_i K_{i,m} \right] = L_1 \prod_{t=2}^{m} (1 + \rho_t) + \cdots + L_m$$

$$a_i \geq 0; \; i \in U$$

If we divide both sides of the last equation by

$$\prod_{t=2}^{m} (1 + \rho_t)$$

we see that the present value of the portfolio's stream of cash flows must be equal to the present value of the stream of liabilities. We can rewrite the above expression in continuous-time notation as

$$\sum_{i=1}^{n} \left[\alpha_i K_{i,1} + \cdots + \alpha_i K_{i,m} e^{-r_m t_m} \right] = L_1 + \cdots + L_m e^{-r_m t_m}$$

As in the case of CFM, if cash flows and liabilities do not occur at the same dates, we can construct an enlarged model with more dates. At these dates, cash flows or liabilities can be zero.

To see under what conditions this expression is insensitive to small parallel shifts of the term structure, we perturb the term structure by a small shift r and compute the derivative with respect to r for $r = 0$. In this way, all rates are written as $r_t + r$. If we compute the derivatives we obtain the following equation:

$$\frac{d \sum_{i=1}^{n} \left[\alpha_i K_{i,1} + \cdots + \alpha_i K_{i,m} e^{-(r_m+r)t_m} \right]}{dr} = \frac{d[L_1 + \cdots + L_m e^{-(r_m+r)t_m}]}{dr}$$

$$-\sum_{i=1}^{n} \left[\alpha_i K_{i,1} + \cdots + \alpha_i K_{i,m} t_m e^{-(r_m+r)t_m} \right] = -[L_1 + \cdots + L_m t_m e^{-(r_m+r)t_m}]$$

which tells us that the first-order conditions for portfolio immunization are that the duration of the cash flows must be equal to the duration of the liabilities. This duration is intended in the sense of effective duration which allows for a shift in the term structure. This condition does not determine univocally the portfolio.

To determine the portfolio, we can proceed in two ways. The first is through optimization. Optimization calls for maximizing some function subject to constraints. In the CFM problem there are two constraints: (1) The initial present value of cash flows must match the initial present value of liabilities, and (2) the duration of cash flows must match the duration of liabilities. A typical objective function is the portfolio's return at the final date. It can be demonstrated that this problem can be approximated by an LP problem.

Optimization might not be ideal as the resulting portfolio might be particularly exposed to the risk of nonparallel shifts of the term structure. In fact, it can be demonstrated that the result of the yield maximization under immunization constraints tends to produce a barbell type of portfolio. A **barbell portfolio** is one in which the portfolio is concentrated at short-term and long-term maturity securities. A portfolio of this type is particularly exposed to yield curve risk, that is, to the risk that the term structure changes its shape.

One way to control yield curve risk is to impose second-order convexity conditions. In fact, reasoning as above and taking the second derivative of both sides, it can be demonstrated that, in order to protect the portfolio from yield curve risk, the convexity of the cash flow stream and the convexity of the liability stream must be equal. (Recall from Chapter 2 that mathematically convexity is the derivative of duration.) This approach can be generalized[10] by assuming that changes of interest rates can be approximated as a linear function of a number of risk factors. Under this assumption we can write

$$\Delta r_t = \sum_{j=1}^{k} \beta_{j,t} \Delta f_j + \varepsilon_t$$

where the f_j are the factors and ε_t is an error term that is assumed to be normally distributed with zero mean and unitary variance. Factors here are a simple discrete-time instance of the factors in the term structure in continuous time. In continuous-time finance, both interest rate processes and factors are Itô processes. Here we assume that changes in interest rates, which are a discrete-time process, are a linear function of other discrete-time processes called "factors." Each path is a vector of real numbers, one for each date.

Ignoring the error term, changes in the present value of the stream of cash flows are therefore given by the following expression:

$$\Delta V = -\sum_{i=1}^{n} [\alpha_i K_{i,1} + \cdots + \alpha_i K_{i,m} t_m e^{-r_m t_m} \Delta r_m]$$

$$= -\sum_{i=1}^{n} \left[\alpha_i K_{i,1} + \cdots + \alpha_i K_{i,m} t_m e^{-r_m t_m} \sum_{j=1}^{k} \beta_{j,t_m} \Delta f_j \right]$$

The derivative of the present value with respect to one of the factors is therefore given by

$$\frac{\partial V}{\partial f_j} = -\sum_{i=1}^{n} [\alpha_i K_{i,1} + \cdots + \alpha_i K_{i,m} t_m \beta_{j,t_m} e^{-r_m t_m}]$$

---

[10]See S. Zenios, *Practical Financial Optimization: Decision Making for Financial Engineers* (Boston: Blackwell-Wiley, 2008)

The factor duration with respect to the jth factor is defined as the relative value sensitivity to that factor:

$$k_j = \frac{1}{V} \frac{\partial V}{\partial f_j}$$

The second derivative represents convexity relative to a factor:

$$Q_j = \frac{1}{V} \frac{\partial^2 V}{\partial f_j^2}$$

First- and second-order immunization conditions become the equality of factor duration and convexity relative to cash flows and liabilities.

Scenario Optimization

The above strategies are based on perturbing the term structure of interest rates with a linear function of one or more factors. We allow stochastic behavior as interest rates can vary (albeit in a controlled way through factors) and impose immunization constraints. We can obtain a more general formulation of a stochastic problem in terms of scenarios.[11] Let the variables be stochastic but assume distributions are discrete. Scenarios are joint paths of all the relevant variables. A probability number is attached to each scenario. A path of interest rates is a scenario. If we consider corporate bonds, a scenario will be formed, for example, by a joint path of interest rates and credit ratings. How scenarios are generated will be discussed later in this chapter.

Suppose that scenarios are given. Using an LP program, one can find the optimal portfolio that (1) matches all the liabilities in each scenario and (2) minimizes initial costs or maximizes final cash positions subject to budget constraints. The CFM problem can be reformulated as follows:

$$\text{Minimize} \sum_{i \in U} \alpha_i P_i, \text{ subject to the constraints,}$$

$$\sum_{i \in U} \alpha_i K_{i,t}^s + (1 + \rho_t^s) r_{t-1}^r + b_t^s = L_t^s + (1 + \beta_t^s) b_{t-1}^s + r_t^s$$

$$b_m^s = 0$$

$$a_i \geq 0; i \in U$$

---

[11] R. Dembo, "Scenario Immunization," in *Financial Optimization*.

In this formulation, all terms are stochastic and scenario-dependent except the portfolio's weights. Each scenario imposes a constraint.

Scenario optimization can also be used in a more general context. One can describe a general objective, for instance expected return or a utility function, which is scenario-dependent. Scenario-dependent constraints can be added. The optimization program maximizes or minimizes the objective function subject to the constraints.

Stochastic Programming

Strategies discussed thus far are static (or myopic) in the sense that decisions are made initially and never changed. As explained in this chapter, stochastic programming (or multistage stochastic optimization) is a more general, flexible framework in which decisions are made at multiple stages, under uncertainty, and on the basis of past decisions and information then available. Both immunization and CFM discussed above can be recast in the framework of stochastic programming. Indeed, multistage optimization is a general framework that allows one to formulate most problems in portfolio management, not only for bonds but also for other asset classes including stocks and derivatives.

Stochastic programming is a computerized numerical methodology to solve variational problems. A **variational principle** is a law expressed as the maximization of a functional, with a functional being a real-valued function defined over other functions. Most classical physics can be expressed equivalently through differential equations or variational principles.

Variational methodologies also have important applications in engineering, where they are used to select a path that maximizes or minimizes a functional given some exogenous dynamics. For example, one might want to find the optimal path that an airplane must follow in order to minimize fuel consumption or flying time. The given dynamics are the laws of motion and eventually specific laws that describe the atmosphere and the behavior of the airplane.

Economics and finance theory have inherited this general scheme. General equilibrium theories can be expressed as variational principles. However, financial applications generally assume that some dynamics are given. In the case of bond portfolios, for example, the dynamics of interest rates are assumed to be exogenously given. The problem is to find the optimal trading strategy that satisfies some specific objective. In the case of immunization an objective might be to match liabilities at the minimum cost with zero exposure to interest rate fluctuations. The solution is a path of portfolio weights. In continuous time, it would be a continuous trading strategy.

Such problems are rarely solvable analytically; numerical techniques, and in particular multistage stochastic optimization, are typically required. The key advantage of stochastic programming is its ability to optimize on the entire path followed by exogenously given quantities. In applications such as bond portfolio optimization, this is an advantage over myopic strategies which optimize looking ahead only one period. However, because stochastic programming works by creating a set of scenarios and choosing the scenario that optimizes a given objective, it involves huge computational costs. Only recently have advances in IT technology made it feasible to create the large number of scenarios required for stochastic optimization. Hence there is a renewed interest in these techniques both at academia and inside financial firms.[12]

The generation of scenarios (i.e., joint paths of the stochastic variables) is key to stochastic programming. Until recently, it was imperative to create a parsimonious system of scenarios. Complex problems could be solved only on supercomputers or massively parallel computers at costs prohibitive for most organizations. While parsimony is still a requirement, systems made of thousands of scenarios can now be solved on desktop machines.

Multistage Stochastic Programming After creating scenarios one can effectively optimize, taking into account that after initial decisions there will be recourses (i.e., new decisions eventually on a smaller set of variables) at each subsequent stage. Here we provide a brief description of multistage stochastic optimization.[13]

The key idea of stochastic programming is that at every stage a decision is made based on conditional probabilities. Scenarios form an information structure so that, at each stage, scenarios are partitioned. Conditional probabilities are evaluated on scenarios that belong to each partition. For this reason, stochastic optimization is a process that runs backwards. Optimization starts from the last period, where variables are certain, and then conditional probabilities are evaluated on each partition.

To apply optimization procedures, an equivalent deterministic problem needs to be formulated. The deterministic equivalent depends on the problem's objective. Taking expectations naturally leads to **deterministic equivalents**. A deterministic equivalent of a stochastic optimization

---

[12]A presentation of stochastic programming in finance can be found in Zenios, *Practical Financial Optimization*.

[13]For a full account of stochastic programming in finance, see Zenios, *Practical Financial Optimization*.

problem might involve maximizing or minimizing the conditional expectation of some quantity at each stage.

We will illustrate stochastic optimization in the case of CFM as a two-stage stochastic optimization problem. The first decision is made under conditions of uncertainty, while the second decision at step 1 is made with certain final values. This problem could be equivalently formulated in a *m*-period setting, admitting perfect foresight after the first period. This two-stage setting can then be extended to a true multistage setting. At the first stage there will be a new set of variables. In this case, the new variables will be the portfolio's weights at stage 1. Call S the set of scenarios. Scenarios are generated from an interest rate model. A probability p_s, $s \in S$ is associated with each scenario s. The quantity to optimize will be the expected value of final cash. The two-stage stochastic optimization problem can be formulated as follows:

$$\text{Maximize } \sum_{s \in S} p_s h_s, \text{ subject to the constraints,}$$

$$\sum_{i \in U} \alpha_i K_{i,0} + b_0 + B = r_0$$

$$\sum_{i \in U} \alpha_i K_{i,t}^s + (1 + \rho_t^s) r_{t-1}^s + b_t^s = L_t^s + (1 + \beta_t^s) b_{t-1}^s + r_t^s$$

$$\sum_{i \in U} \alpha_i P_i^s = \sum_{i \in U} \gamma_i P_i^s$$

$$b_m^s = 0$$

$$r_m^s = h^s$$

$$\alpha_i, \gamma_i \geq 0; \ i \in U$$

The first condition is the initial budget constraint, which tells us that the initial investment (which has a negative sign) plus the initial borrowing plus the initial budget B is equal to the first surplus. The second condition is the liability-matching condition. The third condition is the self-financing condition. Note that as interest rates are known in each scenario, bond prices are also known in each scenario. The fifth and sixth conditions are the statements that there is no borrowing at the final stage and that the objective is the final cash. The seventh condition is the constraint that weights are nonnegative at each stage

This formulation illustrates all the basic ingredients. The problem is formulated as a deterministic equivalent problem, setting as its objective the maximization of final expected cash. The final stage is certain and the process is backward. With this objective, the stochastic optimization problem is recast as an LP problem.

This formulation can be extended to an arbitrary number of stages. Formulating in full generality a multistage stochastic optimization problem is beyond the scope of this chapter. In fact, there are many technical points that need a careful handling.[14]

KEY POINTS

- Optimizing means finding the maxima or minima of a function or of a functional.
- Optimization is a fundamental principle of financial decision-making insofar as financial decisions are an optimal trade-off between risk and return.
- The partial derivatives of an unconstrained function vanish at maxima and minima.
- The maxima and minima of a function subject to equality constraints can be found by equating to zero the derivatives of the corresponding Lagrangian function, which is the sum of the original function and of a linear combination of the constraints.
- If constraints are linear inequalities, the problem can be solved numerically with the techniques of linear programming, quadratic programming, or nonlinear mathematical programming.
- Quadratic and, more in general, nonlinear optimization problems are more difficult to solve and more computationally intensive.
- Functionals are functions defined on other functions.
- Calculus of variations deals with the problem of finding those functions that optimize a functional.
- Control theory deals with the problem of optimizing a functional by controlling some of the variables while other variables are subject to exogenous dynamics.
- Bellmann's Dynamic Programming and Pontryagin's Maximum Principle are the key mathematical tools of control theory.
- Multistage stochastic programming is a set of numerical techniques for finding the maxima and minima of a functional defined on a stochastic process.

---

[14]See, for example, P. Kall and S. W. Wallace, *Stochastic Programming* (Chichester, U.K.: John Wiley & Sons, 1994).

- Multistage stochastic optimization is based on formalizing the rules for recourse, that is, how decisions are made at each stage and on describing possible scenarios.
- Liability-funding strategies are strategies whose objective is to match a given set of liabilities due at future times.
- Cash flow matching in a deterministic environment is the problem of matching a predetermined set of liabilities with an investment portfolio that produces a deterministic stream of cash flows.
- Cash flow matching problems can be solved with linear programming or mixed-integer programming algorithms.
- The objective of an immunization strategy is to construct a portfolio that is insensitive to small parallel shifts of interest rates.
- A given stream of liabilities can be matched with a portfolio whose duration is equal to the duration of the liabilities and whose present value is equal to the present value of the liabilities.
- Matching duration and present value makes portfolios insensitive only to small parallel shifts of interest rates; in order to minimize the effects of nonparallel shifts, optimization procedures are needed.

CHAPTER 8

Difference Equations

In mathematics and statistics, a difference equation refers to a recurrence relation, or an equation that recursively defines a sequence, once one or more initial terms are given. Each further term of the sequence is defined as a function of the preceding terms. Difference equations are extensively used in financial economics. For example, in a theoretical asset pricing framework, one might develop a model of various broad sectors of the economy in which some agents' actions depend on lagged variables. The model would then be solved for current values of key variables (interest rate, output growth, etc.) in terms of exogenous variables and lagged endogenous variables. Difference equations are also useful in financial econometrics. For example, time-series forecasting uses a recursive model to predict future values of financial and economic indicators based on the previously observed values of these variables. In finance, difference equations are also used to model persistence structure of asset returns and asset return volatility. Using difference equations:

- One can determine the serial correlation structure of asset returns in the context of a dynamic econometric model.
- One can examine the stochastic behavior of asset prices expressed as a linear difference equation with random disturbances added.
- One can understand the joint dynamics and dependencies of two persistent financial and macroeconomic variables.
- One can provide a better understanding of the continuous-time processes in a discrete-time framework.

What you will learn after reading this chapter:

- How to use a lag operator to define dependence of future values of a variable on its past values.
- How to define homogeneous difference equations as linear conditions that link the values of variables at different time lags.
- How to solve first- and second-order difference equations.
- How to find real and complex roots of a homogeneous difference equation.
- How to describe and solve nonhomogeneous difference equations.
- How to transform and solve systems of linear difference equations.

INTRODUCTION

A **difference equation** is an equation that involves differences between successive values of a function of a discrete variance. Linear difference equations are important in the context of dynamic econometric models. Understanding the behavior of solutions of linear difference equations helps develop intuition about the behavior of these models. (A related mathematical topic is differential equations covered in the next chapter.) The relationship between difference equations (the subject of this chapter) and differential equations is as follows. Differential equations are great for modeling situations in finance where there is a continually changing value. The problem is that not all changes in value occur continuously. If the change in value occurs incrementally rather than continuously, then differential equations have their limitations. Instead, in financial modeling, one can use difference equations, which are recursively defined sequences.

The theory of linear difference equations covers three areas: (1) solving difference equations, (2) describing the behavior of difference equations, and (3) identifying the equilibrium (or critical value) and stability of difference equations. In this chapter, we cover these areas. Because operations with time series involves a temporal dimension, a convenient notation has been used to denote lags, as well as leads, in time series. A discussion of this notation, the lag operator, begins the chapter.

THE LAG OPERATOR *L*

The **lag operator L** is a linear operator that acts on doubly infinite time series by shifting positions by one place:

$$Lx_t = x_{t-1}$$

The difference operator $\Delta x_t = x_t - x_{t-1}$ can be written in terms of the lag operator as

$$\Delta x_t = (1 - L)x_t$$

Products and thus powers of the lag operator are defined as follows:

$$(L \times L)x_t = L^2 x_t = L(Lx_t) = x_{t-2}$$

From the previous definition, we can see that the *i*th power of the lag operator shifts the series by *i* places:

$$L^i x_t = x_{t-i}$$

The lag operator is linear, that is, given scalars *a* and *b* we have

$$(aL^i + bL^j)x_t = ax_{t-i} + bx_{t-j}$$

Hence we can define the polynomial operator:

$$A(L) = (1 - a_1 L - \cdots - a_P L^P) \equiv \left(1 - \sum_{i=1}^{p} a_i L^i\right)$$

HOMOGENEOUS DIFFERENCE EQUATIONS

Homogeneous difference equations are linear conditions that link the values of variables at different time lags. Using the lag operator L, they can be written as follows:

$$A(L)x_t = (1 - a_1 L - \cdots - a_P L^P)x_t$$
$$= (1 - \lambda_1 L) \times \cdots \times (1 - \lambda_p L)x_t = 0$$

where the λ_i, $i = 1, 2, \ldots, p$ are the solutions of the characteristic equation:

$$z^p - a_1 z^{p-1} - \cdots - a_{P-1}z - a_P$$
$$= (z - \lambda_1) \times \cdots \times (z - \lambda_p) = 0$$

Suppose that time extends from $0 \Rightarrow \infty$, $t = 0, 1, 2, \ldots$ and that the initial conditions $(x_{-1}, x_{-2}, \ldots, x_{-P})$ are given.

Real Roots

Consider first the case of real roots. In this case, as we see later in this chapter, solutions are sums of exponentials. First, suppose that the roots of the characteristic equation are all real and distinct. It can be verified by substitution that any series of the form

$$x_t = C(\lambda_i)^t$$

where C is a constant, solves the homogeneous difference equation. In fact, we can write

$$(1 - \lambda_i L)(C\lambda_i^t) = C\lambda_i^t - \lambda_i C\lambda_i^{t-1} = 0$$

In addition, given the linearity of the lag operator, any linear combination of solutions of the homogeneous difference equation is another solution. We can therefore state that the following series solves the homogeneous difference equation:

$$x_t = \sum_{i=1}^{p} C_i \lambda_i^t$$

By solving the linear system

$$x_{-1} = \sum_{i=1}^{p} C_i \lambda_i^{-1}$$

$$x_{-p} = \sum_{i=1}^{p} C_i \lambda_i^{-p}$$

that states that the p initial conditions are satisfied, we can determine the p constants Cs.

Suppose now that all m roots of the characteristic equation are real and coincident. In this case, we can represent a difference equation in the following way:

$$A(L) = 1 - a_1 L - \cdots - a_P L^P = (1 - \lambda L)^P$$

It can be demonstrated by substitution that, in this case, the general solution of the process is the following:

$$x_t = C_1(\lambda)^t + C_2 t(\lambda)^t + \cdots + C_p t^{p-1}(\lambda)^t$$

In the most general case, assuming that all roots are real, there will be $m < p$ distinct roots φ_i, $i = 1, 2, \ldots, m$ each of order $n_i \geq 1$,

$$\sum_{i=1}^{m} n_i = p$$

and the general solution of the process will be

$$\begin{aligned}
x_t = &\ C_1^1(\lambda_1)^t + C_2^1 t(\lambda_1)^t + \cdots + C_{n_1}^1 t^{n_1-1}(\lambda_1)^t + \cdots \\
&+ C_1^m(\lambda_m)^t + C_2^m t(\lambda_m)^t + \cdots + C_{n_m}^m t^{n_m-1}(\lambda_m)^t
\end{aligned}$$

We can therefore conclude that the solutions of a homogeneous difference equation whose characteristic equation has only real roots is formed by a sum of exponentials. If these roots have modulus greater than unity, then solutions are diverging exponentials; if they have modulus smaller than unity, solutions are exponentials that go to zero. If the roots are unity, solutions are either constants or, if the roots have multiplicity greater than 1, polynomials.

Figure 8.1 illustrates the simple equation

$$\begin{aligned}
A(L)x_t = (1 - 0.8L)x_t = 0, &\quad \lambda = 0.8, \\
t = 1, 2, \ldots, n, \ldots
\end{aligned}$$

whose solution, with initial condition $x_1 = 1$, is

$$x_t = 1.25(0.8)^t$$

The behavior of the solution is that of an exponential decay.

Figure 8.2 illustrates the equation

$$\begin{aligned}
A(L)x_t = (1 + 0.8L)x_t = 0, &\quad \lambda = -0.8, \\
t = 1, 2, \ldots, n, \ldots
\end{aligned}$$

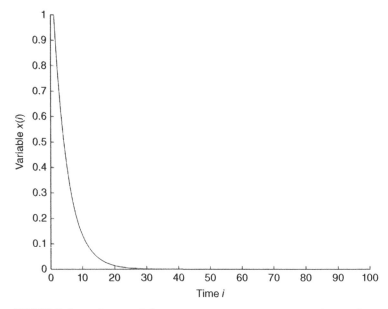

FIGURE 8.1   Solution of the Equation $(1 - 0.8L)x_t = 0$ with Initial Condition $x_1 = 1$

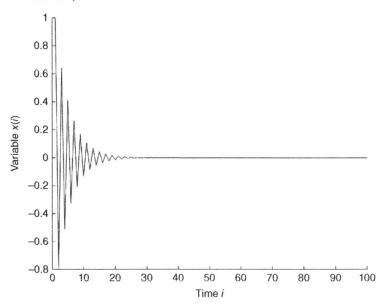

FIGURE 8.2   Solution of the Equation $(1 + 0.8L)x_t = 0$ with Initial Condition $x_1 = 1$

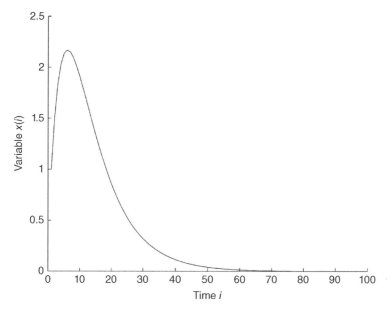

FIGURE 8.3 Solution of the Equation $(1 - 1.7L + 0.72L^2)x_t = 0$ with Initial Conditions $x_1 = 1$, $x_2 = 1.5$

Simulations were run for 100 time steps whose solution, with initial condition $x_1 = 1$, is

$$x_t = -1.25(-0.8)^t$$

The behavior of the solution is that of an exponential decay with oscillations at each step. The oscillations are due to the change in sign of the exponential at odd and even time steps.

If the equation has more than one real root, then the solution is a sum of exponentials. Figure 8.3 illustrates the equation

$$A(L)x_t = (1 - 1.7L + 0.72L^2)x_t = 0, \; \lambda_1 = 0.8,$$
$$\lambda_2 = 0.9, \quad t = 1, 2, \ldots, n, \ldots$$

whose solution, with initial condition $x_1 = 1$, $x_2 = 1.5$, is

$$x_t = -7.5(0.8)^t + 7.7778(0.9)^t$$

The behavior of the solution is that of an exponential decay after a peak.

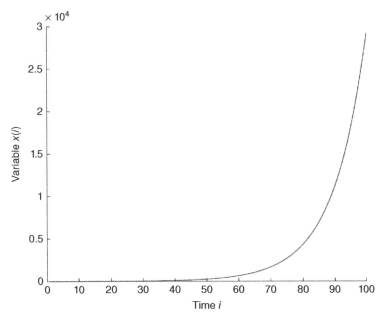

FIGURE 8.4   Solution of the Equation $(1 - 1.9L + 0.88L^2)x_t = 0$
with Initial Conditions $x_1 = 1, x_2 = 1.5$

Figure 8.4 illustrates the equation

$$A(L)x_t = (1 - 1.9L + 0.88L^2)x_t = 0,$$
$$\lambda_1 = 0.8, \quad \lambda_2 = 1.1, \quad t = 1, 2, \ldots, n, \ldots$$

whose solution, with initial condition $x_1 = 1, x_2 = 1.5$, is

$$x_t = -1.6667(0.8)^t + 2.1212(1.1)^t$$

The behavior is that of exponential explosion due to the exponential
with modulus greater than 1.

Complex Roots

Now suppose that some of the roots are complex. In this case, solutions
exhibit an oscillating behavior with a period that depends on the model

coefficients. For simplicity, consider initially a second-order homogeneous difference equation:

$$A(L)x_t = (1 - a_1 L - a_2 L^2)x_t$$

Suppose that its characteristic equation given by

$$A(z) = z^2 - a_1 z - a_s = 0$$

admits the two complex conjugate roots:

$$\lambda_1 = a + ib, \quad \lambda_2 = a - ib$$

Let's write the two roots in polar notation:

$$\lambda_1 = r e^{i\omega}, \qquad \lambda_1 = r e^{-i\omega}$$

$$r = \sqrt{a^2 + b^2}, \quad \omega = \arctan \frac{b}{a}$$

It can be demonstrated that the general solution of the above difference equation has the following form:

$$x_t = r^t(C_1 \cos(\omega t) + C_2 \sin(\omega t)) = C r^t \cos(\omega t + \vartheta)$$

where the C_1 and C_2 or C and ϑ are constants to be determined in function of initial conditions. If the imaginary part of the roots vanishes, then ω vanishes and $a = r$, the two complex conjugate roots become a real root, and we find again the expression $x_t = C r^t$.

Consider now a homogeneous difference equation of order $2n$. Suppose that the characteristic equation has only two distinct complex conjugate roots with multiplicity n. We can write the difference equation as follows:

$$\begin{aligned} A(L)x_t &= (1 - a_1 L - \cdots - a_{2n} L^{2n})x_t \\ &= [(1 - \lambda L)^n (1 - \bar{\lambda} L)^n]x_t = 0 \end{aligned}$$

and its general solution as follows:

$$\begin{aligned} x_t = r^t(C_1^1 \cos(\omega t) + C_2^1 \sin(\omega t)) + \cdots \\ + t^n r^t(C_1^n \cos(\omega t) + C_2^n \sin(\omega t)) \end{aligned}$$

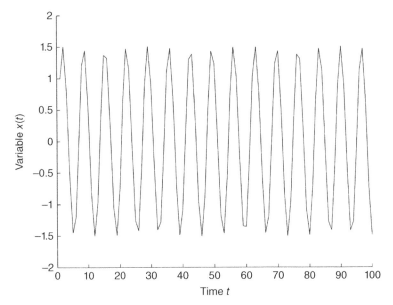

FIGURE 8.5 Solutions of the Equation $(1 - 1.2L + 1.0L^2)x_t = 0$ with Initial Conditions $x_1 = 1$, $x_2 = 1.5$

The general solution of a homogeneous difference equation that admits both real and complex roots with different multiplicities is a sum of the different types of solutions. The above formulas show that real roots correspond to a sum of exponentials while complex roots correspond to oscillating series with exponential dumping or explosive behavior. The above formulas confirm that in both the real and the complex case, solutions decay if the modulus of the roots of the inverse characteristic equation is outside the unit circle and explode if it is inside the unit circle.

Figure 8.5 illustrates the equation

$$A(L)x_t = (1 - 1.2L + 1.0L^2)x_t = 0,$$
$$t = 1, 2, \ldots, n, \ldots$$

which has two complex conjugate roots,

$$\lambda_1 = 0.6 + i0.8, \quad \lambda_2 = 0.6 - i0.8$$

or in polar form,

$$\lambda_1 = e^{i0.9273}, \quad \lambda_2 = e^{i0.9273}$$

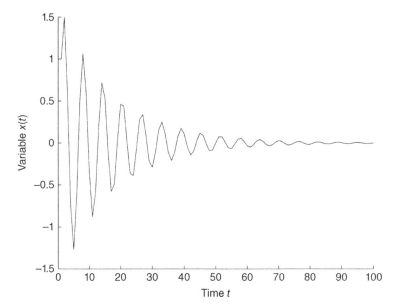

FIGURE 8.6 Solutions of the Equation $(1 - 1.0L + 0.89L^2)x_t = 0$ with Initial Conditions $x_1 = 1$, $x_2 = 1.5$

and whose solution, with initial condition $x_1 = 1$, $x_2 = 1.5$, is

$$x_t = -0.3\cos(0.9273t) + 1.475\ \sin(0.9273t)$$

The behavior of the solutions is that of undamped oscillations with frequency determined by the model.

Figure 8.6 illustrates the equation

$$A(L)x_t = (1 - 1.0L + 0.89L^2)x_t = 0,$$
$$t = 1, 2, \ldots, n, \ldots$$

which has two complex conjugate roots,

$$\lambda_1 = 0.5 + i0.8, \quad \lambda_2 = 0.5 - i0.8$$

or in polar form,

$$\lambda_1 = 0.9434e^{i\,1.0122}, \quad \lambda_2 = 0.9434e^{-i\,1.0122}$$

and whose solution, with initial condition $x_1 = 1, x_2 = 1.5$, is

$$x_t = 0.9434^t(-0.5618 \ \cos(1.0122t)$$
$$+1.6011 \ \sin(1.0122t))$$

The behavior of the solutions is that of damped oscillations with frequency determined by the model.

RECURSIVE CALCULATION OF VALUES OF DIFFERENCE EQUATIONS

In the previous sections, we studied the properties of the solutions of homogeneous difference equations. In this section, we discuss how to simulate the solution of a difference equation and how to determine its parameters. To calculate the values of x for all values of t, it is sufficient to know any p consecutive values of x. These p values are starting values or initial conditions. If we know the starting values $x(1), \ldots, x(p)$ for a difference equation, then we can find $x(p+1), \ldots, x(n)$ recursively by

$$x(p+j) = \sum_{k=1}^{p} a_k x(p+j-k)$$
$$j = 1, \ldots, n-p$$

Note that $x(1), \ldots, x(p)$ are used to find $x(p+1)$, which is in turn used in finding $x(p+2)$, and so on. For example, the homogeneous first-order difference equation $x(t) - a_1 x(t-1) = 0$, thus, $t \geq 1$, can be solved recursively

$$x(t) = a_1 x(t-1) = a_1[a_1 x(t-2)]$$
$$= \cdots = [a_1]^t x(0)$$

that is, $x(t) = [a_1]^t x(0)$, which is a solution to the difference equation. Further, from this expression for $x(t)$, we can see that:

1. If $|a_1| < 1$, then $x(t) \to 0$.
2. If $a_1 = -1$, then $x(t) \to 0$ alternates between $\pm x(0)$ for all t, while if $a_1 = 1$, then $x(t) = x(0)$ for all t.
3. If $a_1 > 1$, then $x(t) \to \infty$.
4. If $a_1 < 0$, then $x(t) \to 0$ alternates between positive and negative values that are getting larger and larger in absolute value.

Solving Homogeneous Higher-Order Difference Equations

Consider the following second-order difference equation:

$$x(t) - a_1 x(t-1) - a_2 x(t-2) = 0$$

Given the findings in the first-order case above, we can conjecture that the homogeneous solution has the form $x(t) = A\beta^t$. Substitution of this trial solution into the second-order difference equation gives

$$A\beta^t - a_1 A\beta^{t-1} - a_2 A\beta^{t-2} = 0$$

Clearly, any arbitrary value of A is satisfactory. If we divide this equation by $A\beta^{t-2}$, the problem is to find the values of β that satisfy

$$\beta^2 - a_1\beta - \alpha_2 = 0$$

Solving this quadratic equation, called the **characteristic equation**, yields two values of β, called the **characteristic roots**. Using the quadratic formula, we find that the two characteristic roots are

$$\beta_1, \beta_2 = \left(a_1 \pm \sqrt{a_1^2 + 4a_2}\right)\Big/2 = \left(a_1 + \sqrt{d}\right)\Big/2$$

Each of these two characteristic roots yields a valid solution for the second-order difference equation. Again, these solutions are not unique. In fact, for any two arbitrary constants A_1 and A_2, the linear combination $A_1(\beta_1)^t + A_2(\beta_2)^t$ also solves the second-order difference equation. As proof, simply substitute $z(t) = A_1(\beta_1)^t + A_2(\beta_2)^t$ into the difference equation to obtain:

$$A_1(\beta_1)^t + A_2(\beta_2)^t = a_1[A_1(\beta_1)^{t-1} + A_2(\beta_2)^{t-1}] + a_2[A_1(\beta_1)^{t-2} + A_2(\beta_2)^{t-2}]$$

Now, regroup terms as follows:

$$A_1[(\beta_1)^t - a_1 A_1(\beta_1)^{t-1} - a_2 A_1(\beta_1)^{t-2}] + A_2[(\beta_2)^t - a_1(\beta_2)^{t-1} - a_2(\beta_2)^{t-2}] = 0$$

Since β_1 and β_2 each solve the difference equation, both terms in brackets must equal zero. As such, the complete homogeneous solution in the second-order case is

$$x(t) = A_1(\beta_1)^t + A_2(\beta_2)^t$$

Without knowing the specific values of α_1 and α_2, we cannot find the two characteristic roots β_1 and β_2. Nevertheless, it is possible to characterize the nature of the solution; there are three possible cases that are dependent on the value of d:

Case 1: If the second-order difference equation is $x(t) - 0.2x(t - 1) - 0.35 x(t - 2) = 0$, we have $a_1 = 0.2$ and $a_2 = 0.35$. Since $d = a_1^2 + 4a_2 = 1.44 > 0$, the characteristic roots will be real and distinct. Let the trial solution have the form $x(t) = \beta^t$. Substitute into the homogeneous equation

$$\beta^t - 0.2\beta^{t-1} - 0.35\beta^{t-2} = 0$$

Divide by β^{t-2} in order to obtain the characteristic equation $\beta^2 - 0.2\beta - 0.35 = 0$. Compute the two characteristic roots:

$$\beta_1 = 0.5 \cdot \left(a_1 + \sqrt{d}\right) = 0.7$$

$$\beta_2 = 0.5 \cdot \left(a_1 - \sqrt{d}\right) = -0.5$$

The homogeneous solution is $A_1(0.7)^t + A_2(-0.5)^t$.

Case 2: If $d = a_1^2 + 4a_2 = 0$, it follows that $\beta_1 = \beta_2 = a_1/2$. Hence, a homogeneous solution is $a_1/2$. However, when $d = 0$, there is a second homogeneous solution given by $t\,(a_1/2)^t$. To demonstrate that $x(t) = t\,(a_1/2)^t$ is a homogeneous solution, substitute it into the second-order difference equation to determine whether

$$t\left(a_1/2\right)^t - a_1\left[(t-1)\left(a_1/2\right)^{t-1}\right] - a_2\left[(t-2)\left(a_1/2\right)^{t-2}\right] = 0$$

Divide by $(a_1/2)^{t-2}$ and form

$$-\left[(a_1^2/4) + a_2\right]t + \left[(a_1^2/2) + 2a_2\right] = 0$$

Since we have $d = a_1^2 + 4a_2 = 0$ each bracketed expression is zero. Hence, $x(t) = t\,(a_1/2)^t$ solves the second-order difference equation. Again, for arbitrary constants A_1 and A_2, the complete homogeneous solution is

$$x(t) = A_1(a_1/2)^t + A_2 t(a_1/2)^t$$

Clearly, the system is explosive if $|a_1| > 2$. If $|a_1| < 2$, the term $A_1(a_1/2)^t$ converges, but one might think that the effect of the term $t(a_1/2)^t$ is ambiguous since the diminishing $(a_1/2)^t$ is multiplied by t. The ambiguity is correct in the limited sense that the behavior of the homogeneous solution is not monotonic.

Case 3: If $d = a_1^2 + 4a_2 < 0$, then the characteristic roots are imaginary. Since $a_1^2 \geq 0$, the imaginary roots can only occur only if $a_2 < 0$. In this case, the characteristic roots are

$$\beta_1 = 0.5 \cdot \left(a_1 + i\sqrt{-d} \right)$$

$$\beta_2 = 0.5 \cdot \left(a_1 - i\sqrt{-d} \right)$$

where $i = \sqrt{-1}$.

NONHOMOGENEOUS DIFFERENCE EQUATIONS

Consider now the following nth order difference equation:

$$A(L)x_t = (1 - a_1 L - \cdots - a_p L^p)x_t = y_t$$

where y_t is a given sequence of real numbers. Recall that we are in a deterministic setting, that is, the y_t are given. The general solution of the above difference equation will be the sum of two solutions $x_{1,t} + x_{2,t}$, where $x_{1,t}$ is the solution of the associated homogeneous equation,

$$A(L)x_t = (1 - a_1 L - \cdots - a_p L^p)x_t = 0$$

and $X_{2,t}$ solves the given **nonhomogeneous equation.**

Real Roots

To determine the general form of $x_{2,t}$ in the case of real roots, we begin by considering the case of a first-order equation:

$$A(L)x_t = (1 - a_1 L)x_t = y_t$$

We can compute the solution as follows:

$$x_{2,t} = \frac{1}{(1 - a_1 L)} y_t = \left(\sum_{j=0}^{\infty} (a_1 L)^j \right) y_t$$

which is meaningful only for $|a_1| < 1$. If, however, y_t starts at $t = -1$, that is, if $y_t = 0$ for $t = -2, -3, \ldots, n$, we can rewrite the above formula as

$$x_{2,t} = \frac{1}{(1 - a_1 L)} y_t = \left(\sum_{j=0}^{t+1} (a_1 L)^j \right) y_t$$

This latter formula, which is valid for any real value of a_1, yields

$$x_{2,0} = y_0 + a_1 y_{-1}$$
$$x_{2,1} = y_1 + a_1 y_0 + a_1^2 y_{-1}$$
$$x_{2,t} = y_t + a_1 y_{t-1} + \cdots + a_1^{t+1} y_{-1}$$

and so on. These formulas can be easily verified by direct substitution. If $y_t = y = $ constant, then

$$x_{2,t} = y(1 + a_1^2 + \cdots + a_1^{t+1})$$

Consider now the case of a second-order equation:

$$A(L)x_t = (1 - a_1 L - a_2 L^2)x_t$$
$$= (1 - \lambda_1 L)(1 - \lambda_2 L)x_t = y_t$$

where λ_1, λ_2 are the solutions of the characteristic equation (the reciprocal of the solutions of the inverse characteristic equation). We can write the solution of the above equation as

$$x_{2,t} = \frac{1}{(1 - a_1 L - a_2 L^2)} y_t = \frac{1}{(1 - \lambda_1 L)(1 - \lambda_2 L)} y_t$$

Recall that, if $|\lambda_i| < 1$, $i = 1, 2$, we can write:

$$\frac{1}{(1 - \lambda_1 L)(1 - \lambda_2 L)} = \frac{1}{\lambda_1 - \lambda_2} \left(\frac{\lambda_1}{(1 - \lambda_1 L)} - \frac{\lambda_2}{(1 - \lambda_2 L)} \right)$$

$$= \frac{\lambda_1}{\lambda_1 - \lambda_2} \left(\sum_{j=0}^{\infty} (\lambda_1 L)^j \right) - \frac{\lambda_2}{\lambda_1 - \lambda_2} \left(\sum_{j=0}^{\infty} (\lambda_2 L)^j \right)$$

so that the solution can be written as

$$x_{2,t} = \frac{\lambda_1}{\lambda_1 - \lambda_2}\left(\sum_{j=0}^{\infty}(\lambda_1 L)^j\right)y_t$$

$$-\frac{\lambda_2}{\lambda_1 - \lambda_2}\left(\sum_{j=0}^{\infty}(\lambda_2 L)^j\right)y_t$$

If the two solutions are coincident, reasoning as in the homogeneous case, we can establish that the general solutions can be written as follows:

$$x_{2,t} = \frac{1}{(1-a_1 L)^2}y_t = \left(\sum_{j=0}^{\infty}(a_1 L)^j\right)y_t$$

$$+t\left(\sum_{j=0}^{\infty}(a_1 L)^j\right)y_t$$

If y_t starts at $t = -2$, that is, if $y_t = 0$ for $t = -3, -4, \ldots, -n, \ldots$, we can rewrite the above formula respectively as

$$x_{2,t} = \frac{\lambda_1}{\lambda_1 - \lambda_2}\left(\sum_{j=0}^{t+2}(\lambda_1 L)^j\right)y_t$$

$$-\frac{\lambda_2}{\lambda_1 - \lambda_2}\left(\sum_{j=0}^{t+2}(\lambda_2 L)^j\right)y_t$$

if the solutions are distinct, and as

$$x_{2,t} = \frac{1}{(1-a_1 L)^2}y_t = \left(\sum_{j=0}^{t+2}(a_1 L)^j\right)y_t$$

$$+t\left(\sum_{j=0}^{t+2}(a_1 L)^j\right)y_t$$

if the solutions are coincident. These formulas are valid for any real value of λ_1.

The above formulas can be generalized to cover the case of an nth order difference equation. In the most general case of an nth order difference equation, assuming that all roots are real, there will be $m < n$ distinct roots λ_i, $i = 1, 2, \ldots, m$, each of order $n_i \geq 1$,

$$\sum_{i=1}^{m} n_i = n$$

and the general solution of the process will be

$$x_{2,t} = \sum_{i=0}^{\infty} ((\lambda_1 L)^i + i(\lambda_1 L)^i + \cdots + i^{n_1-1}(\lambda_1 L)^i + \cdots$$
$$+ (\lambda_m L)^i + i(\lambda_m L)^i + \cdots + i^{n_m-1}(\lambda_m L)^i) y_t$$

if $|\lambda_i| < 1$, $i = 1, 2, \ldots, m$, and

$$x_{2,t} = \sum_{i=0}^{t+m} ((\lambda_1 L)^i + i(\lambda_1 L)^i + \cdots + i^{n_1-1}(\lambda_1 L)^i + \cdots$$
$$+ (\lambda_m L)^i + i(\lambda_m L)^i + \cdots + i^{n_m-1}(\lambda_m L)^i) y_t$$

if y_t starts at $t = -n$, that is, if $y_t = 0$ for $t = -(n + 1), -(n + 2), \ldots$ for any real value of the λ_i.

Therefore, if the roots are all real, the general solution of a difference equation is a sum of exponentials. Figure 8.7 illustrates the case of the same difference equation as in Figure 8.3 with the same initial conditions $x_1 = 1$, $x_2 = 1.5$ but with an exogenous forcing sinusoidal variable:

$$(1 - 1.7L + 0.72L^2)x_t = 0.1 \times \sin(0.4 \times t)$$

The solution of the equation is the sum of $x_{1,t} = -7.5(0.8)^t + 7.7778(0.9)^t$ plus

$$x_{2,t} = \sum [((0.8)^i + (0.9)^i)0.1 \times \sin(0.4 \times (t - i))]$$

After the initial phase dominated by the solution of the homogeneous equation, the forcing term dictates the shape of the solution.

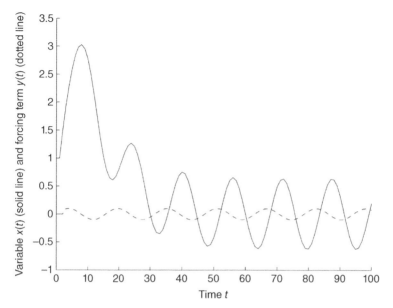

FIGURE 8.7   Solutions of the Equation $(1 - 1.7L + 0.72L^2)x_t = 0.1 \times \sin(0.4 \times t)$ with Initial Conditions $x_1 = 1, x_2 = 1.5$

Complex Roots

Consider now the case of complex roots. For simplicity, consider initially a second-order difference equation:

$$A(L)x_t = (1 - a_1 L - a_2 L^2)x_t = y_t$$

Suppose that its characteristic equation,

$$A(z) = z^2 - a_1 z - a_2 = 0$$

admits the two complex conjugate roots,

$$\lambda_1 = a + ib, \quad \lambda_2 = a - ib$$

We write the two roots in polar notation:

$$\lambda_1 = re^{i\omega}, \quad \lambda_2 = re^{-i\omega}$$
$$r = \sqrt{a^2 + b^2}, \ \omega = \arctan \frac{b}{a}$$

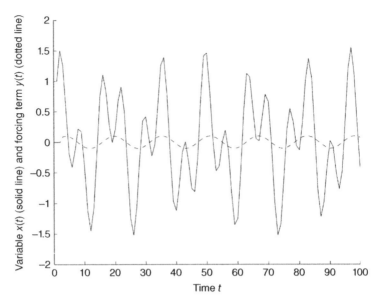

FIGURE 8.8   Solutions of the Equation $(1 - 1.2L + 1.0L^2)x_t = 0.5$
$\times \sin(0.4 \times t)$ with Initial Conditions $x_1 = 1, x_2 = 1.5$

It can be demonstrated that the general form of the $x_{2,t}$ of the above
difference equation has the following form:

$$x_{2,t} = \sum_{i=1}^{\infty} (r^i(\cos(\omega i) + \sin(\omega i))y_{t-i})$$

which is meaningful only if $|r| < 1$. If y_t starts at $t = -2$, that is, if $y_t = 0$
for $t = -3, -4, \ldots, -n, \ldots$ we can rewrite the previous formula as

$$x_{2,t} = \sum_{i=1}^{t+2} (r^i(\cos(\omega i) + \sin(\omega i))y_{t-i})$$

This latter formula is meaningful for any real value of r. Note that the
constant ω is determined by the structure of the model while the constants
C_1, C_2 that appear in $x_{1,t}$ need to be determined in the function of initial
conditions. If the imaginary part of the roots vanishes, then ω vanishes and
$a = r$, the two complex conjugate roots become a real root, and we again
find the expression $x_t = Cr^t$.

Figure 8.8 illustrates the case of the same difference equation as in Figure 8.7 with the same initial conditions $x_1 = 1, x_2 = 1.5$ but with an exogenous forcing sinusoidal variable:

$$(1 - 1.2L + 1.0L^2)x_t = 0.5 \times \sin(0.4 \times t)$$

The solution of the equation is the sum of $x_{1,t} = -0.3\cos(0.9273t) + 1.475\sin(0.9273t)$ plus

$$x_{2,t} = \sum_{i=0}^{t-1} [(\cos(0.9273i) + \sin(0.9273i))0.5\sin(0.4 \times (t - i))]$$

After the initial phase dominated by the solution of the homogeneous equation, the forcing term dictates the shape of the solution. Note the model produces amplification and phase shift of the forcing term $0.1 \times \sin(0.4 \times t)$ represented by a dotted line.

SYSTEMS OF LINEAR DIFFERENCE EQUATIONS

In this section, we discuss **systems of linear difference equations** of the type

$$x_{1,t} = a_{11}x_{1,t-1} + \cdots + a_{1k}x_{k,t-1} + y_{1,t}$$
$$x_{k,t} = a_{k1}x_{1,t-1} + \cdots + a_{kk}x_{k,t-1} + y_{k,t}$$

or in vector notation:

$$\mathbf{x}_t = \mathbf{A}\mathbf{x}_{t-1} + \mathbf{y}_t$$

Observe that we need to consider only first-order systems, that is, systems with only one lag. In fact, a system of an arbitrary order can be transformed into a first-order system by adding one variable for each additional lag. For example, a second-order system of two difference equations,

$$x_{1,t} = a_{11}x_{1,t-1} + a_{12}x_{2,t-1} + b_{11}x_{1,t-2}$$
$$+ b_{12}x_{2,t-2} + y_{1,t}$$
$$x_{2,t} = a_{21}x_{1,t-1} + a_{22}x_{2,t-1} + b_{21}x_{1,t-2}$$
$$+ b_{22}x_{2,t-2} + y_{2,t}$$

can be transformed in a first-order system adding two variables:

$$x_{1,t} = a_{11}x_{1,t-1} + a_{12}x_{2,t-1} + b_{11}x_{1,t-1}$$
$$+ b_{12}x_{2,t-1} + y_{1,t}$$
$$x_{2,t} = a_{21}x_{1,t-1} + a_{22}x_{2,t-1} + b_{21}x_{1,t-1}$$
$$+ b_{22}x_{2,t-1} + y_{2,t}$$
$$z_{1,t} = x_{1,t-1}$$
$$z_{2,t} = x_{2,t-1}$$

Transformations of this type can be generalized to systems of any order and any number of equations.

A system of difference equations is called **homogeneous** if the exogenous variable $\mathbf{y}_t$ is zero, that is, if it can be written as

$$\mathbf{x}_t = \mathbf{A}\mathbf{x}_{t-1}$$

while it is called **nonhomogeneous** if the exogenous term is present.

There are different ways to solve first-order systems of difference equations. One method consists in eliminating variables as in ordinary algebraic systems. In this way, the original first-order system in k equations is solved by solving a single difference equation of order k with the methods explained above. This observation implies that solutions of systems of linear difference equations are of the same nature as those of difference equations (i.e., sums of exponential and/or sinusoidal functions). In the following section, we will show a direct method for solving systems of linear difference equations. This method could be used to solve equations of any order, as they are equivalent to first-order systems. In addition, it gives a better insight into vector autoregressive processes.

SYSTEMS OF HOMOGENEOUS LINEAR DIFFERENCE EQUATIONS

Consider a homogeneous system of the following type:

$$\mathbf{x}(t) = \mathbf{A}\mathbf{x}(t-1), \quad t = 0, 1, \ldots, n, \ldots$$

where $\mathbf{A}$ is a $k \times k$, real-valued, nonsingular matrix of constant coefficients. Using the lag operator notation, we can also write the above systems in the following form:

$$(\mathbf{I} - \mathbf{A}L)\mathbf{x}_t = 0, \quad t = 1, \ldots, n, \ldots$$

If a vector of initial conditions $\mathbf{x}(0)$ is given, the above system is called an **initial value problem**.

Through recursive computation, that is, starting at $t = 0$ and computing forward, we can write

$$\begin{aligned}
\mathbf{x}(1) &= \mathbf{A}\mathbf{x}(0) \\
\mathbf{x}(2) &= \mathbf{A}\mathbf{x}(1) = \mathbf{A}^2\mathbf{x}(0) \\
\mathbf{x}(t) &= \mathbf{A}^t\mathbf{x}(0)
\end{aligned}$$

The following theorem can be demonstrated: Any homogeneous system of the type $\mathbf{x}(t) = \mathbf{A}\mathbf{x}(t - 1)$, where $\mathbf{A}$ is a $k \times k$, real-valued, nonsingular matrix, coupled with given initial conditions $\mathbf{x}(0)$ admits one and only one solution.

A set of k solutions $\mathbf{x}_i(t)$, $i = 1, \ldots, k$, $t = 0,1, 2, \ldots$ are said to be linearly independent if

$$\sum_{i=1}^{k} c_i\mathbf{x}_i(t) = 0$$

$t = 0, 1, 2, \ldots$ implies $c_i = 0$, $i = 1, \ldots, k$. Suppose now that k linearly independent solutions $\mathbf{x}_i(t)$, $i = 1, \ldots, k$ are given. Consider the matrix

$$\boldsymbol{\Phi}(t) = [\mathbf{x}_1(t) \cdots \mathbf{x}_k(t)]$$

The following matrix equation is clearly satisfied:

$$\boldsymbol{\Phi}(t) = \mathbf{A}\boldsymbol{\Phi}(t - 1)$$

The solutions $\mathbf{x}_i(t)$, $i = 1, \ldots, n$ are linearly independent if and only if the matrix $\boldsymbol{\Phi}(t)$ is nonsingular for every value $t \geq 0$, that is, if $\det[\boldsymbol{\Phi}(t)] \neq 0$, $t = 0, 1, \ldots$. Any nonsingular matrix $\boldsymbol{\Phi}(t)$, $t = 0, 1, \ldots$ such that the matrix equation

$$\boldsymbol{\Phi}(t) = \mathbf{A}\boldsymbol{\Phi}(t - 1)$$

is satisfied is called a **fundamental matrix** of the system $\mathbf{x}(t) = \mathbf{A}\mathbf{x}(t-1)$, $t = 1, \ldots, n, \ldots$ and it satisfies the equation

$$\Phi(t) = \mathbf{A}^t \Phi(0)$$

In order to compute an explicit solution of this system, we need an efficient algorithm to compute the matrix sequence $\mathbf{A}^t$. We will discuss one algorithm for this computation.[1] Recall that an eigenvalue of the $k \times k$ real valued matrix $\mathbf{A} = (a_{ij})$ is a real or complex number λ that satisfies the matrix equation:

$$(\mathbf{A} - \lambda \mathbf{I})\xi = 0$$

where $\xi \in \mathbb{C}^k$ is a k-dimensional complex vector. The above equation has a nonzero solution if and only if

$$|(\mathbf{A} - \lambda \mathbf{I})| = 0$$

or

$$\det \begin{pmatrix} a_{11} - \lambda & \cdots & a_{1k} \\ \vdots & \ddots & \vdots \\ a_{k1} & \cdots & a_{kk} - \lambda \end{pmatrix} = 0$$

The above condition can be expressed by the following algebraic equation:

$$z^k + a_1 z^{k-1} + \cdots + a_{k-1} z + a_k$$

which is called the characteristic equation of the matrix $\mathbf{A} = (a_{ij})$.

To see the relationship of this equation with the characteristic equations of single equations, consider the k-order equation:

$$(1 - a_1 L - \cdots - a_k L^k)x(t) = 0$$
$$x_t = a_1 x(t-1) + \cdots + a_k x(t-k)$$

---

[1]This discussion of systems of difference equations draws on S. Elaydi, *An Introduction to Difference Equations* (New York: Springer Verlag, 2002).

which is equivalent to the first-order system,

$$
\begin{aligned}
x_t &= a_1 x_{t-1} + \cdots + a_k z_{t-1}^{k-1} \\
z_t^1 &= x_{t-1} \\
&\vdots \\
z_{t-1}^{k-1} &= x_{t-k}
\end{aligned}
$$

The matrix

$$
\mathbf{A} = \begin{bmatrix}
a_1 & a_2 & \cdots & a_{k-1} & a_k \\
1 & 0 & \cdots & 0 & 0 \\
0 & 1 & \cdots & 0 & 0 \\
\vdots & \vdots & \ddots & \vdots & \vdots \\
0 & 0 & \cdots & 1 & 0
\end{bmatrix}
$$

is called the **companion matrix**. By induction, it can be demonstrated that the characteristic equation of the system $\mathbf{x}(t) = \mathbf{A}\mathbf{x}(t-1)$, $t = 1, \ldots, n, \ldots$ and of the k-order equation above coincide.

Given a system $\mathbf{x}(t) = \mathbf{A}\mathbf{x}(t-1)$, $t = 1, \ldots, n, \ldots$, we now consider separately two cases: (1) All, possibly complex, eigenvalues of the real-valued matrix $\mathbf{A}$ are distinct, and (2) two or more eigenvalues coincide.

Recall that if λ is a complex eigenvalue with corresponding complex eigenvector ξ, the complex conjugate number $\bar{\lambda}$ is also an eigenvalue with corresponding complex eigenvector $\bar{\xi}$.

If the eigenvalues of the real-valued matrix $\mathbf{A}$ are all distinct, then the matrix can be diagonalized. This means that $\mathbf{A}$ is similar to a diagonal matrix, according to the matrix equation

$$
\mathbf{A} = \Xi \begin{bmatrix}
\lambda_1 & \cdots & 0 \\
\vdots & \ddots & \vdots \\
0 & \cdots & \lambda_n
\end{bmatrix} \Xi^{-1}
$$
$$
\Xi = [\xi_1 \cdots \xi_n]
$$

and

$$
\mathbf{A}^t = \Xi \begin{bmatrix}
\lambda_1^t & \cdots & 0 \\
\vdots & \ddots & \vdots \\
0 & \cdots & \lambda_n^t
\end{bmatrix} \Xi^{-1}
$$

We can therefore write the general solution of the system $x(t) = Ax(t - 1)$ as follows:

$$x(t) = c_1\lambda_1^t\xi_1 + \cdots + c_n\lambda_1^n\xi_n$$

The c_i are complex numbers that need to be determined for the solutions to be real and to satisfy initial conditions. We therefore see the parallel between the solutions of first-order systems of difference equations and the solutions of k-order difference equations that we have determined above. In particular, if solutions are all real they exhibit exponential decay if their modulus is less than 1 or exponential growth if their modulus is greater than 1. If the solutions of the characteristic equation are real, they can produce oscillating damped or undamped behavior with period equal to two time steps. If the solutions of the characteristic equation are complex, then solutions might exhibit damped or undamped oscillating behavior with any period.

To illustrate the above, consider the following second-order system:

$$x_{1,t} = 0.6x_{1,t-1} - 0.1x_{2,t-1} - 0.7x_{1,t-2} + 0.15x_{2,t-2}$$
$$x_{2,t} = -0.12x_{1,t-1} + 0.7x_{2,t-1} + 0.22x_{1,t-2} - 0.85x_{2,t-2}$$

This system can be transformed in the following first-order system:

$$x_{1,t} = 0.6x_{1,t-1} - 0.1x_{2,t-1} - 0.7x_{1,t-2} + 0.15x_{2,t-2}$$
$$x_{2,t} = -0.12x_{1,t-1} + 0.7x_{2,t-1} + 0.22x_{1,t-2} + 0.85x_{2,t-2}$$
$$z_{1,t} = x_{1,t-1}$$
$$z_{2,t} = x_{2,t-1}$$

with matrix

$$A = \begin{bmatrix} 0.6 & -0.1 & -0.7 & 0.15 \\ -0.12 & 0.7 & 0.22 & -0.8 \\ 1 & 0 & 0 & 0 \\ 0 & 1 & 0 & 0 \end{bmatrix}$$

The eigenvalues of the matrix A are distinct and complex:

$$\lambda_1 = 0.2654 + 0.7011i, \quad \lambda_2 = \bar{\lambda}_1 = 0.2654 - 0.7011i$$
$$\lambda_3 = 0.3846 + 0.8887i, \quad \lambda_4 = \bar{\lambda}_3 = 0.3846 - 0.8887i$$

The corresponding eigenvector matrix Ξ is

$$\Xi = \begin{bmatrix} 0.1571 + 0.4150i & 0.1571 - 0.4150i & -0.1311 - 0.3436i & -0.1311 + 0.3436i \\ -0.0924 + 0.3928i & 0.0924 - 0.3928i & 0.2346 + 0.5419i & 0.2346 - 0.5419i \\ 0.5920 & 0.5920 & -0.3794 - 0.0167i & -0.3794 + 0.0167i \\ 0.5337 + 0.0702i & 0.5337 - 0.0702i & 0.6098 & 0.6098 \end{bmatrix}$$

Each column of the matrix is an eigenvector. The solution of the system is given by

$$\mathbf{x}(t) = c_1 \lambda_1^t \xi_1 + c_2 \bar{\lambda}_1^t \bar{\xi}_1 + c_3 \lambda_3^t \xi_3 + c_4 \bar{\lambda}_3^t \bar{\xi}_3$$

$$= c_1 (0.2654 + 0.7011i)^t \begin{pmatrix} 0.1571 + 0.4150i \\ 0.0924 + 0.3928i \\ 0.5920 \\ 0.5337 + 0.0702i \end{pmatrix} \xi_1$$

$$+ c_2 (0.2654 - 0.7011i)^t \begin{pmatrix} 0.1571 - 0.4150i \\ 0.0924 - 0.3928i \\ 0.5920 \\ 0.5337 - 0.0702i \end{pmatrix}$$

$$+ c_3 (0.3846 + 0.8887i)^t \begin{pmatrix} -0.1311 + 0.3436i \\ 0.2346 + 0.5419i \\ -0.3794 + 0.0167i \\ 0.6098 \end{pmatrix} \xi_3$$

$$+ c_4 (0.3846 - 0.8887i)^t \begin{pmatrix} -0.1311 - 0.3436i \\ 0.2346 - 0.5419i \\ -0.3794 - 0.0167i \\ 0.6098 \end{pmatrix}$$

The four constants c can be determined using the initial conditions: $(1) = 1$; $x(2) = 1.2$; $y(1) = 1.5$; $y(2) = -2$. Figure 8.9 illustrates the behavior of solutions.

Now consider the case in which two or more solutions of the characteristic equation are coincident. In this case, it can be demonstrated that the matrix $\mathbf{A}$ can be diagonalized only if it is normal, that is if

$$\mathbf{A}^T \mathbf{A} = \mathbf{A} \mathbf{A}^T$$

If the matrix $\mathbf{A}$ is not normal, it cannot be diagonalized. However, it can be put in **Jordan canonical form**. In fact, it can be demonstrated that any

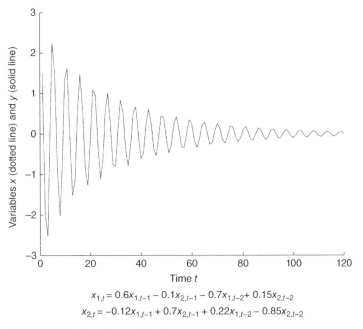

$$x_{1,t} = 0.6x_{1,t-1} - 0.1x_{2,t-1} - 0.7x_{1,t-2} + 0.15x_{2,t-2}$$
$$x_{2,t} = -0.12x_{1,t-1} + 0.7x_{2,t-1} + 0.22x_{1,t-2} - 0.85x_{2,t-2}$$

FIGURE 8.9   Solution of the System

nonsingular real-valued matrix $\mathbf{A}$ is similar to a matrix in Jordan canonical form,

$$\mathbf{A} = \mathbf{P}\mathbf{J}\mathbf{P}^{-1}$$

where the matrix $\mathbf{J}$ has the form $\mathbf{J} = \mathrm{diag}[\mathbf{J}_1, \ldots, \mathbf{J}k]$, that is, it is formed by **Jordan diagonal blocks**:

$$\mathbf{J} = \begin{bmatrix} \mathbf{J}_1 & \cdots & 0 \\ \vdots & \ddots & \vdots \\ 0 & \cdots & \mathbf{J}_k \end{bmatrix}$$

where each Jordan block has the form

$$\mathbf{J}_i = \begin{bmatrix} \lambda_1 & 1 & \cdots & 0 \\ 0 & \lambda_i & \cdots & \vdots \\ \vdots & \vdots & \ddots & 1 \\ 0 & 0 & \cdots & \lambda_i \end{bmatrix}$$

The Jordan canonical form is characterized by two sets of multiplicity parameters, the algebraic multiplicity and the geometric multiplicity. The geometric multiplicity of an eigenvalue is the number of Jordan blocks corresponding to that eigenvalue, while the algebraic multiplicity of an eigenvalue is the number of times the eigenvalue is repeated. An eigenvalue that is repeated s times can have from 1 to s Jordan blocks. For example, suppose a matrix has only one eigenvalue $\lambda = 5$ that is repeated three times. There are four possible matrices with the following Jordan representation:

$$\begin{pmatrix} 5 & 0 & 0 \\ 0 & 5 & 0 \\ 0 & 0 & 5 \end{pmatrix}, \begin{pmatrix} 5 & 1 & 0 \\ 0 & 5 & 0 \\ 0 & 0 & 5 \end{pmatrix}, \begin{pmatrix} 5 & 0 & 0 \\ 0 & 5 & 1 \\ 0 & 0 & 5 \end{pmatrix}, \begin{pmatrix} 5 & 1 & 0 \\ 0 & 5 & 1 \\ 0 & 0 & 5 \end{pmatrix}$$

These four matrices have all algebraic multiplicity 3 but geometric multiplicity from left to right 1, 2, 2, 3, respectively.

KEY POINTS

- Homogeneous difference equations are linear conditions that link the values of variables at different time lags.
- In the case of real roots, solutions are sums of exponentials. Any linear combination of solutions of the homogeneous difference equation is another solution.
- When some of the roots are complex, the solutions of a homogeneous difference equation exhibit an oscillating behavior with a period that depends on the model coefficients.
- The general solution of a homogeneous difference equation that admits both real and complex roots with different multiplicities is a sum of the different types of solutions.
- A system of difference equations is called homogeneous if the system's exogenous variable is zero, and nonhomogeneous if the exogenous term is present.
- One method of solving first-order systems of difference equations is by eliminating variables as in ordinary algebraic systems; another way is a direct method that can be used to solve systems of linear difference equations of any order.

CHAPTER 9

Differential Equations

A differential equation is a mathematical equation for an unknown function of one or several variables that relates the values of the function itself and its derivatives of various orders. Differential equations play a prominent role in financial economics. Differential equations arise in many areas of financial economics, that is, whenever a deterministic relation involving some continuously varying quantities (modeled by functions) and their rates of change in time or some other variable (expressed as derivatives) is known or postulated. Differential equations are mathematically studied from several different perspectives, mostly concerning their solutions—the set of functions that satisfy the equation. Only the simplest differential equations admit solutions given by explicit formulas; however, some properties of solutions of a given differential equation may be determined without finding their exact form. If a self-contained formula for the solution is not available, the solution can be numerically approximated using computer algorithms. Using differential equations:

- One can come up with a closed-form solution for the prices of options, as in the case of the Black-Scholes model.
- One can introduce the key idea behind the Black-Scholes model to perfectly hedge the option by buying and selling the underlying asset in just the right way and consequently eliminate risk.
- One can compute the quantities (popularly referred to as the "Greeks") representing the sensitivities of the price of options to a change in underlying parameters on which the value of an instrument or portfolio of financial instruments is dependent.
- One can deal with Itô calculus to find the differential of a time-dependent function of a stochastic process.

What you will learn after reading this chapter:

- How to define a differential equation.
- How to define an ordinary differential equation, and the order and degree of an ordinary differential equation.
- How to solve an ordinary differential equation.
- How to combine differential equations to form systems of differential equations.
- How to find a closed-form solution to an ordinary differential equation.
- How to find a numerical solution to an ordinary differential equation.
- How to apply the finite difference method to find a solution to an ordinary differential equation.
- How to find a closed form and numerical solution to partial differential equations.

INTRODUCTION

In nontechnical terms, **differential equations** are equations that express a relationship between a function and one or more derivatives (or differentials) of that function. The highest order of derivatives included in a differential equation is referred to as its **order**. In financial modeling, differential equations are used to specify the laws governing the evolution of price distributions, deriving solutions to simple and complex options, and estimating term structure models. In most applications in finance, only first- and second-order differential equations are used.

Differential equations are classified as ordinary differential equations and partial differential equations depending on the type of derivatives included in the differential equation. When there is only an ordinary derivative (i.e., a derivative of a mathematical function with only one independent variable), the differential equation is called an **ordinary differential equation**. For differential equations where there are partial derivatives (i.e., a derivative of a mathematical function with more than one independent variable), then the differential equation is called a **partial differential equation**. Typically in differential equations, one of the independent variables is time. A differential equation may have a derivative of a mathematical function where one or more of the independent variables is a random variable or a stochastic process. In such instances, the differential equation is referred to as a **stochastic differential equation**.

The solutions to a differential equation or system of differential equations can be as simple as explicit formulas. When an explicit formula is not possible to obtain, various numerical methods can be used to approximate a solution. Even in the absence of an exact solution, properties of solutions of a differential equation can be determined. A large number of properties of differential equations have been established over the last three centuries. In this chapter, we provide only a brief introduction to the concept of differential equations and their properties, limiting our discussion to the principal concepts. We do not cover stochastic differential equations.

DIFFERENTIAL EQUATIONS DEFINED

A differential equation is a condition expressed as a functional link between one or more functions and their derivatives. It is expressed as an equation (that is, as an equality between two terms).

A solution of a differential equation is a function that satisfies the given condition. For example, the condition

$$Y''(x) + \alpha Y'(x) + \beta Y(x) - b(x) = 0$$

equates to zero a linear relationship between an unknown function $Y(x)$, its first and second derivatives $Y'(x)$, $Y''(x)$, and a known function $b(x)$. (In some equations, we denote the first and second derivatives by a single and double prime, respectively.) The unknown function $Y(x)$ is the solution of the equation that is to be determined.

There are two broad types of differential equations: ordinary differential equations and partial differential equations. Ordinary differential equations are equations or systems of equations involving only one independent variable. Another way of saying this is that ordinary differential equations involve only total derivatives. In contrast, partial differential equations are differential equations or systems of equations involving partial derivatives. That is, there is more than one independent variable.

ORDINARY DIFFERENTIAL EQUATIONS

In full generality, an ordinary differential equation (ODE) can be expressed as the following relationship:

$$F[x, \ Y(x), \ Y^1(x), \dots, Y^{(n)}(x)] = 0$$

where $Y^{(m)}(x)$ denotes the mth derivative of an unknown function $Y(x)$. If the equation can be solved for the nth derivative, it can be put in the form:

$$Y^{(n)}(x) = G[x,\ Y(x),\ Y^{(1)}(x), \ldots, Y^{(n-1)}(x)]$$

Order and Degree of an ODE

A differential equation is classified in terms of its order and its degree. The order of a differential equation is the order of the highest derivative in the equation. For example, the above differential equation is of order n since the highest order derivative is $Y^{(n)}(x)$. The degree of a differential equation is determined by looking at the highest derivative in the differential equation. The degree is the power to which that derivative is raised.

For example, the following ordinary differential equations are first-degree differential equations of different orders:

$$Y^{(1)}(x) - 10Y(x) + 40 = 0 \qquad (\text{order } 1)$$
$$4Y^{(3)}(x) + Y^{(2)}(x) + Y^{(1)}(x) - 0.5Y(x) + 100 = 0$$
$$(\text{order } 3)$$

The following ordinary differential equations are of order 3 and fifth degree:

$$4[Y^{(3)}(x)]^5 + [Y^{(2)}(x)]^2 + Y^{(1)}(x) - 0.5Y(x) + 100 = 0$$
$$4[Y^{(3)}(x)]^5 + [Y^{(2)}(x)]^3 + Y^{(1)}(x) - 0.5Y(x) + 100 = 0$$

When an ordinary differential equation is of the first degree, it is said to be a **linear ordinary differential equation.**

Solution to an ODE

Let's return to the general ODE. A solution of this equation is any function $y(x)$ such that:

$$F[x,\ y(x),\ y^{(1)}(x), \ldots, y^{(n)}(x)] = 0$$

In general there will be not one but an infinite family of solutions. For example, the equation

$$Y^{(1)}(x) = \alpha Y(x)$$

admits, as a solution, all the functions of the form

$$y(x) = C \exp(\alpha x)$$

To identify one specific solution among the possible infinite solutions that satisfy a differential equation, additional restrictions must be imposed. Restrictions that uniquely identify a solution to a differential equation can be of various types. For instance, one could impose that a solution of an nth order differential equation passes through n given points. A common type of restriction—called an *initial condition*—is obtained by imposing that the solution and some of its derivatives assume given initial values at some initial point.

Given an ODE of order n, to ensure the uniqueness of solutions it will generally be necessary to specify a starting point and the initial value of $n - 1$ derivatives. It can be demonstrated, given the differential equation

$$F[x, \ Y(x), \ Y^{(1)}(x), \dots, \ Y^{(n)}(x)] = 0$$

that if the function F is continuous and all of its partial derivatives up to order n are continuous in some region containing the values $y_0, \dots, y_0^{(n-1)}$, then there is a unique solution $y(x)$ of the equation in some interval $I = (M \le x \le L)$ such that $y_0 = Y(x_0), \dots, y_0^{(n-1)} = Y^{(n-1)}(x_0)$.[1] Note that this theorem states that there is an interval in which the solution exists. Existence and uniqueness of solutions in a given interval is a more delicate matter and must be examined for different classes of equations.

The general solution of a differential equation of order n is a function of the form

$$y = \varphi(x, C_1, \dots, C_n)$$

that satisfies the following two conditions:

Condition 1. The function $y = \varphi(x, C_1, \dots, C_n)$ satisfies the differential equation for any n-tuple of values $(C_1, \dots, C_n)$.

Condition 2. Given a set of initial conditions $y(x_0) = y_0, \dots,$ $y^{(n-1)}(x_0) = y_0^{(n-1)}$ that belong to the region where solutions of the equation exist, it is possible to determine n constants in such a way that the function $y = \varphi(x, C_1, \dots, C_n)$ satisfies these conditions.

---

[1] The condition of existence and continuity of derivatives is stronger than necessary. The Lipschitz condition, which requires that the incremental ratio be uniformly bounded in a given interval, suffices.

The coupling of differential equations with initial conditions embodies the notion of universal determinism of classical physics. Given initial conditions, the future evolution of a system that obeys those equations is completely determined. This notion was forcefully expressed by Pierre-Simon Laplace in the eighteenth century: A supernatural mind who knows the laws of physics and the initial conditions of each atom could perfectly predict the future evolution of the universe with unlimited precision.

In the twentieth century, the notion of universal determinism was challenged twice in the physical sciences. First, in the 1920s, the development of quantum mechanics introduced the so-called "indeterminacy principle" that established explicit bounds to the precision of measurements. Later, in the 1970s, the development of nonlinear dynamics and chaos theory showed how arbitrarily small initial differences might become arbitrarily large: The flapping of a butterfly's wings in the southern hemisphere might cause a tornado in the northern hemisphere.

SYSTEMS OF ORDINARY DIFFERENTIAL EQUATIONS

Differential equations can be combined to form systems of differential equations. These are sets of differential conditions that must be satisfied simultaneously. A **first-order system of differential equations** is a system of the following type:

$$
\begin{cases}
\dfrac{dy_1}{dx} = f_1(x, y_1, \ldots, y_n) \\[2mm]
\dfrac{dy_2}{dx} = f_2(x, y_1, \ldots, y_n) \\[2mm]
\quad \cdot \\
\quad \cdot \\
\quad \cdot \\
\dfrac{dy_n}{dx} = f_n(x, y_1, \ldots, y_n)
\end{cases}
$$

Solving this system means finding a set of functions $y_1, \ldots, y_n$ that satisfy the system as well as the initial conditions:

$$
y_1(x_0) = y_{10}, \ldots, y_n(x_0) = y_{n0}
$$

Systems of orders higher than 1 can be reduced to first-order systems in a straightforward way by adding new variables defined as the derivatives of existing variables. As a consequence, an *n*th order differential equation can be transformed into a first-order system of *n* equations. Conversely, a system of first-order differential equations is equivalent to a single *n*th order equation.

To illustrate this point, let's differentiate the first equation to obtain

$$\frac{d^2 y_1}{dx^2} = \frac{\partial f_1}{\partial x} + \frac{\partial f_1}{\partial y_1}\frac{dy_1}{dx} + \cdots + \frac{\partial f_1}{\partial y_n}\frac{dy_n}{dx}$$

Replacing the derivatives

$$\frac{d_{y1}}{dx}, \ldots, \frac{d_{yn}}{dx}$$

with their expressions $f_1, \ldots, f_n$ from the system's equations, we obtain

$$\frac{d^2 y_1}{dx^2} = F_2(x, y_1, \ldots, y_n)$$

If we now reiterate this process, we arrive at the *n*th order equation:

$$\frac{d^{(n)} y_1}{dx^{(n)}} = F_n(x, y_1, \ldots, y_n)$$

We can thus write the following system:

$$\begin{cases} \dfrac{dy_1}{dx} = f_1(x, y_1, \ldots, y_n) \\ \dfrac{d^2 y_1}{dx^2} = F_2(x, y_1, \ldots, y_n) \\ \quad . \\ \quad . \\ \quad . \\ \dfrac{d^{(n)} y_1}{dx^{(n)}} = F_n(x, y_1, \ldots, y_n) \end{cases}$$

We can express $y_2, \ldots, y_n$ as functions of $x, y_1, y_1', \ldots, y_1^{(n-1)}$ by solving, if possible, the system formed with the first $n - 1$ equations:

$$\begin{cases} y_2 = \varphi_2(x, y_1, y_1', \ldots, y_1^{(n-1))} \\ y_3 = \varphi_3(x, y_1, y_1', \ldots, y_1^{(n-1))} \\ \cdot \\ \cdot \\ \cdot \\ y_n = \varphi_n(x, y_1, y_1', \ldots, y_1^{(n-1)}) \end{cases}$$

Substituting these expressions into the nth equation of the previous system, we arrive at the single equation:

$$\frac{d^{(n)} y_1}{dx^{(n)}} = \Phi(x, y_1', \ldots, y_1^{(n-1)})$$

Solving, if possible, this equation, we find the general solution

$$y_1 = y_1(x, C_1, \ldots, C_n)$$

Substituting this expression for y_1 into the previous system, $y_2, \ldots, y_n$ can be computed.

CLOSED-FORM SOLUTIONS OF ORDINARY DIFFERENTIAL EQUATIONS

Let's now consider the methods for solving two types of common differential equations: equations with separable variables and equations of linear type. Let's start with equations with separable variables. Consider the equation

$$\frac{dy}{dx} = f(x)g(y)$$

This equation is said to have separable variables because it can be written as an equality between two sides, each depending on only y or only x. We can rewrite our equation in the following way:

$$\frac{dy}{g(y)} = f(x)dx$$

This equation can be regarded as an equality between two differentials in y and x respectively. Their indefinite integrals can differ only by a constant. Integrating the left side with respect to y and the right side with respect to x, we obtain the general solution of the equation:

$$\int \frac{dy}{g(y)} = \int f(x)dx + C$$

For example, if $g(y) = y$, the previous equation becomes

$$\frac{dy}{y} = f(x)dx$$

whose solution is

$$\int \frac{dy}{y} = \int f(x)dx + C \Rightarrow$$

$$\log y = \int f(x)dx + C \Rightarrow y = A \exp\left(\int f(x)dx\right)$$

where $A = \exp(C)$.

A differential equation of this type describes the continuous compounding of time-varying interest rates. Consider, for example, the growth of capital C deposited in a bank account that earns the variable but deterministic rate $r = f(t)$. When interest rates R_i are constant for discrete periods of time Δt_i, compounding is obtained by purely algebraic formulas as follows:

$$R_i \Delta t_i = \frac{C(t_i) - C(t_{i-\Delta t_i})}{C(t_{i-\Delta t_i})}$$

Solving for $C(t_i)$:

$$C(t_i) = (1 + R_i \Delta t_i)C(t_i - \Delta t_i)$$

By recursive substitution we obtain

$$C(t_i) = (1 + R_i \Delta t_i)(1 + R_{i-1}\Delta t_{i-1})\ldots$$
$$(1 + R_1 \Delta t_1)C(t_0)$$

However, market interest rates are subject to rapid change. In the limit of very short time intervals, the instantaneous rate $r(t)$ would be defined as the limit, if it exists, of the discrete interest rate:

$$r(t) = \lim_{\Delta t \to 0} \frac{C(t + \Delta t) - C(t)}{\Delta t C(t)}$$

The above expression can be rewritten as a simple first-order differential equation in C:

$$r(t)C(t) = \frac{dC(t)}{dt}$$

In a simple intuitive way, the above equation can be obtained considering that in the elementary time dt the bank account increments by the amount $dC = C(t)r(t)dt$. In this equation, variables are separable. It admits the family of solutions:

$$C = A \ \exp\left(\int r(t)dt \right)$$

where A is the initial capital.

Linear Differential Equation

Linear differential equations are equations of the following type:

$$a_n(x)y^{(n)} + a_{n-1}(x)y^{(n-1)} + \cdots + a_1(x)y^{(1)} + a_0(x)y + b(x) = 0$$

If the function b is identically zero, the equation is said to be homogeneous.

In cases where the coefficients a's are constant, Laplace transforms provide a powerful method for solving linear differential equations. Laplace transforms are one of two popular integral transforms—the other being Fourier transforms—used in financial modeling. Integral transforms are operations that take any function into another function of a different variable through an improper integral. (Laplace and Fourier transforms are described in Chapter 3.)

Consider, without loss of generality, the following linear equation with constant coefficients:

$$a_n y^{(n)} + a_{n-1} y^{(n-1)} + \cdots + a_1 y^{(1)} + a_0 y = b(x)$$

together with the initial conditions: $y_0 = y0, \ldots, y^{(n-1)}(0) = y_0^{(n-1)}$. In cases in which the initial point is not the origin, by a variable transformation we can shift the origin.

Laplace Transform Recall from Chapter 3 that for one-sided Laplace transforms the following formulas hold:

$$\mathcal{L}\left(\frac{df(x)}{dx}\right) = s\mathcal{L}[f(x)] - f(0)$$

$$\mathcal{L}\left(\frac{d^n f(x)}{dx^n}\right) = s^n\mathcal{L}[f(x)] - s^{n-1}f(0) - \cdots - f^{(n-1)}(0)$$

Suppose that a function $y = y(x)$ satisfies the previous linear equation with constant coefficients and that it admits a Laplace transform. Apply one-sided Laplace transform to both sides of the equation. If $Y(s) = \mathcal{L}[y(x)]$, the following relationships hold:

$$L\left(a_n y^{(n)} + a_{n-1} y^{(n-1)} + \cdots + a_1 y^{(1)} + a_0 y\right) = L[b(x)]$$
$$a_n[s^n Y(s) - s^{n-1} y^{(1)}(0) - \cdots - y^{(n-1)}(0)]$$
$$+ a_{n-1}[s^{n-1} Y(s) - s^{n-2} y^{(1)}(0) - \cdots - y^{(n-2)}(0)]$$
$$+ \cdots + a0 Y(s) = B(s)$$

Solving this equation for $Y(s)$, that is, $Y(s) = g[s, y^{(t)}(0), \ldots, y^{(n-1)}(0)]$, the inverse Laplace transform $y(t) = \mathcal{L}^{-1}[Y(s)]$ uniquely determines the solution of the equation.

Because inverse Laplace transforms are integrals, with this method, when applicable, the solution of a differential equation is reduced to the determination of integrals. Laplace transforms and inverse Laplace transforms are known for large classes of functions. Because of the important role that Laplace transforms play in solving ordinary differential equations in engineering problems, there are published reference tables. Laplace transform methods also yield closed-form solutions of many ordinary differential equations of interest in economics and finance.

NUMERICAL SOLUTIONS OF ORDINARY DIFFERENTIAL EQUATIONS

Closed-form solutions are solutions that can be expressed in terms of known functions such as polynomials or exponential functions. Before the advent of computers, the search for closed-form solutions of differential equations was an important task. Today, thanks to the availability of high-performance computing, most problems are solved numerically. This section looks at methods for solving ordinary differential equations numerically.

The Finite Difference Method

Among the methods used to numerically solve ordinary differential equations subject to initial conditions, the most common is the finite difference method. The finite difference method is based on replacing derivatives with difference equations; differential equations are thereby transformed into recursive difference equations.

Key to this method of numerical solution is the fact that ODEs subject to initial conditions describe phenomena that evolve from some starting point. In this case, the differential equation can be approximated with a system of difference equations that compute the next point based on previous points. This would not be possible should we impose boundary conditions instead of initial conditions. In this latter case, we have to solve a system of linear equations.

To illustrate the finite difference method, consider the following simple ordinary differential equation and its solution in a finite interval:

$$f'(x) = f(x)$$
$$\frac{df}{f} = dx$$
$$\log f(x) = x + C$$
$$f(x) = \exp(x + C)$$

As shown, the closed-form solution of the equation is obtained by separation of variables, that is, by transforming the original equation into another equation where the function f appears only on the left side and the variable x only on the right side.

Suppose that we replace the derivative with its forward finite difference approximation and solve

$$\frac{f(x_{i+1}) - f(x_i)}{x_{i+1} - x_i} = f(x_i)$$
$$f(x_{i+1}) = [1 + (x_{i+1} - x_i)] f(x_i)$$

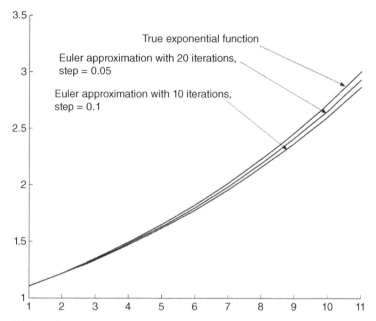

FIGURE 9.1 Numerical Solutions of the Equation $f' = f$ with the Euler Approximation for Different Step Sizes

If we assume that the step size is constant for all i:

$$f(x_i) = [1 + \Delta x]^i \, f(x_0)$$

The replacement of derivatives with finite differences is often called the **Euler approximation**. The differential equation is replaced by a recursive formula based on approximating the derivative with a finite difference. The ith value of the solution is computed from the $i - 1$th value. Given the initial value of the function f, the solution of the differential equation can be arbitrarily approximated by choosing a sufficiently small interval. Figure 9.1 illustrates this computation for different values of Δx.

In the previous example of a first-order linear equation, only one initial condition was involved. Let's now consider a second-order equation:

$$f''(x) = kf(x) = 0$$

This equation describes oscillatory motion, such as the elongation of a pendulum or the displacement of a spring.

To approximate this equation we must approximate the second derivative. This could be done, for example, by combining difference quotients as follows:

$$f'(x) \approx \frac{f(x + \Delta x) - f(x)}{\Delta x}$$

$$f'(x + \Delta x) \approx \frac{f(x + 2\Delta x) - f(x + \Delta x)}{\Delta x}$$

$$f''(x) \approx \frac{f'(x + \Delta x) - f'(x)}{\Delta x}$$

$$= \frac{\dfrac{f(x + 2\Delta x) - f(x - \Delta x)}{\Delta x} - \dfrac{f(x - \Delta x) - f(x)}{\Delta x}}{\Delta x}$$

$$= \frac{f(x + 2\Delta x) - 2f(x + \Delta x) + f(x)}{(\Delta x)^2}$$

With this approximation, the original equation becomes

$$f''(x) + kf(x) \approx$$
$$\frac{f(x + 2\Delta x) - 2f(x + \Delta x) + f(x)}{(\Delta x)^2} + kf(x) = 0$$
$$f(x + 2\Delta x) - 2f(x + \Delta x) + (1 + k(\Delta x)^2)f(x) = 0$$

We can thus write the approximation scheme:

$$f(x + \Delta x) = f(x) + \Delta x f'(x)$$
$$f(x + 2\Delta x) = 2f(x + \Delta x) - (1 + k(\Delta x)^2)f(x)$$

Given the increment Δx and the initial values $f(0)$, $f'(0)$, using the above formulas we can recursively compute $f(0 + \Delta x)$, $f(0 + 2\Delta x)$, and so on. Figure 9.2 illustrates this computation.

In practice, the Euler approximation scheme is often not sufficiently precise and more sophisticated approximation schemes are used. For example, a widely used approximation scheme is the **Runge-Kutta method.** We give an example of the Runge-Kutta method in the case of the equation $f'' + f = 0$ which is equivalent to the linear system:

$$x' = y$$
$$y' = -x$$

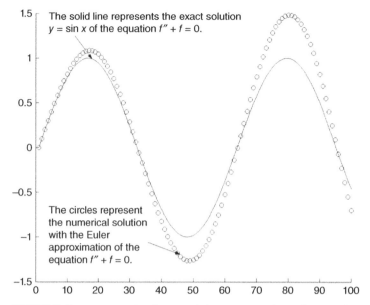

FIGURE 9.2 Numerical Solution of the Equation $f'' + f = 0$ with the Euler Approximation

In this case the Runge-Kutta approximation scheme is the following:

$$k_1 = hy(i)$$
$$h_1 = -hx(i)$$
$$k_2 = h\left[y(i) + \frac{1}{2}h_1\right]$$
$$h_2 = -h\left[x(i) + \frac{1}{2}k_1\right]$$
$$k_3 = h\left[y(i) + \frac{1}{2}h_2\right]$$
$$h_3 = -h\left[x(i) + \frac{1}{2}k_2\right]$$
$$k_4 = h[y(i) + h_3]$$
$$h_4 = -h[x(i) + k_3]$$
$$x(i+1) = x(i) + \frac{1}{6}(k_1 + 2k_2 + 2k_3 + k_4)$$
$$y(i+1) = y(i) + \frac{1}{6}(h_1 + 2h_2 + 2h_3 + h_4)$$

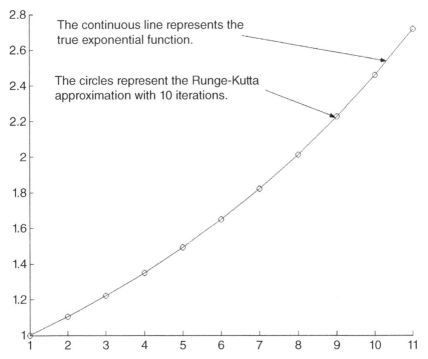

FIGURE 9.3 Numerical Solution of the Equation $f' = f$ with the Runge-Kutta Method After 10 Steps

Figures 9.3 and 9.4 illustrate the results of this method in the two cases $f' = f$ and $f' + f = 0$.

As mentioned above, this numerical method depends critically on our having as givens (1) the initial values of the solution, and (2) its first derivative. Suppose that instead of initial values two boundary values were given, for instance the initial value of the solution and its value 1,000 steps ahead, that is, $f(0) = f_0, f(0 + 1{,}000\Delta x) = f_{1{,}000}$. Conditions like these are rarely used in the study of dynamical systems as they imply foresight, that is, knowledge of the future position of a system. However, they often appear in static systems and when trying to determine what initial conditions should be imposed to reach a given goal at a given date.

In the case of boundary conditions, one cannot write a direct recursive scheme; it's necessary to solve a system of equations. For instance, we could introduce the derivative $f'(x) = \delta$ as an unknown quantity. The difference

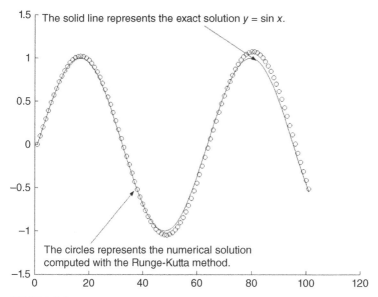

FIGURE 9.4 Numerical Solution of the Equation $f' + f = 0$ with the Runge-Kutta Method

quotient that approximates the derivative becomes an unknown. We can now write a system of linear equations in the following way:

$$\begin{cases} f(\Delta x) = f_0 + \delta \Delta x \\ f(2\Delta x) = 2 f(\Delta x) - (1 + k(\Delta x)^2) f_0 \\ f(3\Delta x) = 2 f(2\Delta x) - (1 + k(\Delta x)^2 f(\Delta x) \\ \quad \cdot \\ \quad \cdot \\ \quad \cdot \\ f_{1000} = 2 f(999\Delta x) - (1 + k(\Delta x)^2 f(998\Delta x) \end{cases}$$

This is a system of 1,000 equations in 1,000 unknowns. Solving the system we compute the entire solution. In this system two equations, the first and the last, are linked to boundary values; all other equations are transfer equations that express the dynamics (or the law) of the system. This is a general feature of boundary value problems. We encounter it again when discussing numerical solutions of partial differential equations.

In the previous example, we chose a forward scheme where the derivative is approximated with the forward difference quotient. One might use a different approximation scheme, computing the derivative in intervals centered around the point x. When derivatives of higher orders are involved, the choice of the approximation scheme becomes critical. Recall that when we approximated first and second derivatives using forward differences, we were required to evaluate the function at two points (i, $i + 1$) and three points (i, $i + 1$, $i + 2$) ahead respectively. If purely forward schemes are employed, computing higher-order derivatives requires many steps ahead. This fact might affect the precision and stability of numerical computations.

We saw in the examples that the accuracy of a finite difference scheme depends on the discretization interval. In general, a finite difference scheme works, that is, it is consistent and stable, if the numerical solution converges uniformly to the exact solution when the length of the discretization interval tends to zero. Suppose that the precision of an approximation scheme depends on the length of the discretization interval Δx. Consider the difference $\delta f = \hat{f}(x) - f(x)$ between the approximate and the exact solutions. We say that $\delta f \to 0$ uniformly in the interval $[a,b]$ when $\Delta x \to 0$ if, given any ε arbitrarily small, it is possible to find a Δx such that $|\delta f| < \varepsilon$, $\forall x \in [a, b]$.

NONLINEAR DYNAMICS AND CHAOS

Systems of differential equations describe dynamical systems that evolve starting from initial conditions. A fundamental concept in the theory of dynamical systems is that of the stability of solutions. This topic has become of paramount importance with the development of nonlinear dynamics and with the discovery of chaotic phenomena. We can only give a brief introductory account of this subject whose role in economics is still the subject of debate.

Intuitively, a dynamical system is considered stable if its solutions do not change much when the system is only slightly perturbed. There are different ways to perturb a system: changing parameters in its equations, changing the known functions of the system by a small amount, or changing the initial conditions.

Consider an equilibrium solution of a dynamical system, that is, a solution that is time invariant. If a stable system is perturbed when it is in a position of equilibrium, it tends to return to the equilibrium position or, in any case, not to diverge indefinitely from its equilibrium position. For example, a damped pendulum—if perturbed from a position of equilibrium—will tend to go back to an equilibrium position. If the pendulum is not damped it will continue to oscillate forever.

Consider a system of n equations of first order. (As noted above, systems of higher orders can always be reduced to first-order systems by enlarging the set of variables.) Suppose that we can write the system explicitly in the first derivatives as follows:

$$\begin{cases} \dfrac{dy_1}{dx} = f_1(x, y_1, \ldots, y_n) \\[2mm] \dfrac{dy_2}{dx} = f_2(x, y_1, \ldots, y_n) \\ \\ \\ \\ \dfrac{dy_n}{dx} = f_n(x, y_1, \ldots, y_n) \end{cases}$$

If the equations are all linear, a complete theory of stability has been developed. Essentially, linear dynamical systems are stable except possibly at singular points where solutions might diverge. In particular, a characteristic of linear systems is that they incur only small changes in the solution as a result of small changes in the initial conditions.

However, during the 1970s, it was discovered that nonlinear systems have a different behavior. Suppose that a nonlinear system has at least three degrees of freedom (that is, it has three independent nonlinear equations). The dynamics of such a system can then become chaotic in the sense that arbitrarily small changes in initial conditions might diverge. This sensitivity to initial conditions is one of the signatures of chaos. Note that while discrete systems such as discrete maps can exhibit chaos in one dimension, continuous systems require at least three degrees of freedom (that is, three equations).

Sensitive dependence from initial conditions was first observed in 1960 by the meteorologist Edward Lorenz of the Massachusetts Institute of Technology. Lorenz remarked that computer simulations of weather forecasts starting, apparently, from the same meteorological data could yield very different results. He argued that the numerical solutions of extremely sensitive differential equations such as those he was using produced diverging results due to rounding-off errors made by the computer system. His discovery was published in a meteorological journal where it remained unnoticed for many years.

Fractals

While in principle deterministic chaotic systems are unpredictable because of their sensitivity to initial conditions, the statistics of their behavior can be studied. Consider, for example, the chaos laws that describe the evolution of weather: While the weather is basically unpredictable over long periods of time, long-run simulations are used to predict the statistics of weather.

It was discovered that probability distributions originating from chaotic systems exhibit fat tails in the sense that very large, extreme events have non-negligible probabilities.[2] It was also discovered that chaotic systems exhibit complex unexpected behavior. The motion of chaotic systems is often associated with self-similarity and fractal shapes.

Fractals were introduced in the 1960s by Benoit Mandelbrot, a mathematician working at the IBM research center in Yorktown Heights, New York. Starting from the empirical observation that cotton price time-series are similar at different time scales, Mandelbrot developed a powerful theory of fractal geometrical objects. Fractals are geometrical objects that are geometrically similar to part of themselves. Stock prices exhibit this property insofar as price time-series look the same at different time scales.

Chaotic systems are also sensitive to changes in their parameters. In a chaotic system, only some regions of the parameter space exhibit chaotic behavior. The change in behavior is abrupt and, in general, it cannot be predicted analytically. In addition, chaotic behavior appears in systems that are apparently very simple.

While the intuition that chaotic systems might exist is not new, the systematic exploration of chaotic systems started only in the 1970s. The discovery of the existence of nonlinear chaotic systems marked a conceptual crisis in the physical sciences: It challenges the very notion of the applicability of mathematics to the description of reality. Chaos laws are not testable on a large scale; their applicability cannot be predicted analytically. Nevertheless, the statistics of chaos theory might still prove to be meaningful.

The economy being a complex system, the expectation was that its apparently random behavior could be explained as a deterministic chaotic system of low dimensionality. Despite the fact that tests to detect low-dimensional chaos in the economy have produced a substantially negative response, it is easy to make macroeconomic and financial econometric models exhibit chaos.[3] As a matter of fact, most macroeconomic models are nonlinear. Though chaos has not been detected in economic time-series, most economic dynamic models are nonlinear in more than three dimensions and

---

[2]See W. Brock, D. Hsieh, and B. LeBaron, *Nonlinear Dynamics, Chaos, and Instability* (Cambridge, MA: MIT Press, 1991); and D. Hsieh, "Chaos and Nonlinear Dynamics: Application to Financial Markets," *Journal of Finance* 46 (1991): 1839–1877.

[3]See W. A. Brock, W. D. Dechert, J. A. Scheinkman, and B. LeBaron, "A Test for Independence Based on the Correlation Dimension," *Econometric Reviews* 15 (1996): 197–235; and W. Brock and C. Hommes, "A Rational Route to Randomness," *Econometrica* 65 (1997): 1059–1095.

thus potentially chaotic. At this stage of the research, we might conclude that if chaos exists in economics it is not of the low-dimensional type.

PARTIAL DIFFERENTIAL EQUATIONS

To illustrate the notion of a **partial differential equation** (PDE), let's start with equations in two dimensions. An *n*-order PDE in two dimensions *x,y* is an equation of the form

$$F\left(x, y, \frac{\partial f}{\partial x}, \frac{\partial f}{\partial y}, \ldots, \frac{\partial^{(i)} f}{\partial^{(k)} x \partial^{(i-k)} y}\right) = 0, 0 \leq k \leq i, 0 \leq i \leq n$$

A solution of the previous equation will be any function that satisfies the equation.

In the case of PDEs, the notion of initial conditions must be replaced with the notion of boundary conditions or initial plus boundary conditions. Solutions will be defined in a multidimensional domain. To identify a solution uniquely, the value of the solution on some subdomain must be specified. In general, this subdomain will coincide with the boundary (or some portion of the boundary) of the domain.

Diffusion Equation

Different equations will require and admit different types of boundary and initial conditions. The question of the existence and uniqueness of solutions of PDEs is a delicate mathematical problem. We can only give a brief account by way of an example.

Let's consider the **diffusion equation.** This equation describes the propagation of the probability density of stock prices under the random-walk hypothesis:

$$\frac{\partial f}{\partial t} = a^2 \frac{\partial^2 f}{\partial x^2}$$

The Black-Scholes equation, which describes the evolution of option prices, can be reduced to the diffusion equation.

The diffusion equation describes propagating phenomena. Call *f(t,x)* the probability density that prices have value *x* at time *t*. In finance theory, the diffusion equation describes the time-evolution of the probability density function $f(t,x)$ of stock prices that follow a random walk.[4] It is therefore natural to impose initial and boundary conditions on the distribution of prices.

In general, we distinguish two different problems related to the diffusion equation: the first boundary value problem and the **Cauchy initial value problem,** named after the French mathematician Augustin Cauchy who first formulated it. The two problems refer to the same diffusion equation but consider different domains and different initial and boundary conditions. It can be demonstrated that both problems admit a unique solution.

The first boundary value problem seeks to find in the rectangle $0 \leq x \leq 1, 0 \leq t \leq T$ a continuous function $f(t,x)$ that satisfies the diffusion equation in the interior Q of the rectangle plus the following initial condition,

$$f(0, x) = \phi(x), 0 \leq x \leq l$$

and boundary conditions,

$$f(t, 0) = f_1(t), \quad f(t, l) = f_2(t), \quad 0 \leq t \leq T$$

The functions f_1, f_2 are assumed to be continuous and $f_1(0) = \phi(0)$, $f_2(0) = \phi(l)$.

The Cauchy problem is related to an infinite half plane instead of a finite rectangle. It is formulated as follows. The objective is to find for any x and for $t \geq 0$ a continuous and bounded function $f(t,x)$ that satisfies the diffusion equation and which, for $t = 0$, is equal to a continuous and bounded function $f(0, x) = \phi(x)$, $\forall x$.

Solution of the Diffusion Equation

The first boundary value problem of the diffusion equation can be solved exactly. We illustrate here a widely used method based on the separation of variables, which is applicable if the boundary conditions on the vertical sides vanish (that is, if $f_1(t) = f_2(t) = 0$). The method involves looking for a tentative solution in the form of a product of two functions, one that depends only on t and the other that depends only on x: $f(t,x) = h(t)g(x)$.

---

[4]In physics, the diffusion equation describes phenomena such as the diffusion of particles suspended in some fluid. In this case, the diffusion equation describes the density of particles at a given moment at a given point.

If we substitute the previous tentative solution in the diffusion equation

$$\frac{\partial f}{\partial t} = a^2 \frac{\partial^2 f}{\partial x^2}$$

we obtain an equation where the left side depends only on t while the right side depends only on x:

$$\frac{dh(t)}{dt} g(x) = a^2 h(t) \frac{d^2 g(x)}{dx^2}$$

$$\frac{dh(t)}{dt} \frac{1}{h(t)} = a^2 \frac{d^2 g(x)}{dx^2} \frac{1}{g(x)}$$

This condition can be satisfied only if the two sides are equal to a constant. The original diffusion equation is therefore transformed into two ordinary differential equations:

$$\frac{1}{a^2} \frac{dh(t)}{dt} = bh(t)$$

$$\frac{d^2 g(x)}{dx^2} = bg(x)$$

with boundary conditions $g(0) = g(l) = 0$. From the above equations and boundary conditions, it can be seen that b can assume only the negative values,

$$b = -\frac{k^2 \pi^2}{l^2}, k = 1, 2, \ldots$$

while the functions g can only be of the form

$$g(x) = B_k \sin \frac{k\pi}{l} x$$

Substituting for h, we obtain

$$h(t) = B'_k \exp \left(-\frac{a^2 k^2 \pi^2}{l^2} t \right)$$

Therefore, we can see that there are denumerably infinite solutions of the diffusion equation of the form

$$f_x(t, x) = C_k \exp\left(-\frac{a^2 k^2 \pi^2}{l^2} t\right) \sin \frac{k\pi}{l} x$$

All these solutions satisfy the boundary conditions $f(t,0) = f(t,l) = 0$. By linearity, we know that the infinite sum

$$f(t, x) = \sum_{k=1}^{\infty} f_k(t, x)$$

$$= \sum_{k=1}^{\infty} C_k \exp\left(-\frac{a^2 k^1 \pi^2}{l^2} t\right) \sin \frac{k\pi}{l} x$$

will satisfy the diffusion equation. Clearly $f(t,x)$ satisfies the boundary conditions $f(t,0) = f(t,l) = 0$. In order to satisfy the initial condition, given that $\phi(x)$ is bounded and continuous and that $\phi(0) = \phi(l) = 0$, it can be demonstrated that the coefficients Cs can be uniquely determined through the following integrals, which are called the Fourier integrals:

$$C_k = \frac{2}{L} \int_0^L \phi(\xi) \sin\left(\frac{\pi k}{L} \xi\right) d\xi$$

The previous method applies to the first boundary value problem but cannot be applied to the Cauchy problem, which admits only an initial condition. It can be demonstrated that the solution of the Cauchy problem can be expressed in terms of a convolution with a Green's function. In particular, it can be demonstrated that the solution of the Cauchy problem can be written in closed form as follows:

$$f(t, x) = \frac{1}{2\sqrt{\pi}} \int_{-\infty}^{\infty} \frac{\phi(\xi)}{\sqrt{t}} \exp\left\{-\frac{(x-\xi)^2}{4t}\right\} d\xi$$

for $t > 0$ and $f(0,x) = \phi(x)$. It can be demonstrated that the Black-Scholes equation, which is an equation of the form

$$\frac{\partial f}{\partial t} + \frac{1}{2}\sigma^2 x^2 \frac{\partial^2 f}{\partial x^2} + rx\frac{\partial f}{\partial x} - rf = 0$$

can be reduced through transformation of variables to the standard diffusion equation to be solved with the Green's function approach.

Numerical Solution of PDEs

There are different methods for the numerical solution of PDEs. We illustrate the finite difference methods, which are based on approximating derivatives with finite differences. Other discretization schemes such as finite elements and spectral methods are possible but, being more complex, they go beyond the scope of this book.

Finite difference methods result in a set of recursive equations when applied to initial conditions. When finite difference methods are applied to boundary problems, they require the solution of systems of simultaneous linear equations. PDEs might exhibit boundary conditions, initial conditions, or a mix of the two.

The Cauchy problem of the diffusion equation is an example of initial conditions. The simplest discretization scheme for the diffusion equation replaces derivatives with their difference quotients. As for ordinary differential equations, the discretization scheme can be written as follows:

$$\frac{\partial f}{\partial t} \approx \frac{f(t + \Delta t,\ x) - f(t,\ x)}{\Delta t}$$
$$\frac{\partial^2 f}{\partial x^2} \approx \frac{f(t, x + \Delta x) - 2 f(t,\ x) + f(t,\ x - \Delta x)}{(\Delta x)^2}$$

In the case of the Cauchy problem, this approximation scheme defines the forward recursive algorithm. It can be proved that the algorithm is stable only if the Courant-Friedrichs-Lewy (CFL) conditions

$$\Delta t < \frac{(\Delta x)^2}{2a^2}$$

are satisfied.

Different approximation schemes can be used. In particular, the forward approximation to the derivative used above could be replaced by centered approximations. Figure 9.5 illustrates the solution of a Cauchy problem for initial conditions that vanish outside of a finite interval. The simulation shows that solutions diffuse in the entire half space.

Applying the same discretization to a first boundary problem would require the solution of a system of linear equations at every step. Figure 9.6 illustrates this case.

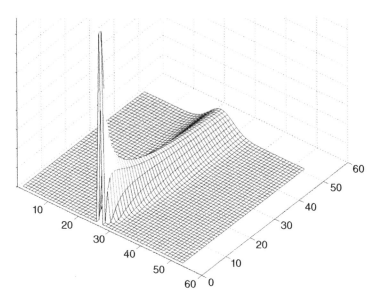

FIGURE 9.5 Solution of the Cauchy Problem by the Finite Difference Method

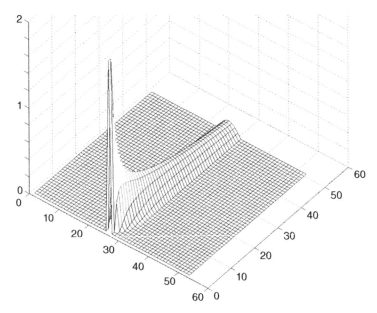

FIGURE 9.6 Solution of the First Boundary Problem by the Finite Difference Method

KEY POINTS

- Basically, differential equations are equations that express a relationship between a function and one or more derivatives (or differentials) of that function.
- The two classifications of differential equations are ordinary differential equations and partial differential equations. The classification depends on the type of derivatives included in the differential equation: ordinary differential equation when there is only an ordinary derivative and partial differential equation where there are partial derivatives.
- Typically in differential equations, one of the independent variables is time.
- The term stochastic differential equation refers to a differential equation in which a derivative of one or more of the independent variables is a random variable or a stochastic process.
- Differential equations are conditions that must be satisfied by their solutions. Differential equations generally admit infinite solutions. Initial or boundary conditions are needed to identify solutions uniquely.
- Differential equations are the key mathematical tools for the development of modern science; in finance they are used in arbitrage pricing, to define stochastic processes, and to compute the time evolution of averages.
- Differential equations can be solved in closed form or with numerical methods. Finite difference methods approximate derivatives with difference quotients. Initial conditions yield recursive algorithms.
- Boundary conditions require the solution of linear equations.

CHAPTER 10

Stochastic Integrals

S tochastic calculus is a branch of mathematics that operates on stochastic processes. It allows a consistent theory of integration to be defined for integrals of stochastic processes with respect to stochastic processes. It is used to model variables that behave randomly. The best-known stochastic process to which stochastic calculus is applied is the Wiener process, which is used for modeling Brownian motion and other diffusion processes subject to random fluctuations. Since the 1970s, the Wiener process has been widely applied in mathematical finance to model the evolution in time of stock prices and interest rates. While an ordinary integral is either a number or a function, a stochastic integral is a random variable or a stochastic process. Stochastic integrals allow financial modelers to differentiate the time-varying behavior of asset returns from the stochastic behavior of asset returns. Using stochastic integrals:

- One can define random movements and state-dependent nature of asset prices more rigorously.
- One can convert the physical measure which describes the probability that an underlying instrument (such as a stock price or interest rate) will take a particular value or values to the risk-neutral measure which is a useful tool for pricing derivatives on the underlying asset.
- One can convert a financial asset into a martingale, which is useful for defining expected future prices of underlying assets that determine the value of derivative products written on these underlying assets.
- One can take the observed discrete-time stochastic process to continuous-time Brownian motion by pushing the length of time

interval to close to zero. The continuous-time stochastic processes are used to generate closed-form solutions for option prices.

■ One can convert a complicated continuous-time stochastic process with a nonlinear drift and diffusion to a new, simplified Brownian motion that can easily be implemented to find a closed-form solution for option prices.

What you will learn after reading this chapter:

■ What the differences are between ordinary and stochastic integrals.

■ How to define stochastic integrals and the intuition behind them.

■ How to define a Brownian motion and its stochastic properties.

■ How to prove the existence of the standard Brownian motion using the Kolmogorov extension theorem.

■ How to relate the diffusion function of a continuous-time stochastic process to an instantaneous volatility function.

■ How to convert a discrete-time stochastic process to a continuous-time process as the length of the time interval approaches zero.

■ What the properties of Itô stochastic integrals are.

■ What the properties of continuous-time martingales are.

■ How to convert the physical measure to the risk-neutral measure using Girsanov theorem.

■ How to convert a financial asset into a martingale measure using Novikov theorem.

INTRODUCTION

In elementary calculus, integration is an operation performed on single, deterministic functions; the end product is another single, deterministic function. Integration defines a process of **cumulation**: The integral of a function represents the area below the function. However, the usefulness of deterministic functions in financial modeling is limited. Given the amount of uncertainty, few laws in financial theory can be expressed through them. It is necessary to adopt an ensemble view, where the path of economic variables must be considered a realization of a stochastic process, not a deterministic path. We must therefore move from deterministic integration to **stochastic integration**. In doing so we have to define how to cumulate random shocks in a continuous-time environment. These concepts require rigorous definition. In this chapter we define the concept and the properties of stochastic integration. Based on the concept of stochastic integration, an important tool used in finance, stochastic differential equations, the subject of the next chapter, can be understood.

Two observations are in order. First, although ordinary integrals and derivatives operate on functions and yield either individual numbers or other functions, stochastic integration operates on stochastic processes and yields either random variables or other stochastic processes. Therefore, while a definite integral is a number and an indefinite integral is a function, a stochastic integral is a random variable or a stochastic process. A differential equation—when equipped with suitable initial or boundary conditions—admits as a solution a single function while a stochastic differential equation admits as a solution a stochastic process.

Second, moving from a deterministic to a stochastic environment does not necessarily require leaving the realm of standard calculus. In fact, all the stochastic laws of financial theory could be expressed as laws that govern the distribution of transition probabilities. An example of this mathematical strategy is the application of the forward Komogorov differential equation or the Fokker-Planck differential equation to term structure modeling, which are deterministic partial differential equations that govern the probability distributions of prices. Nevertheless it is often convenient to represent uncertainty directly through stochastic integration and stochastic differential equations. This approach is not limited to finance theory: It is also used in the domain of the physical sciences. In finance theory, stochastic differential equations have the advantage of being intuitive: Thinking in terms of a deterministic path plus an uncertain term is easier than thinking in terms of abstract probability distributions. There are other reasons why stochastic calculus is the methodology of choice in economics and finance but easy intuition plays a key role.

For example, a risk-free bank account, which earns a deterministic instantaneous interest rate $f(t)$, evolves according to the deterministic law:

$$y = A \exp\left(\int f(t)dt\right)$$

which is the general solution of the differential equation:

$$\frac{dy}{y} = f(t)dt$$

The solution of this differential equation tells us how the bank account cumulates over time.

However, if the rate is not deterministic but is subject to volatility—that is, at any instant the rate is $f(t)$ plus a random disturbance—then the bank account evolves as a stochastic process. That is to say, the bank account might follow any of an infinite number of different paths: Each path cumulates the rate $f(t)$ plus the random disturbance. In a sense that will be made precise in this chapter and, with an understanding of stochastic differential equations covered in the next chapter, we must solve the following equation:

$$\frac{dy}{y} = f(t)dt \text{ plus random distrubance}$$

Here is where stochastic integration comes into play: It defines how the stochastic rate process is transformed into the stochastic account process. This is the direct stochastic integration approach.

It is possible to take a different approach. At any instant t, the instantaneous interest rate and the cumulated bank account have two probability distributions. We could use a partial differential equation to describe how the probability distribution of the cumulated bank account is linked to the interest rate probability distribution.

Similar reasoning applies to stock and derivative price processes. In continuous-time finance, these processes are defined as stochastic processes that are the solution of a stochastic differential equation. Hence, the importance of stochastic integrals in continuous-time finance theory should be clear.

Following some remarks on the informal intuition behind stochastic integrals, we proceed to define Brownian motion and outline the formal mathematical process through which stochastic integrals are defined. A number of properties of stochastic integrals are then established. After introducing stochastic integrals informally, we go on to define more rigorously the mathematical process for defining stochastic integrals.[1]

---

[1] A history of stochastic integrations and financial mathematics is provided by R. Jarrow and P. Protter, "A Short History of Stochastic Integration and Mathematical Finance: The Early Years, 1880–1970," *IMS Lecture Notes Monograph* 45 (2004): 1–17. For a more detailed discussion of stochastic integration, see P. Protter, *Stochastic Integration and Differential Equations* (New York: Springer, 1990).

THE INTUITION BEHIND STOCHASTIC INTEGRALS

Let's first contrast ordinary integration with stochastic integration. A definite integral

$$A = \int_a^b f(x)dx$$

is a number A associated to each function $f(x)$ while an indefinite integral

$$y(x) = \int_a^x f(s)ds$$

is a function y associated to another function f. The integral represents the cumulation of the infinite terms $f(s)ds$ over the integration interval. A stochastic integral, which we will denote by

$$W = \int_a^b X_t dB_t$$

or

$$W = \int_a^b X_t \circ dB_t$$

is a random variable W associated to a stochastic process if the time interval is fixed or, if the time interval is variable, is another stochastic process W_t. The stochastic integral represents the cumulation of the stochastic products $X_t dB_t$. As we will see in the next chapter when we discuss stochastic differential equations, the rationale for this approach is that we need to represent how random shocks feed back into the evolution of a process. We can cumulate separately the deterministic increments and the random shocks only for linear processes. In nonlinear cases, as in the simple example of the bank account, random shocks feed back into the process. For this reason, we define stochastic integrals as the cumulation of the product of a process X by the random increments of a Brownian motion.

Consider a stochastic process X_t over an interval $[S,T]$. Recall that a stochastic process is a real variable $X(\omega)_t$ that depends on both time and the state of the economy ω. For any given ω, $X(\cdot)_t$ is a path of the process from the origin S to time T. A stochastic process can be identified with the set of its paths equipped with an appropriate probability measure. A stochastic integral is an integral associated to each path; it is a random variable that associates a real number, obtained as a limit of a sum, to each path. If we fix the origin and let the interval vary, then the stochastic integral is another stochastic process.

It would seem reasonable, *prima facie*, to define the stochastic integral of a process $X(\omega)_t$ as the definite integral in the sense of Riemann-Stieltjes associated to each path $X(\cdot)_t$ of the process. If the process $X(\omega)_t$ has continuous paths $X(\cdot, \omega)$, the integrals

$$W(\omega) = \int_s^T X(s, \omega)ds$$

exist for each path. However, as discussed in the previous section, this is not the quantity we want to represent. In fact, we want to represent the cumulation of the stochastic products $X_t dB_t$. Defining the integral

$$W = \int_a^b X_t d B_t$$

pathwise in the sense of Riemann-Stieltjes would be meaningless because the paths of a Brownian motion are not of finite variation. If we define stochastic integrals simply as the limit of $X_t dB_t$ sums, the stochastic integral would be infinite (and therefore useless) for most processes.

However, Brownian motions have bounded **quadratic variation**. Using this property, we can define stochastic integrals pathwise through an approximation procedure. The approximation procedure to arrive at such a definition is far more complicated than the definition of the Riemann-Stieltjes integrals. Two similar but not equivalent definitions of stochastic integral have been proposed, the first by the Japanese mathematician Kiyoshi Itô, the second by the Russian physicist Ruslan Stratonovich in the 1960s.[2] The definition of stochastic integral in the sense of Itô integral or of Stratonovich

---

[2] See K. Itô, "On Stochastic Differential Equations," *Memoirs, American Mathematical Society* 4 (1951): 1–51. The publications of Stratonovich can be found in Y. M. Romanovski, *Professor R. L. Stratonovich: Reminiscences of Relatives, Colleagues and Friends* (Moscow-Izhevsk: Publishing House of Computer Research Institute, 2007).

stochastic replaces the increments Δx_i with the increments ΔB_i of a fundamental stochastic process called Brownian motion. The increments ΔB_i represent the "noise" of the process.

The definition proceeds in the following three steps:

Step 1. The first step consists in defining a fundamental stochastic process—the **Brownian motion**. In intuitive terms, a Brownian motion $B_t(\omega)$ is a continuous limit (in a sense that will be made precise in the following sections) of a simple random walk. A simple random walk is a discrete-time stochastic process defined as follows. A point can move one step to the right or to the left. Movement takes place only at discrete instants of time, say at time $1,2,3,\ldots$. At each discrete instant, the point moves to the right or to the left with probability $\frac{1}{2}$.

The random walk represents the cumulation of completely uncertain random shocks. At each point in time, the movement of the point is completely independent from its past movements. Hence, the Brownian motion represents the cumulation of random shocks in the limit of continuous time and of continuous states. It can be demonstrated that a.s. each path of the Brownian motion is not of bounded total variation but it has bounded quadratic variation.

Recall that the total variation of a function $f(x)$ is the limit of the sums

$$\sum |f(x_i) - f(x_{i-1})|$$

while the quadratic variation is defined as the limit of the sums

$$\sum |f(x_i) - f(x_{i-1})|^2$$

Quadratic variation can be interpreted as the **absolute volatility** of a process. Thanks to this property, the ΔB_i of the Brownian motion provides the basic increments of the stochastic integral, replacing the Δx_i of the Riemann-Stieltjes integral.

Step 2. The second step consists in defining the stochastic integral for a class of simple functions called **elementary functions**. Consider the time interval $[S,T]$ and any partition of the interval $[S,T]$ in N subintervals: $S \equiv t_0 < t_1 < \ldots t_i < \ldots t_N \equiv T$. An elementary function ϕ is a function defined on the time t and the outcome ω such that it assumes a constant value on the ith subinterval. Call $I[t_{i+1}, t_i)$ the indicator function of the interval $[t_{i+1}, t_i)$. The indicator function of a given set is a function that assumes value 1 on the points of the set and 0 elsewhere. We can then write an elementary function ϕ as follows:

$$\phi(t, \omega) = \sum_i \varepsilon_i(\omega) I[t_{i+1}, \ t_i)$$

In other words, the constants $\varepsilon_i(\omega)$ are random variables and the function $\phi(t,\omega)$ is a stochastic process made up of paths that are constant on each ith interval.

We can now define the stochastic integral, in the sense of Itô, of elementary functions $\phi(t,\omega)$ as follows:

$$W = \int_S^T \phi(t, \omega) d\, B_t(\omega)$$

$$= \sum_i \varepsilon_i(\omega)[B_{i+1}(\omega) - B_i(\omega)]$$

where B is a Brownian motion.

It is clear from this definition that W is a random variable $\omega \to W(\omega)$. Note that the *Itô integral* thus defined for elementary functions cumulates the products of the elementary functions $\phi(t,\omega)$ and of the increments of the Brownian motion $B_t(\omega)$.

It can be demonstrated that the following property called **Itô isometry,** holds for Itô stochastic integrals defined for bounded elementary functions as above:

$$E\left[\left(\int_S^T \phi(t, \omega) d\, B_t(\omega)\right)^2\right] = E\left[\int_S^T \phi(t, \omega)^2 dt\right]$$

The Itô isometry will play a fundamental role in Step 3.

Step 3. The third step consists in using the Itô isometry to show that each function g which is square-integrable (plus other conditions that will be made precise in the next section) can be approximated by a sequence of elementary functions $\phi_n(t,\omega)$ in the sense that

$$E\left[\int_S^T [g - \phi_n(t, \omega)]^2 dt\right] \to 0$$

If g is bounded and has a continuous time-path, the functions $\phi_n(t,\omega)$ can be defined as follows:

$$\phi_n(t, \omega) = \sum_i g(t_i, \omega) I[t_{i+1}, t_i)$$

where I is the indicator function. We can now use the Itô isometry to define the stochastic integral of a generic function $f(t, \omega)$ as follows:

$$\int_S^T f(t, \omega) d\, B_t(\omega) = \lim_{n \to \infty} \int_S^T \phi_n(t, \omega) d\, B_t(\omega)$$

The Itô isometry ensures that the Cauchy condition is satisfied and that the above sequence thus converges.

In outlining the above definition, we omitted an important point that will be dealt with in the next section: The definition of the stochastic integral in the sense of Itô requires that the elementary functions be without anticipation—that is, they depend only on the past history of the Brownian motion. In fact, in the case of continuous paths, we wrote the approximating functions as follows:

$$\phi_n(t, \omega) = \sum_i g(t_i, \omega) [B_{i+1}(\omega) - B_i(\omega)]$$

taking the function g in the left extreme of each subinterval.

However, the definition of stochastic integrals in the sense of Stratonovich admits anticipation. In fact, the stochastic integral in the sense of Stratonovich, written as follows

$$\int_S^T f(t, \omega) \circ d\, B_t(\omega)$$

uses the following approximation under the assumption of continuous paths:

$$\phi_n(t, \omega) = \sum_i g(t_i^*, \omega) [B_{i+1}(\omega) - B_i(\omega)]$$

where

$$t_i^* = \frac{t_{i+1} - t_i}{2}$$

is the midpoint of the ith subinterval.

Whose definition—Itô's or Stratonovich's—is preferable? Note that neither can be said to be correct or incorrect. The choice of the one over the other is a question of which one best represents the phenomena under study. The lack of anticipation is one reason why the Itô integral is generally preferred in finance theory.

We have just outlined the definition of stochastic integrals leaving aside mathematical details and rigor. The following two sections will make the above process mathematically rigorous and will discuss the question of anticipation of information. While these sections are a bit technical and might be skipped by those not interested in the mathematical details of stochastic calculus, they explain a number of concepts that are key to the modern development of finance theory.

BROWNIAN MOTION DEFINED

The previous section introduced Brownian motion informally as the limit of a simple random walk when the step size goes to zero. This section defines Brownian motion formally. The term "Brownian motion" is due to the Scottish botanist Robert Brown who in 1828 observed that pollen grains suspended in a liquid move irregularly. This irregular motion was later explained by the random collision of the molecules of the liquid with the pollen grains. It is therefore natural to represent Brownian motion as a continuous-time stochastic process that is the limit of a discrete random walk.

Let's now formally define Brownian motion and demonstrate its existence. Let's first go back to the probabilistic representation of the economy explained in Chapter 4. The economy can be represented as a probability space $(\Omega, \Im, P)$, where Ω is the set of all possible economic states, $\Im$ is the event σ-algebra, and P is a probability measure. The economic states $\omega \in \Omega$ are not instantaneous states but represent full histories of the economy for the time horizon considered, which can be a finite or infinite interval of time. In other words, the economic states are the possible realization outcomes of the economy.

In this probabilistic representation of the economy, time-variable economic quantities—such as interest rates, security prices, or cash flows as well as aggregate quantities such as economic output—are represented as stochastic processes $X_t(\omega)$. In particular, the price and dividend of each stock are represented as two stochastic processes $S_t(\omega)$ and $d_t(\omega)$.

Stochastic processes are time-dependent random variables defined over the set Ω. It is critical to define stochastic processes so that there is no anticipation of information, that is, at time t no process depends on variables that will be realized later. Anticipation of information is possible only within a deterministic framework. However, the space Ω in itself does not contain any coherent specification of time. If we associate random variables $X_t(\omega)$ to a time index without any additional restriction, we might incur the problem of anticipation of information. Consider, for instance, an arbitrary family of time-indexed random variables $X_t(\omega)$ and suppose that, for some instant t, the relationship $X_t(\omega) = X_{t+1}(\omega)$ holds. In this case, there is clearly anticipation of information as the value of the variable $X_{t+1}(\omega)$ at time $t+1$ is known at an earlier time t. All relationships that lead to anticipation of information must be treated as deterministic.

The formal way to specify in full generality the evolution of time and the propagation of information without anticipation is through the concept of **filtration** that was introduced in Chapter 5. Recall from Chapter 4, the concept of filtration is based on identifying all events that are known at any given instant. It is the propagation of information assuming that it is possible to associate to each moment t a σ-algebra of events $\mathfrak{I}_t \subset \mathfrak{I}$ formed by all events that are known prior to or at time t. It is assumed that events are never "forgotten," that is, that $\mathfrak{I}_t \subset \mathfrak{I}_s$, if $t < s$. An increasing sequence of σ-algebras, each associated to the time at which all its events are known, represents the propagation of information. This sequence (called a filtration) is typically indicated as $\mathfrak{I}_t$.

The economy is therefore represented as a probability space $(\Omega, \mathfrak{I}, P)$ equipped with a filtration $\{\mathfrak{I}_t\}$. The key point is that every process $X_t(\omega)$ that represents economic or financial quantities must be *adapted* to the filtration $\{\mathfrak{I}_t\}$, that is, the random variable $X_t(\omega)$ must be measurable with respect to the σ-algebras $\mathfrak{I}_t$. In simple terms, this means that each event of the type $X_t(\omega) \leq x$ belongs to $\mathfrak{I}_t$ while each event of the type $X_s(\omega) \leq y$ for $t \leq s$ belongs to $\mathfrak{I}_s$. For instance, consider a process $P_t(\omega)$, which might represent the price of a stock. Any coherent representation of the economy must ensure that events such as $\{\omega: P_s(\omega) \leq c\}$ are not known at any time $t < s$. The filtration $\{\mathfrak{I}_t\}$ prescribes all events admissible at time t.

Why do we have to use the complex concept of filtration? Why can't we simply identify information at time t with the values of all the variables known at time t as opposed to identifying a set of events? The principal reason is that in a continuous-time continuous-state environment any individual value has probability zero; we cannot condition on single values as the standard definition of conditional probability would become meaningless. In fact, in the standard definition of conditional probability (see Chapter 4), the probability of the conditioning event appears in the denominator and cannot be zero.

It is possible, however, to reverse this reasoning and construct a filtration starting from a process. Suppose that a process $X_t(\omega)$ does not admit any anticipation of information, for instance because the $X_t(\omega)$ are all mutually independent. We can therefore construct a filtration $\mathfrak{F}_t$ as the strictly increasing sequence of σ-algebras generated by the process $X_t(\omega)$. Any other process must be adapted to $\mathfrak{F}_t$.

Let's now go back to the definition of the Brownian motion. Suppose that a probability space $(\Omega, \mathfrak{F}, P)$ equipped with a filtration $\mathfrak{F}_t$ is given. A **one-dimensional standard Brownian motion** is a stochastic process $B_t(\omega)$ with the following properties:

- $B_t(\omega)$ is defined over the probability space $(\Omega, \mathfrak{F}, P)$.
- $B_t(\omega)$ is continuous for $0 < t < \infty$.
- $B_0(\omega) = 0$.
- $B_t(\omega)$ is adapted to the filtration $\mathfrak{F}_t$.
- The increments $B_t(\omega) - B_s(\omega)$ are independent and normally distributed with variance $(t - s)$ and zero mean.

The above conditions state that the standard Brownian motion is a stochastic process that starts at zero, has continuous paths and normally distributed increments whose variance grows linearly with time.[3] Note that in the last condition the increments are independent of the σ-algebra $\mathfrak{F}_S$ and not of the previous values of the process. As noted above, this is because any single realization of the process has probability zero and it is therefore impossible to use the standard concept of conditional probability: Conditioning must be with respect to a σ-algebra $\mathfrak{F}_S$. Once this concept has been firmly established, one might speak loosely of independence of the present values of a process from its previous values. It should be clear, however, that what is meant is independence with respect to a σ-algebra $\mathfrak{F}_S$.

Note also that the filtration $\mathfrak{F}_t$ is an integral part of the above definition of the Brownian motion. This does not mean that, given any probability space and any filtration, a standard Brownian motion with these characteristics exists. For instance, the filtration generated by a discrete-time continuous-state random walk is insufficient to support a Brownian motion. The definition states only that we call a one-dimensional standard Brownian motion a mathematical object (if it exists) made up of a probability space, a filtration, and a time dependent random variable with the properties specified in the definition.

However, it can be demonstrated that Brownian motions exist by constructing them. Several construction methodologies have been proposed,

---

[3]The set of conditions defining a Brownian motion can be more parsimonious. If a process has stationary, independent increments and continuous paths almost surely it must have normally distributed increments. A process with stationary independent increments and with paths that are continuous to the right and limited to the left (the *cadlag* functions) is called a Lévy process.

including methodologies based on the Kolmogorov extension theorem or on constructing the Brownian motion as the limit of a sequence of discrete random walks. To prove the existence of the standard Brownian motion, we will use the **Kolmogorov extension theorem**.

The Kolmogorov theorem can be summarized as follows. Consider the following family of probability measures

$$\mu_{t_1 \ldots t_m}(H_1 \times \ldots \times H_m) = P[(X_{t_1} \in H_1, \ldots, X_{t_m} \in H_m), \ H_i \in -\mathcal{B}^n]$$

for all $t_1, \ldots, t_k \in [0, \infty)$, $k \in N$ and where the Hs are n-dimensional Borel sets. Suppose that the following two consistency conditions are satisfied

$$\mu_{t_{\sigma(1)}, \ldots, t_{\sigma(m)}}(H_1 \times \ldots \times H_m) = \mu_{t_1 \ldots t_m}(H_{\sigma^{-1}(1)} \times \ldots \times H_{\sigma^{-1}(m)})$$

for all permutations σ on $\{1, 2, \ldots, k\}$, and

$$\mu_{t_1, \ldots, t_k}(H_1 \times \ldots \times H_k)$$
$$= \mu_{t_1, \ldots, t_k, t_{k+1}, \ldots, t_m}(H_1 \times \ldots \times H_k \times R^n \times \ldots \times R^n)$$

for all m. The Kolmogorov extension theorem states that, if the above conditions are satisfied, then there is (1) a probability space $(\Omega, \tilde{\mathfrak{J}}, P)$ and (2) a stochastic process that admits the probability measures

$$\mu_{t_1 \ldots t_m}(H_1 \times \ldots \times H_m)$$
$$= P[(X_{t_1} \in H_1, \ldots, X_{tm} \in H_m), \ H_i \in -\mathcal{B}^n]$$

as finite dimensional distributions.

The construction is lengthy and technical and we omit it here, but it should be clear how, with an appropriate selection of finite-dimensional distributions, the Kolmogorov extension theorem can be used to prove the existence of Brownian motions. The finite-dimensional distributions of a one-dimensional Brownian motion are distributions of the type

$$\mu_{t_1, \ldots, t_k}(H_1 \times \ldots \times H_k)$$
$$= \int p(t, x, x_1) p(t_2 - t_1, x_1, x_2) \ldots$$
$$p(t_k - t_{k-1}, x_{k-1}, x_k) dx_1 \ldots dx_k H_1 \times \ldots \times H_k$$

where

$$p(t, x, y) = (2\pi t)^{-\frac{1}{2}} \exp\left(-\frac{|x - y|^2}{2t}\right)$$

and with the convention that the integrals are taken with respect to the Lebesgue measure. The distribution $p(t, x, x_1)$ in the integral is the initial distribution. If the process starts at zero, $p(t, x, x_1)$ is a Dirac delta, that is, it is a distribution of mass 1 concentrated in one point.

It can be verified that these distributions satisfy the above consistency conditions; the Kolmogorov extension theorem therefore ensures that a stochastic process with the above finite dimensional distributions exists. It can be demonstrated that this process has normally distributed independent increments with variance that grows linearly with time. It is therefore a one-dimensional Brownian motion. These definitions can be easily extended to an n-dimensional Brownian motion.

In the initial definition of a Brownian motion, we assumed that a filtration $\Im_t$ was given and that the Brownian motion was adapted to the filtration. In the present construction, however, we reverse this process. Given that the process we construct has normally distributed, stationary, independent increments, we can define the filtration $\Im_t$ as the filtration $\Im_t^B$ generated by $B_t(\omega)$. The independence of the increments of the Brownian motion guarantees the absence of anticipation of information. Note that if we were given a filtration $\Im_t$ larger than the filtration $\Im_t^B$, $B_t(\omega)$ would still be a Brownian motion with respect to $\Im_t$.

In stochastic differential equations, there are two types of solutions of stochastic differential equations—strong and weak—depending on whether the filtration is given or generated by the Brownian motion. The implications of these differences for economics and finance will be discussed in the same section.

The above construction does not specify uniquely the Brownian motion. In fact, there are infinite stochastic processes that start from the same point and have the same finite dimensional distributions but have totally different paths. However, it can be demonstrated that only one Brownian motion has continuous paths a.s. (**a.s.** means almost surely; i.e., for all paths except a set of measure zero). This process is called the **canonical Brownian motion**. Its paths can be identified with the space of continuous functions.

The Brownian motion can also be constructed as the continuous limit of a discrete random walk. Consider a simple random walk W_i where i are discrete time points. The random walk is the motion of a point that moves Δx to the right or to the left with equal probability $\frac{1}{2}$ at each time increment Δx. The total displacement X_i at time i is the sum of i independent increments each distributed as a Bernoulli variable. Therefore, the random variable X has a binomial distribution with mean zero and variance:

$$\frac{\Delta^2 x}{\Delta t}$$

Suppose that both the time increment and the space increment approach zero: $\Delta t \to 0$ and $\Delta x \to 0$. Note that this is a very informal statement. In fact what we mean is that we can construct a sequence of random walk processes W_i^n, each characterized by a time step and by a time displacement. It can be demonstrated that if

$$\frac{\Delta^2 x}{\Delta t} \to \sigma$$

(i.e., the square of the spaced interval and the time interval are of the same order) then the sequence of random walks approaches a Brownian motion. Though this is intuitive as the binomial distributions approach normal distributions, it should be clear that it is far from being mathematically obvious.

Figure 10.1 illustrates 100 realizations of a Brownian motion approximated as a random walk. The exhibit clearly illustrates that the standard deviation grows with the square root of the time as the variance grows linearly with time. In fact, as illustrated, most paths remain confined within a parabolic region.

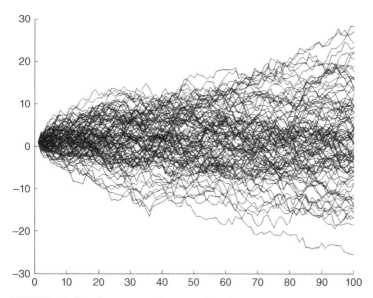

FIGURE 10.1 Illustration of 100 Paths of a Brownian Motion Generated as an Arithmetic Random Walk

PROPERTIES OF BROWNIAN MOTION

The paths of a Brownian motion are rich structures with a number of surprising properties. It can be demonstrated that the paths of a canonical Brownian motion, though continuous, are nowhere differentiable. It can also be demonstrated that they are fractals of fractal dimension $\frac{1}{2}$. The fractal dimension is a concept that measures quantitatively how a geometric object occupies space. A straight line has fractal dimension one, a plane has fractal dimension two, and so on. Fractal objects might also have intermediate dimensions. This is the case, for example, of the path of a Brownian motion, which is so jagged that, in a sense, it occupies more space than a straight line.

The fractal nature of Brownian motion paths implies that each path is a self-similar object. This property can be illustrated graphically. If we generate random walks with different time steps, we obtain jagged paths. If we allow paths to be graphically magnified, all paths look alike regardless of the time step with which they have been generated. In Figure 10.2, sample paths are generated with different time steps and then portions of the paths are magnified. Note that they all look perfectly similar.

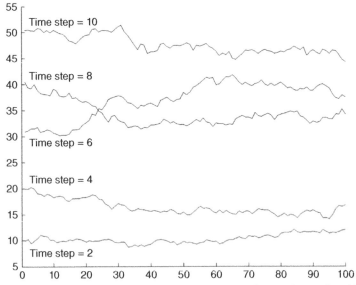

Note: Five paths of a Brownian motion are generated as random walks with different time steps and then magnified.

FIGURE 10.2   Illustration of the Fractal Properties of the Paths of a Brownian Motion

This property was first observed by Mandelbrot in sequences of cotton prices in the 1960s.[4] In general, if one looks at asset or commodity price time series, it is difficult to recognize their time scale. For instance, weekly or monthly time series look alike. (Recent empirical and theoretical research work has made this claim more precise.)

Let's consider a one-dimensional standard Brownian motion. If we wait a sufficiently long period of time, every path except a set of paths of measure zero will return to the origin. The path between two consecutive passages through zero is called an **excursion** of the Brownian motion. The distribution of the maximum height attained by an excursion and of the time between two passages through zero or through any level have interesting properties. The distribution of the time between two passages through zero has infinite mean. This is at the origin of the so-called St. Petersburg paradox described by the Swiss mathematician Bernoulli. The paradox consists of the following. Suppose a player bets increasing sums on a game that can be considered a realization of a random walk. As the return to zero of a random walk is a sure event, the player is certain to win—but while the probability of winning is one, the average time before winning is infinite. To stay the game, the capital required is also infinite. Difficult to imagine a banker ready to put up the money to back the player.

The distribution of the time to the first passage through zero of a Brownian motion is not Gaussian. In fact, the probability of a very long waiting time before the first return to zero is much higher than in a normal distribution. It is a fat-tailed distribution in the sense that it has more weight in the tail regions than a normal distribution. The distribution of the time to the first passage through zero of a Brownian motion is an example of how fat-tailed distributions can be generated from Gaussian variables.

STOCHASTIC INTEGRALS DEFINED

Let's now go back to the definition of stochastic integrals, starting with one-dimensional stochastic integrals. Suppose that a probability space $(\Omega, \Im, P)$ equipped with a filtration $\Im_t$ is given. Suppose also that a Brownian motion $B_t(\omega)$ adapted to the filtration $\Im_t$ is given. We will define Itô integrals following the three-step procedure outlined earlier in this chapter. We have just completed the first step defining Brownian motion. The second step consists in defining the Itô integral for elementary functions.

---

[4]B. Mandelbrot, "The Variation of Certain Speculative Prices," *Journal of Business* 36 (1963): 394–419.

Let's first define the set $\Phi(S, T)$ of functions $\Phi(S, T) \equiv \{f(t, \omega): [(0, \infty) \times \Omega \to R]\}$ with the following properties:

- Each f is jointly $-\mathcal{B} \times \mathfrak{J}$ measurable.
- *Each $f(t,\omega)$ is adapted to $\mathfrak{J}_t$.*
- $E\left[\int\limits_S^T f^2(t, \omega)dt\right] < \infty$ (this condition can be weakened).

This is the set of paths for which we define the Itô integral.

Consider the time interval $[S,T]$ and, for each integer n, partition the interval $[S,T]$ in subintervals: $t_0 < t_1 < \ldots t_1 < \ldots t_n < \ldots t_N \equiv T$ in this way:

$$t_k = t_k^n = \begin{cases} k2^{-n} & \text{if} \quad S \le k2^{-n} \le T \\ S & \text{if} \quad k2^{-n} < S \\ T & \text{if} \quad k2^n > T \end{cases}$$

This rule provides a family of partitions of the interval $[S,T]$ which can be arbitrarily refined.

Consider the elementary functions $\phi(t,\omega) \in \Phi$ which we write as

$$\phi(t, \omega) = \sum_i \varepsilon_i(\omega) I[t_{i+1} - t_i)$$

As $\phi(t,\omega) \in \Phi$, $\varepsilon_i(\omega)$ are $\mathfrak{J}_{t_i}$ measurable random variables.

We can now define the stochastic integral, in the sense of Itô, of elementary functions $\phi(t, \omega)$ as

$$W = \int\limits_S^T \phi(t, \omega)d\, B_t(\omega) = \sum_{i \ge 0} \varepsilon_i(\omega)[B_{i+1}(\omega) - B_i(\omega)]$$

where B is a Brownian motion. Note that the $\varepsilon_i(\omega)$ and the increments $B_j(\omega) - B_i(\omega)$ are independent for $j > i$. The key aspect of this definition that was not included in the informal outline is the condition that the $\varepsilon_i(\omega)$ are $\mathfrak{J}_{t_i}$ measurable.

For bounded elementary functions $\phi(t,\omega) \in \Phi$ the Itô isometry holds

$$E\left[\left(\int\limits_S^T \phi(t, \omega)d\, B_t(\omega)\right)^2\right] = E\left[\int\limits_S^T \phi(t, \omega)^2 dt\right]$$

The demonstration of the Itô isometry rests on the fact that

$$E[\varepsilon_i\, \varepsilon_j (B_{t_{i+1}} - B_{t_i})(B_{t_{j+1}} - B_{t_j})] = \begin{cases} 0 & \text{if } i \neq j \\ E(\varepsilon_i^2) & \text{if } i \neq j \end{cases}$$

This completes the definition of the stochastic integral for elementary functions.

We have now completed the introduction of Brownian motions and defined the Itô integral for elementary functions. Let's next introduce the approximation procedure that allows us to define the stochastic integral for any $\phi(t,\omega)$. We will develop the approximation procedure in the following three additional steps that we will state without demonstration:

Step 1. Any function $g(t,\omega) \in \Phi$ that is bounded and such that all its time paths $\phi(\cdot, \omega)$ are continuous functions of time can be approximated by

$$\phi_n(t, \omega) = \sum_i g(t_i, \omega) I [t_{i+1} - t_i)$$

in the sense that:

$$E \int_S^T [(g - \phi_n)^2 dt] \to 0, \quad n \to \infty, \ \forall \omega$$

where the intervals are those of the partition defined above. Note that $\phi_n(t, \omega) \in \Phi$ given that $g(t, \omega) \in \Phi$.

Step 2. We release the condition of time-path continuity of the $\phi_n(t, \omega)$. It can be demonstrated that any function $h(t, \omega) \in \Phi$ which is bounded but not necessarily continuous can be approximated by functions $g_n(t, \omega) \in \Phi$, which are bounded and continuous in the sense that

$$E \left[\int_S^T (h - g_n)^2 dt \right] \to 0$$

Step 3. It can be demonstrated that any function $f(t, \omega) \in \Phi$, not necessarily bounded or continuous, can be approximated by a sequence of bounded functions $h_n(t, \omega) \in \Phi$ in the sense that

$$E\left[\int_S^T (f - h_n)^2 dt\right] \to 0$$

We now have all the building blocks to complete the definition of Itô stochastic integrals. In fact, by virtue of the above three-step approximation procedure, given any function $f(t, \omega) \in \Phi$, we can choose a sequence of elementary functions $\phi_n(t, \omega) \in \Phi$ such that the following property holds:

$$E\left[\int_S^T (f - \phi_n)^2 dt\right] \to 0$$

Hence we can define the Itô stochastic integral as follows:

$$I[f](w) = \int_S^T f(t, \omega) d\, B_t(\omega) = \lim_{n \to \infty}\left[\int_S^T \phi_n(t, \omega) dt\right]$$

The limit exists as

$$\int_S^T \phi_n(t, \omega) d\, B_t(\omega)$$

forms a Cauchy sequence by the Itô isometry which holds for every bounded elementary function.

Let's now summarize the definition of the Itô stochastic integral: Given any function $f(t, \omega) \in \Phi$, we define the Itô stochastic integral by

$$I[f](w) = \int_S^T f(t, \omega) d\, B_t(\omega) = \lim_{n \to \infty}\left[\int_S^T \phi_n(t, \omega) dt\right]$$

where the functions $\phi_n(t, \omega) \in \Phi$ are a sequence of elementary functions such that

$$E\left[\int_S^T (f - \phi_n)^2 dt\right] \to 0$$

The multistep procedure outlined above ensures that the sequence $\phi_n(t, \omega) \in \Phi$ exists. In addition, it can be demonstrated that the Itô isometry holds in general for every $f(t, \omega) \in \Phi$

$$E\left[\left(\int_S^T f(t, \omega)d\,B_t(\omega)\right)^2\right] = E\left[\int_S^T f(t, \omega)^2 dt\right]$$

SOME PROPERTIES OF ITÔ STOCHASTIC INTEGRALS

Suppose that $f, g \in \Phi(S, T)$ and let $0 < S < U < T$. It can be demonstrated that the following properties of Itô stochastic integrals hold:

$$\int_S^T f d\,B_t = \int_S^U f d\,B_t + \int_U^T f d\,B_t \text{ for a.a.}\omega$$

$$E\left[\int_S^T f d\,B_t\right] = 0$$

$$\int_S^T (cf + dg)d\,B_t = c\int_S^T f d\,B_t + d\int_S^T g d\,B_t$$

for a.a. ω, c, d constants

If we let the time interval vary, say $(0, t)$, then the stochastic integral becomes a stochastic process:

$$I_t(\omega) \int_0^t f d\,B_t$$

It can be demonstrated that a continuous version of this process exists. The following three properties can be demonstrated from the definition of integral:

$$\int_0^t d B_s = B_t$$

$$\int_0^t sd\, B_s = t B_t - \int_0^t B_s ds$$

$$\int_0^t B_s d\, B_s = \frac{1}{2} B_t^2 - \frac{1}{2}t$$

The last two properties show that, after performing stochastic integration, deterministic terms might appear.

MARTINGALE MEASURES AND THE GIRSANOV THEOREM

In probability theory, the **Girsanov theorem** (named after Igor Vladimirovich Girsanov) describes how the dynamics of stochastic processes change when the original measure is changed to an equivalent probability measure.[5] The theorem is especially important in the theory of financial mathematics as it tells how to convert from the physical measure which describes the probability that an underlying instrument (such as a stock price or interest rate) will take a particular value or values to the risk-neutral measure which is a very useful tool for pricing derivatives on the underlying asset.

---

[5]I. V. Girsanov, "On Transforming a Certain Class of Stochastic Processes by Absolutely Continuous Substitution of Measures," *Theory of Probability and its Applications* 5, no. 3 (1960): 285–301; and M. Musiela and M. Rutkowski, *Martingale Methods in Financial Modeling*, 2nd ed. (New York: Springer, 2005).

The theorem was first proved by Cameron and Martin in the 1940s and by Girsanov in 1960.[6] They have been subsequently extended to more general classes of process by Lenglart.[7] Girsanov's theorem is important in the general theory of stochastic processes since it enables the key result that if Q is a measure absolutely continuous with respect to P then every P-semimartingale is a Q-semimartingale.

Risk-Neutral Measure

A risk-neutral measure is used in the pricing of financial derivatives due to the fundamental theorem of asset pricing, which implies that in a complete market a derivative's price is the discounted expected value of the future payoff under the risk-neutral measure.[8]

Prices of assets depend crucially on their risk as investors typically demand more return for bearing more risk. Therefore, today's price of a claim on a risky amount realized tomorrow will generally differ from its expected value. Typically, investors are risk-averse and today's price is below the expectation. To price assets, the calculated expected values need to be adjusted for an investor's risk preferences. Unfortunately, the discount rates would vary among investors and an individual's risk preference is difficult to quantify.

It turns out that in a complete market with no arbitrage opportunities there is an alternative way to do this calculation. Instead of first taking the expectation and then adjusting for an investor's risk preference, one can adjust the probabilities of future outcomes such that they incorporate all investors' risk premia, and then take the expectation under this new probability distribution. The resulting expectation is the **risk-neutral measure**. The main benefit of the risk-neutral measure stems from the fact that once the risk-neutral probabilities are found, every asset can be priced by simply taking its expected payoff. Note that if we used the actual real-world probabilities, every asset would require a different adjustment (as they differ in riskiness).

---

[6]R. H. Cameron and W. T. Martin, "Transformations of Wiener Integrals under Translations," *Annals of Mathematics* 45 (1940): 386–396.

[7]E. Lenglart, "Transformation de martingales locales par changement absolue continu de probabilities [Transformation of Local Martingales for Changing Continuous Absolutes of Probability]," *Zeitschrift für Wahrscheinlichkeit* 39 (1944): 65–70.

[8]As explained in Chapter 4, a complete market is one in which the complete set of possible gambles on future states-of-the-world can be constructed with existing assets.

The lack of arbitrage is crucial for the existence of a risk-neutral measure. In fact, by the fundamental theorem of asset pricing, the condition of no-arbitrage is equivalent to the existence of a risk-neutral measure. Completeness of the market is also important because in an incomplete market there are a multitude of possible prices for an asset corresponding to different risk-neutral measures. It is usual to argue that market efficiency implies that there is only one price; the correct risk-neutral measure to price with must be selected using economic, rather than purely mathematical, arguments.

Continuous-Time Martingales

Let's begin with two definitions. Let S_t be a random price process during a finite time interval $t \in [0, T]$. S_t is said to be adapted to the filtration if S_t is a F_t-measurable function $\forall t \in T$. It is also said to be a nonanticipating process, or one that cannot see into the future.

Definition

A process S_t is said to be a martingale with respect to F_t and probability measure P if $\forall t > 0$:

Property 1: S_t is I_t–adapted.

Property 2: $E|S_t| < \infty$.

Property 3: $E_t[S_T] = S_t \forall t < T$ with probability 1.

Property 3 is of vast importance. It means that the best forecast of an unobserved future value of a martingale is its last observation. This will turn out to be extremely useful if we can convert a financial asset into a martingale. There are two general steps:

Step 1: Find a probability distribution $\tilde{P}$ such that bond or stock prices discounted by the risk-free rate become martingales. This can be done with Doob-Meyer decomposition and similar detrending techniques.

Step 2: Transform the probability distribution.

For example, in Step 2 if one had

$$E_t^P \left[\exp\left(-ru\right) S_{t+u} \right] > S_t$$

we can try to find an equivalent probability $\tilde{P}$ such that

$$E_t^{\tilde{P}} \left[\exp\left(-ru\right) S_{t+u} \right] = S_t$$

and thus we have a martingale. These are called **equivalent martingale measures** and can be done by using the Girsanov theorem.

Girsanov Theorem Before stating the theorem, some additional background needs to be provided. We can summarize two methods for changing the mean of a random variable.

1. *Subtraction.* For example, given a random variable $Z \sim N(\mu, 1)$, we can define

$$\tilde{Z} = \frac{Z - \mu}{1} \sim N(0, 1)$$

   a transformed variable with zero mean and standard deviation of unity.

2. *Using equivalent measure.* Given a random variable Z with probability measure P, $Z \sim P = N(\mu, 1)$, we obtain a new probability via the Radon-Nikodym derivative $\zeta(Z)$ and obtain a new probability $\tilde{P}$ such that $Z \sim \tilde{P} = N(0, 1)$.[9]

   The Girsanov theorem attempts to do both by defining the conditions under which the Radon-Nikodym derivative exists. It then constructs a new probability distribution and a new transformed variable that eliminates the stochastic drift term. The Girsanov theorem and the Radon-Nikodym derivative are defined in the next sections.

Girsanov Theorem Defined

Let W_t be a Wiener process on the probability space $\{\Omega, F, P\}$. Let X_t be a measurable process adapted to the natural filtration of the Wiener process $\{F_t^W\}$. Given an adapted process X_t with $X_0 = 0$ define the stochastic exponential of X with respect to W:

$$\zeta_t = \Psi\left(X\right)_t = \exp\left(\int_0^t X_u dW_u - \frac{1}{2} \int_0^t X_u^2 du \right)$$

---

[9]O. Nikodym, "Sur une Généralisation des Intégrales de M. J. Radon [On the Generalization of Integrals]," *Fundamenta Mathematicae* 15 (1930): 131–179.

Under certain conditions, ζ_t is a martingale. Then, the probability measure $\tilde{P}$ can be defined on $\{\Omega, F\}$ such that we have Radon-Nikodym derivative:

$$\frac{d\tilde{P}}{dP} = \zeta_t$$

Then $\tilde{W}_t = W_t - \int_0^t X_u du$ is a Wiener process with repsect to F_t and the probability measure $\tilde{P}_T$ given by $\tilde{P}_T(A) = E^P[1_A \zeta_T]$, with A being an event determined by F_T and 1_A the indicator function for the event.

Novikov Theorem Defined

If the condition

$$E\left[\exp\left(\frac{1}{2}\int_0^T |X_u|^2 \, du\right)\right] < \infty$$

is true then the stochastic exponential

$$\zeta_t = \Psi(X)_t = \exp\left(\int_0^t X_u dW_u - \frac{1}{2}\int_0^t X_u^2 du\right)$$

is a martingale under the probability measure P and filtration F.[10]

The Girsanov theorem implies that if we are given a Wiener process W_t, multiplying the probability distribution of this process by the stochastic exponential, we can obtain a new Wiener process $\tilde{W}_t$ with probability distribution $\tilde{P}$. The two processes are related to each other through the following partial differential equation:

$$d\tilde{W}_t = dW_t - X_t dt$$

That is, the new Wiener process is the same as the old one minus an I_t-adapted drift. Note that this drift term is stochastic, in contrast to the overly simple subtraction of means we saw in the first example in this section.

---

[10]A. Pascucci, *PDE and Martingale Methods in Option Pricing* (Berlin: Springer-Verlag, 2011).

Application of Girsanov Theorem to a Brownian Motion   Assume that S_t is modeled as Brownian motion with constant drift and constant diffusion function,

$$dS_t = \mu dt + \sigma dW_t \, (W_0 = 0)$$

where W_t is assumed to have the following probability distribution:

$$dP(W_t) = \frac{1}{\sqrt{2\pi t}} \exp\left(-\frac{1}{2t}\left(W_t^2\right)\right) dW_t$$

Clearly S_t is not a martingale if its drift term $\mu \neq 0$. Taking the integrals of both sides, we have

$$S_t = \mu t + \sigma W_t$$

and hence we can write

$$E[S_{t+s}|S_t] = \mu(t+s) + \sigma E[W_{t+s} - W_t|S_t] + \sigma W_t$$
$$= S_t + \mu s$$

The drift term is deterministic and the middle term indicates the expected change in the diffusion process W_t while under F_t. Hence, S_t is not a martingale, but this suggests the variable $\tilde{S}_t = S_t - \mu t$ is a martingale.

We could also come up with a function $\zeta(S_t)$ and multiply it with the original probability measure associated with S_t such that while S_t is a sub-martingale under P, that is,

$$E^P[S_{t+s}|S_t] > S_t$$

it will be a martingale under $\tilde{P}$, that is,

$$E^{\tilde{P}}[S_{t+s}|S_t] = S_t$$

We calculate $\zeta(S_t)$, the stochastic exponential:

$$\zeta(S_t) = \exp\left(\int_0^t S_u dW_u - \frac{1}{2}\int_0^t S_u^2 du\right)$$
$$= -\frac{1}{\sigma^2} \exp\left(\mu S_t - \frac{1}{2}\mu^2 t\right)$$

This is the Radon-Nikodym derivative, and thus

$$
\begin{aligned}
d\tilde{P}\,(S_t) &= \zeta\,(S_t)\,dP\,(S_t) \\
&= -\frac{1}{\sigma^2}\exp\left(\mu S_t - \frac{1}{2}\mu^2 t\right) \times \frac{1}{\sqrt{2\pi\sigma^2 t}}\exp\left(-\frac{1}{2\sigma^2 t}\,(S_t - \mu t)^2\right)dS_t \\
&= \frac{1}{\sqrt{2\pi\sigma^2 t}}\exp\left(-\frac{1}{2\sigma^2 t}\,(S_t)^2\right)dS_t
\end{aligned}
$$

which is the probability measure of a normally distributed process with zero drift and diffusion term σ. Basically, we have arrived at a new Wiener variable $d\tilde{W}$ subject to $dS = \sigma\,d\tilde{W}_t$ using Girsanov theorem.

KEY POINTS

- Stochastic integration provides a coherent way to represent that instantaneous uncertainty (or volatility) cumulates over time. It is thus fundamental to the representation of financial processes such as interest rates, security prices, or cash flows as well as aggregate quantities such as economic output.
- Stochastic integration operates on stochastic processes and produces random variables or other stochastic processes.
- Stochastic integration is a process defined on each path as the limit of a sum. However, these sums are different from the sums of the Riemann-Lebesgue integrals because the paths of stochastic processes are generally not of bounded variation.
- Stochastic integrals in the sense of Itô are defined through a three-step process that involves (1) defining Brownian motion (which is the continuous limit of a random walk), (2) defining stochastic integrals for elementary functions as the sums of the products of the elementary functions multiplied by the increments of the Brownian motion, and (3) extending this definition to any function through approximating sequences.
- A risk-neutral measure is used in the pricing of financial derivatives. The lack of arbitrage is crucial for the existence of a risk-neutral measure.
- A derivative's price is the discounted expected value of the future payoff under the risk-neutral measure.
- Physical probability measures are converted to risk-neutral probability measures using the Girsanov theorem.
- A financial asset is converted into a martingale measure using the Novikov Theorem.

CHAPTER 11

Stochastic Differential Equations

In the previous chapter, we explained stochastic integrals, a mathematical concept used for defining stochastic differential equations, the subject of this chapter. Stochastic differential equations solve the problem of giving meaning to a differential equation where one or more of its terms are subject to random fluctuations. In nontechnical terms, differential equations are equations that express a relationship between a function and one or more derivatives (or differentials) of that function. It would be difficult to overemphasize the importance of differential equations in financial economics where they are used to express laws that govern the evolution of price probability distributions, intertemporal portfolio optimization, and conditions for continuous hedging such as in the Black-Scholes option pricing model.

The two broad types of differential equations are ordinary differential equations and partial differential equations. The former are equations or systems of equations involving only one independent variable; the latter are differential equations or systems of equations involving partial derivatives. When one or more of the variables is a stochastic process, we have the case of stochastic differential equations and the solution is also a stochastic process. An assumption must be made about a noise term (or random variable) in a stochastic differential equation. In most applications in financial economics, it is assumed that the noise term follows a Gaussian random variable, although different types of random variables can be assumed.

Using stochastic differential equations:

- One can model the evolution of price probability distributions.
- One can deal with portfolio optimization in an intertemporal asset pricing framework.

- One can introduce the idea of a replicating portfolio that is made up of a risky asset plus a risk-free asset whose payoff perfectly replicates the payoff of an option. Forming a replicating portfolio is the backbone of no-arbitrage conditions in an option pricing framework. The Black-Scholes model is developed based on the absence of arbitrage implying that the price of the original financial instrument coincides with the price of the replicating portfolio.
- One can use the idea of delta hedging in a continuous-time framework to derive the well celebrated Black-Scholes option pricing model.
- One can compute the arbitrage-free value of an option.
- One can determine how the option prices change as the variables or the parameters that impact an option's value change.
- One can monitor the sensitivity of option positions with respect to changes in the underlying asset's price, volatility, interest rate, and time.

What you will learn after reading this chapter:

- The differences between ordinary and stochastic differential equations.
- The uses of stochastic differential equations.
- How to define a stochastic differential equation and the intuition behind it.
- How to define Itô processes and their stochastic properties.
- How to generalize a one-dimensional Itô formula.
- How to solve stochastic differential equations.
- The differences between arithmetic and geometric Brownian motion.
- How to derive Itô's lemma.
- How to derive the Black-Scholes option pricing formula using stochastic differential equations.

INTRODUCTION

Stochastic differential equations solve the problem of giving meaning to a differential equation where one or more of its terms are subject to random fluctuations. For instance, consider the following deterministic equation:

$$\frac{dy}{dt} = f(t)y$$

We know from differential equations that, by separating variables, the general solution of this equation can be written as follows:

$$y = A \exp\left[\int f(t)dt\right]$$

A stochastic version of this equation might be obtained, for instance, by perturbing the term f, thus resulting in the stochastic differential equation

$$\frac{dy}{y} = [f(t) + \varepsilon]dt$$

where ε is a random noise process.

As with stochastic integrals, in defining stochastic differential equations it is necessary to adopt an ensemble view: The solution of a stochastic differential equation is a stochastic process, not a single function. In this chapter, we first provide the basic intuition behind stochastic differential equations and then proceed to formally define the concept and the properties.

THE INTUITION BEHIND STOCHASTIC DIFFERENTIAL EQUATIONS

Let's go back to the equation

$$\frac{dy}{dt} = [f(t) + \varepsilon]y$$

where ε is a continuous-time noise process. It would seem reasonable to define a continuous-time noise process informally as the continuous-time limit of a zero-mean, IID sequence, that is, a sequence of independent and identically distributed variables with zero mean. In a discrete time setting, a zero-mean, IID sequence is called a **white noise**. We could envisage defining a continuous-time white noise as the continuous-time limit of a discrete-time white noise. Each path of ε is a function of time $\varepsilon(\cdot, \omega)$. It would therefore seem reasonable to define the solution of the equation pathwise, as the family of functions that are solutions of the equations

$$\frac{dy}{dt} = [f(t) + \varepsilon(t, \omega)]y$$

where each equation corresponds to a specific white noise path.

However, this definition would be meaningless in the domain of ordinary functions. In other words, it would generally not be possible to find a family of functions $y(\cdot, \omega)$ that satisfy the above equations for each white-noise path and that form a reasonable stochastic process.

The key problem is that it is not possible to define a white-noise process as a zero-mean stationary stochastic process with independent increments and continuous paths. Such a process does not exist in the domain of ordinary functions. In discrete time the white noise process is obtained as the first-difference process of a random walk. Random walk is an integrated nonstationary process, while its first-difference process is a stationary IID sequence.

The continuous-time limit of the random walk is the Brownian motion. However, the paths of a Brownian motion are not differentiable. As a consequence, it is not possible to take the continuous-time limit of first differences and to define the white noise process as the derivative of a Brownian motion. In the domain of ordinary functions in continuous time, the white noise process can be defined only through its integral, which is the Brownian motion. The definition of stochastic differential equations must therefore be recast in integral form.

A sensible definition of a stochastic differential equation must respect a number of constraints. In particular, the solution of a stochastic differential equation should be a "perturbation" of the associated deterministic equation. In the above example, for instance, we want the solution of the stochastic equation

$$\frac{dy}{dt} = [f(t) + \varepsilon(t, \omega)]dt$$

to be a perturbation of the solution

$$y = A \exp\left(\int f(t)dt\right)$$

of the associated deterministic equation

$$\frac{dy}{y} = f(t)dt$$

In other words, the solution of a stochastic differential equation should tend to the solution of the associated deterministic equation in the limit of zero noise. In addition, the solutions of a stochastic differential equation should be the continuous-time limit of some discrete-time process obtained by discretization of the stochastic equation.

A formal solution of this problem was proposed by Kiyoshi Itô and, in a different setting, by Ruslan Stratonovich in the 1960s.[1] Itô and Stratonovich proposed to give meaning to a stochastic differential equation through its integral equivalent. The Itô definition proceeds in two steps: In the first step, Itô processes are defined; in the second step, stochastic differential equations are defined.

Step 1: Definition of Itô processes. Given two functions $\varphi(t, \omega)$ and $\psi\varphi(t, \omega)$ that satisfy usual conditions to be defined later, an **Itô process**— also called a **stochastic integral**—is a stochastic process of the form:

$$Z(t, \omega) = \int_0^t \varphi(s, \omega)ds + \int_0^t \psi(s, \omega)dB_s(s, \omega)$$

An Itô process is a process that is the result of the sum of two summands: The first is an ordinary integral, the second an Itô integral. Itô processes are stable under smooth maps, that is, any smooth function of an Itô process is an Itô process that can be determined through the Itô formula (discussed in the next section).

Step 2: Definition of stochastic differential equations. As we have seen, it is not possible to write a differential equation plus a white-noise term that admits solutions in the domain of ordinary functions. However, we can meaningfully write an integral stochastic equation of the form

$$X(t, \omega) = \int_0^t \varphi(s, X)ds + \int_0^t \psi(s, X)dB_s$$

---

[1] See K. Itô, "On Stochastic Differential Equations," *Memoirs, American Mathematical Society* 4 (1951): 1–51. The publications of Stratonovich can be found in Y. M. Romanovski, *Professor R. L. Stratonovich: Reminiscences of Relatives, Colleagues and Friends* (Moscow-Izhevsk: Publishing House of Computer Research Institute, 2007).

It can be demonstrated that this equation admits solutions in the sense that, given two functions φ and ψ, there is a stochastic process X that satisfies the above equation. We stipulate that the above integral equation can be written in differential form as follows:

$$dX(t, \omega) = \varphi(t, X)dt + \psi(t, X)dB_t$$

Note that this is a definition; a stochastic differential equation acquires meaning only through its integral form. In particular, we *cannot* divide both terms by dt and rewrite the equation as follows:

$$\frac{dX(t, \omega)}{dt} = \varphi(t, X) + \psi(t, X)\frac{dB_t}{dt}$$

The above equation would be meaningless because the Brownian motion is not differentiable.

This is the difficulty that precludes writing stochastic differential equations adding white noise pathwise. The differential notation of a stochastic differential equation is just a shorthand for the integral notation.

However, we can consider a discrete approximation:

$$\Delta X(t, \omega) = \varphi^*(t, X)\Delta t + \psi^*(t, X)\Delta B_t$$

Note that in this approximation the functions $\varphi^*(t, X)$, $\psi^*(t, X)$ will not coincide with the functions $\varphi(t, X)$, $\psi(t, X)$. Using the latter would (in general) result in a poor approximation.

The following section defines Itô processes and stochastic differential equations and studies their properties.

ITÔ PROCESSES

Let's now formally define Itô processes and establish key properties, in particular the Itô formula. In the previous section, we stated that an Itô process is a stochastic process of the form

$$Z(t, \omega) = \int_0^t a(s, \omega)ds + \int_0^t b(s, \omega)dB(s, \omega)$$

To make this definition rigorous, we have to state the conditions under which (1) the integrals exist, and (2) there is no anticipation of information.

Note that the two functions a and b might represent two stochastic processes and that the Riemann-Stieltjes integral might not exist for the paths of a stochastic process. We have therefore to demonstrate that both the Itô integral and the ordinary integral exist. To this end, we define Itô processes as follows.

Suppose that a one-dimensional Brownian motion B_t is defined on a probability space $(\Omega, \mathfrak{J}, P)$ equipped with a filtration $\mathfrak{J}_t$. The filtration might be given or might be generated by the Brownian motion B_t. Suppose that both a and b are adapted to $\mathfrak{J}_t$ and jointly measurable in $\mathfrak{J} \times \mathfrak{R}$. Suppose, in addition, that the following two integrability conditions hold:

$$
P\left[\int_0^t b^2(s, \omega)ds < \infty \text{ for all } t \geq 0 \right] = 1
$$

and

$$
P\left[\int_0^t |a(s, \omega)|ds < \infty \text{ for all } t \geq 0 \right] = 1
$$

These conditions ensure that both integrals in the definition of Itô processes exist and that there is no anticipation of information. We can therefore define the Itô process as the following stochastic process:

$$
Z(t, \omega) = \int_0^t a(s, \omega)ds + \int_0^t b(s, \omega)dB_s(s, \omega)
$$

Itô processes can be written in the shorter differential form as

$$
d\,Z_t = adt + bdB_t
$$

It should be clear that the latter formula is just a shorthand for the integral definition.

STOCHASTIC DIFFERENTIAL EQUATIONS

An Itô process defines a process $Z(t, \omega)$ as the sum of the time integral of the process $a(t, \omega)$ plus the Itô integral of the process $b(t, \omega)$. Suppose that two functions $\varphi(t, x)$, $\psi(t, x)$ that satisfy conditions established below are given. Given an Itô process $X(t, \omega)$, the two processes $\varphi(t, X)$, $\psi(t, X)$ admit respectively a time integral and an Itô integral. It therefore makes sense to consider the following Itô process:

$$Z(t, \omega) = \int_0^t \varphi[s, X(s, \omega)]ds + \int_0^t \psi[s, X(s, \omega)]dB_s$$

The term on the right side transforms the process X into a new process Z. We can now ask if there are stochastic processes X that are mapped into themselves such that the following stochastic equation is satisfied:

$$X(t, \omega) = \int_0^t \varphi[s, X(s, \omega)]ds + \int_0^t \psi[s, X(s, \omega)]dB_s$$

The answer is positive under appropriate conditions. It is possible to prove the following theorem of existence and uniqueness. Suppose that a one-dimensional Brownian motion B_t is defined on a probability space (Ω, $\Im$, P) equipped with a filtration $\Im_t$ and that B_t is adapted to the filtration $\Im_t$. Suppose also that the two measurable functions $\varphi(t, x)$, $\psi(t, x)$ map $[0,T] \times R \to R$ and that they satisfy the following conditions:

$$|\varphi(t, x)|^2 + |\psi(t, x)|^2 \leq C(1 + |x|)^2,$$
$$t \in [0, T], \ x \in R$$

and

$$|\varphi(t, x)| - \varphi(t, y) + |\psi(t, x)| - \psi(t, y)$$
$$\leq D(|x - y|), \ t \in [0, T], \ x \in R$$

for appropriate constants C, D. The first condition is known as the linear growth condition, the last condition is the Lipschitz condition. Suppose that Z is a random variable indepenent of the σ-algebra $\Im_\infty$ generated by B_t for $t \geq 0$ such that $E(|Z|^2) < \infty$. Then there is a unique stochastic process X, defined for $0 \leq t \leq T$, with time-continuous paths such that $X_0 = Z$ and such that the following equation is satisfied:

$$X(t, \omega) = X_0 + \int_0^t \varphi[s, X(s, \omega)]ds + \int_0^t \psi[s, X(s, \omega)]dB_s$$

The process X is called a strong solution of the above equation.

The above equation can be written in differential form as follows:

$$dX(t, \omega) = \varphi[t, X(t, \omega)]dt + \psi[t, X(t, \omega)]dB_t$$

The differential form does not have an independent meaning; a differential stochastic equation is just a short albeit widely used way to write the integral equation.

The key requirement of a strong solution is that the filtration $\mathfrak{J}_t$ is given and that the functions φ, ψ are adapted to the filtration $\mathfrak{J}_t$. From the economic (or physics) point of view, this requirement translates the notion of causality. In simple terms, a strong solution is a functional of the driving Brownian motion and of the "inputs" φ, ψ. A strong solution at time t is determined only by the "history" up to time t of the inputs and of the random shocks embodied in the Brownian motion.

These conditions can be weakened. Suppose that we are given only the two functions $\varphi(t, x)$, $\psi(t, x)$ and that we must construct a process X_t, a Brownian motion B_t, and the relative filtration so that the above equation is satisfied. The equation still admits a unique solution with respect to the filtration generated by the Brownian motion B. It is, however, only a weak solution in the sense that, though there is no anticipation of information, it is not a functional of a given Brownian motion.[2] Weak and strong solutions do not necessarily coincide. However, any strong solution is also a weak solution with respect to the same filtration.

Note that the solution of a differential equation is a stochastic process. Initial conditions must therefore be specified as a random variable and not as a single value as for ordinary differential equations. In other words, there is an initial value for each state. It is possible to specify a single initial value as the initial condition of a stochastic differential equation. In this case the initial condition is a random variable where the probability mass is concentrated in a single point.

We omit the detailed proof of the theorem of uniqueness and existence. Uniqueness is proved using the Itô isometry and the Lipschitz condition. One assumes that there are two different solutions and then demonstrates that their difference must vanish. The proof of existence of a solution is similar to the proof of existence of solutions in the domain of ordinary equations.

---

[2]See, for example, I. Karatzas and S. E. Shreve, *Brownian Motion and Stochastic Calculus* (New York: Springer, 1991).

The solution is constructed inductively by a recursive relationship of the type

$$
X^{(k+1)}(t, \omega) = \int_0^t \varphi[s, X^k(s, \omega)]ds
$$

$$
+ \int_0^t \psi[s, X^k(s, \omega)]dB_s
$$

It can be shown that this recursive relationship produces a sequence of processes that converge to the unique solution.

GENERALIZATION TO SEVERAL DIMENSIONS

The concepts and formulas established so far for Itô (and Stratonovich) integrals and processes can be extended in a straightforward but often cumbersome way to multiple variables. The first step is to define a d-dimensional Brownian motion.

Given a probability space $(\Omega, \mathfrak{J}, P)$ equipped with a filtration $\{\mathfrak{J}_t\}$, a d-dimensional standard Brownian motion $B_t(\omega)$, is a stochastic process with the following properties:

- $B_t(\omega)$ is a d-dimensional process defined over the probability space $(\Omega, \mathfrak{J}, P)$ that takes values in R^d.
- $B_t(\omega)$ has continuous paths for $0 \leq t \leq \infty$.
- $B_t(\omega) = 0$.
- $B_t(\omega)$ is adapted to the filtration $\mathfrak{J}_t$.
- The increments $B_t(\omega) - B_s(\omega)$ are independent of the σ-algebra $\mathfrak{J}_s$ and have a normal distribution with mean zero and covariance matrix $(t - s)I_d$, where I_d is the identity matrix.

These properties state that the standard Brownian motion is a stochastic process that starts at zero, has continuous paths, and has normally distributed increments whose variances grow linearly with time.

The next step is to extend the definition of the Itô integral in a multi-dimensional environment. This is again a straightforward but cumbersome extension of the one-dimensional case. Suppose that the following $r \times d$-dimensional matrix is given:

$$\mathbf{v} = \begin{bmatrix} v_{11} & \cdot & v_{1d} \\ \cdot & \cdot & \cdot \\ v_{r1} & \cdot & v_{rd} \end{bmatrix}$$

where each entry $v_{ij} = v_{ij}, (t,\omega)$ satisfies the following conditions:

1. V_{ij} are $\mathfrak{B}^d \times \mathfrak{I}$ measurable.
2. V_{ij} are $\mathfrak{I}_t$-adapted.
3. $P\left[\int\limits_0^t (v_{ij})^2 ds < \infty \text{ for all } t \geq 0 \right] = 1.$

Then, we define the multidimensional Itô integral

$$\int\limits_0^t \mathbf{v} dB = \int\limits_0^t \begin{bmatrix} v_{11} & \cdot & v_{1d} \\ \cdot & \cdot & \cdot \\ v_{r1} & \cdot & v_{rd} \end{bmatrix} \begin{bmatrix} dB_1 \\ \cdot \\ dB_d \end{bmatrix}$$

as the r-dimensional column vector whose components are the following sums of one-dimensional Itô integrals:

$$\sum\limits_{i=1}^{d} \int\limits_0^t v_{ij}(s,\ \omega) dB_j(s,\ \omega)$$

Note that the entries of the matrix are functions of time and state: They form a vector of stochastic processes. Given the previous definition of Itô integrals, we can now extend the definition of Itô processes to the multidimensional case. Suppose that the functions u and v satisfy the conditions established for the one-dimensional case. We can then form a multidimensional Itô process as the following vector of Itô processes:

$$dX_1 = u_1 dt + v_{11} dB_1 + \cdots + v_{1d} dB_d$$
$$\cdots$$
$$dX_{1r} = u_r dt + v_{r1} dB_1 + \cdots + v_{rd} dB_d$$

or, in matrix notation,

$$d\mathbf{X} = \mathbf{u} dt + \mathbf{v} dB$$

After defining the multidimensional Itô process, multidimensional stochastic equations are defined in differential form in matrix notation as follows:

$$dX(t, \omega) = \mathbf{u}[t, X_1(t, \omega), \ldots, X_d(t, \omega)]dt$$
$$+\mathbf{v}[t, X_1(t, \omega), \ldots, X_d(t, \omega)]dB$$

Consider now the multidimensional map: $g(t, x) \equiv [g_1(t, x), \ldots, g_d(t, x)]$, which maps the process X into another process $Y = g(t, X)$. It can be demonstrated that Y is a multidimensional Itô process whose components are defined according to the following rules:

$$dY_k = \frac{\partial g_k(t, X)}{\partial t}dt + \sum_i \frac{\partial g_k(t, X)}{\partial X_i}dX_i$$
$$+\frac{1}{2}\sum_{i.j} \frac{\partial^2 g_k(t, X)}{\partial X_i \partial X_j}dX_i dX_j$$

$$dB_i dB_j = 1 \text{ if } i = j, \ 0 \text{ if } i \neq j, \ dB_i dt = dt dB_i = 0$$

SOLUTION OF STOCHASTIC DIFFERENTIAL EQUATIONS

It is possible to determine an explicit solution of stochastic differential equations in the linear case and in a number of other cases that can be reduced to linear equations through functional transformations. Let's first consider linear stochastic equations of the form:

$$dX_t = [A(t)X_t + a(t)]dt + \sigma(t)dB_t, \ 0 \leq t < \infty$$
$$X_0 = \xi$$

where B is an r-dimensional Brownian motion independent of the d-dimensional initial random vector ξ and the $(d \times d), (d \times d), (d \times r)$ matrices $A(t), a(t), \sigma(t)$ are nonrandom and time dependent.

The simplest example of a linear stochastic equation is the equation of an arithmetic Brownian motion with drift, written as follows:

$$dX_t = \mu dt + \sigma dB_t$$
$$0 \leq t < \infty$$
$$X_0 = \xi, \mu, \sigma \text{ constants}$$

In linear equations of this type, the stochastic part enters only in an additive way through the terms $\sigma_{ij}(t)dB_t$. The functions $\sigma(t)$ are sometimes called the instantaneous variances and covariances of the process. In the example of the arithmetic Brownian motion, μ, is the drift of the process and σ the volatility of the process.

It is intuitive that the solution of this equation is given by the solution of the associated deterministic equation, that is, the ordinary differential equation obtained by removing the stochastic part, plus the cumulated random disturbances. Let's first consider the associated deterministic differential equation

$$\frac{dx}{dt} = A(t)x + a(t), \ 0 \le t < \infty$$

where $x(t)$ is a d-dimensional vector with initial conditions $x(0) = \xi$.

It can be demonstrated that this equation has an absolutely continuous solution in the domain $0 \le t < \infty$. To find its solution, let's first consider the matrix differential equation

$$\frac{d\Phi}{dt} = A(t)\Phi, 0 \le t < \infty$$

This matrix differential equation has an absolutely continuous solution in the domain $0 \le t < \infty$. The matrix $\Phi(t)$ that solves this equation is the fundamental solution of the equation. It can be demonstrated that $\Phi(t)$ is a nonsingular matrix for each t. Lastly, it can be demonstrated that the solution of the equation:

$$\frac{dx}{dt} = A(t)x + a(t), \ 0 \le t < \infty$$

with initial condition $x(0) = \xi$, can be written in terms of the fundamental solution as follows:

$$x(t) = \Phi(t) \left[x(0) + \int_0^t \Phi^{-1}(s)a(s)ds \right], \ 0 \le t < \infty$$

Let's now go back to the stochastic equation

$$dX_t = [A(t)X_t + a(t)]dt + \sigma(t)dB_t, \ 0 \le t < \infty$$
$$X_0 = \xi$$

Using Itô's formula, it can be demonstrated that the above linear stochastic equation admits the following unique solution:

$$X(t) = \Phi(t) \left[\xi + \int_0^t \Phi^{-1}(s)a(s)ds \right.$$
$$\left. + \int_0^t \Phi^{-1}(s)\sigma(s)dB_s \right], \ 0 \le t < \infty$$

This effectively demonstrates that the solution of the linear stochastic equation is the solution of the associated deterministic equation plus the cumulated stochastic term

$$\int_0^t \Phi^{-1}(s)\sigma(s)dB_s$$

To illustrate this, we now specialize the above solutions in the case of arithmetic Brownian motion, Ornstein-Uhlenbeck processes, and geometric Brownian motion:

The Arithmetic Brownian Motion

The **arithmetic Brownian motion** in one dimension is defined by the following equation:

$$dX_t = \mu dt + \sigma dB_t$$

In this case, $\mathbf{A}(t) = 0$, $\mathbf{a}(t) = \mu$, $\sigma(t) = \sigma$ and the solution becomes

$$X = \mu t + \sigma B$$

The Ornstein-Uhlenbeck Process

The **Ornstein-Uhlenbeck process** in one dimension is a mean-reverting process defined by the following equation:

$$dX_t = -\alpha X_t dt + \sigma dB_t$$

It is a mean-reverting process because the drift is pulled back to zero by a term proportional to the process itself. In this case, $A(t) = -\alpha$, $a(t) = 0$, $\sigma(t) = \sigma$ and the solution becomes

$$X_t = X_0 + e^{-\alpha t} + \sigma \int_0^t e^{-\alpha(t-s)} d B_s$$

The Geometric Brownian Motion

The **geometric Brownian motion** in one dimension is defined by the following equation:

$$dX = \mu X dt + \sigma X dB$$

This equation can be easily reduced to the previous linear case by the transformation:

$$Y = \log X$$

Let's apply Itô's formula

$$dY_t = \left(\frac{\partial g}{\partial t} + \frac{\partial g}{\partial x} a + \frac{1}{2}\frac{\partial^2 g}{\partial x^2} b^2\right) dt + \frac{\partial g}{\partial x} b dB_t$$

where

$$g(t, x) = \log x, \quad \frac{\partial g}{\partial t} = 0, \quad \frac{\partial g}{\partial t} = \frac{1}{x}, \quad \frac{\partial^2 g}{\partial x^2} = -\frac{1}{x^2}$$

We can then verify that the logarithm of the geometric Brownian motion becomes an arithmetic Brownian motion with drift

$$\mu' = \mu = \frac{1}{2}\sigma^2$$

The geometric Brownian motion evolves as a lognormal process:

$$X_t = x_0 \exp\left\{\left(\mu - \frac{1}{2}\sigma^2\right) t + \sigma B_t\right\}$$

DERIVATION OF ITÔ'S LEMMA

In mathematics, **Itô's lemma** is an identity used in Itô calculus to find the differential of a time-dependent function of a stochastic process. It serves as the stochastic calculus counterpart of the chain rule. It is best described using the Taylor series expansion of the function up to its second derivatives and identifying the square of an increment in the stochastic process with an increment in time.[3] The lemma is widely employed in mathematical finance, and its best known application is in the derivation of the Black-Scholes formula for option prices.

Consider a continuous and differentiable function, G, of a variable x. If Δx is a small change in x and ΔG is the resulting small change in G, a well-known result from ordinary calculus is

$$\Delta G \approx \frac{dG}{dx} \Delta x \tag{11.1}$$

In other words, ΔG is approximately equal to the rate of change of G with respect to x multiplied by Δx. The error involves terms of order Δx^2. If more precision is required, a Taylor series expansion of ΔG can be used:

$$\Delta G = \frac{dG}{dx} \Delta x + \frac{1}{2} \frac{d^2 G}{dx^2} \Delta x^2 + \frac{1}{6} \frac{d^3 G}{dx^3} \Delta x^3 + \cdots \tag{11.2}$$

For a continuous and differentiable function, G, of two variables, x and y, the result analogous to equation (11.1) is

$$\Delta G \approx \frac{dG}{dx} \Delta x + \frac{dG}{dy} \Delta y \tag{11.3}$$

and the Taylor series expansion of ΔG is

$$\Delta G = \frac{\partial G}{\partial x} \Delta x + \frac{\partial G}{\partial y} \Delta y + \frac{1}{2} \frac{\partial^2 G}{\partial x^2} \Delta x^2 + \frac{1}{2} \frac{\partial^2 G}{\partial y^2} \Delta y^2 + \frac{\partial^2 G}{\partial x \partial y} \Delta x \Delta y + \cdots \tag{11.4}$$

In the limit as Δx and Δy tend to zero, equation (11.4) becomes

$$dG = \frac{\partial G}{\partial x} dx + \frac{\partial G}{\partial y} dy \tag{11.5}$$

---

[3] See Chapter 2 for the Taylor series expansion.

We now extend equation (11.5) to cover functions of variables following Itô processes. Suppose that a variable, x, follows the Itô process in equation (11.5):

$$dx = a(x, t)dt + b(x, t)dW \tag{11.6}$$

and that G is some function of x and of time t. By analogy with equation (11.4), we can write:

$$\Delta G = \frac{\partial G}{\partial x}\Delta x + \frac{\partial G}{\partial t}\Delta t + \frac{1}{2}\frac{\partial^2 G}{\partial x^2}\Delta x^2 + \frac{1}{2}\frac{\partial^2 G}{\partial t^2}\Delta t^2 + \frac{\partial^2 G}{\partial x \partial t}\Delta x \Delta t + \cdots \tag{11.7}$$

Equation (11.6) can be discretized to

$$\Delta x = a(x, t)\Delta t + b(x, t)\varepsilon\sqrt{\Delta t} \tag{11.8}$$

where $\Delta W = \varepsilon\sqrt{\Delta t}$ is the Wiener process with ε is a standard normal random variable, that is, $\varepsilon \sim N(0,1)$. If we drop arguments in equation (11.8), we have

$$\Delta x = a\Delta t + b\varepsilon\sqrt{\Delta t} \tag{11.9}$$

This equation reveals an important difference between the situation in equation (11.7) and the situation in equation (11.4). When limiting arguments are used to move from equation (11.4) to equation (11.5), terms in Δx^2 are ignored because they are second-order terms. From equation (11.9), we have

$$\Delta x^2 = b^2\varepsilon^2\Delta t + \text{terms of higher order in } \Delta t \tag{11.10}$$

This shows that the term involving Δx^2 in equation (11.7) has a component that is order of Δt and cannot be ignored.

The variance of a standardized normal distribution is one, that is,

$$E(\varepsilon) = 0, \text{ var}(\varepsilon) = E(\varepsilon^2) - [E(\varepsilon)]^2 = 1$$

where E denotes expected value. The expected value of $\varepsilon^2\Delta t$ is, therefore, Δt. It can be shown that the variance of $\varepsilon^2\Delta t$ is of order Δt^2 and that as a result of this, we can treat $\varepsilon^2\Delta t$ as nonstochastic and equal to its expected value of Δt as Δt tends to zero. It follows from equation (11.10) that Δx^2 becomes nonstochastic and equal to $b^2 dt$ as Δt tends to zero. Taking limits as Δx and Δt tend to zero in equation (11.7), and using this last result, we obtain

$$dG = \frac{\partial G}{\partial x}dx + \frac{\partial G}{\partial t}dt + \frac{1}{2}\frac{\partial^2 G}{\partial x^2}b^2 dt \qquad (11.11)$$

This is Itô's lemma. Substituting for dx from equation (11.6), equation (11.11) becomes

$$dG = \left(\frac{\partial G}{\partial x}a + \frac{\partial G}{\partial t} + \frac{1}{2}\frac{\partial^2 G}{\partial x^2}b^2\right)dt + \frac{\partial G}{\partial x}bd\,W \qquad (11.12)$$

DERIVATION OF THE BLACK-SCHOLES OPTION PRICING FORMULA

The first formal solution of the option pricing model was developed independently by Fischer Black and Myron Scholes in 1976, working together, and in the same year by Robert Merton.[4] The solution of the option pricing problem proposed by Black, Scholes, and Merton was simple and elegant. Suppose that a market contains a risk-free bond, a stock, and an option. Suppose also that the market is arbitrage-free and that stock price processes follow a continuous-time geometric Brownian motion as described in the previous section.[5] Black, Scholes, and Merton demonstrated that it is possible to construct a portfolio made up of the stock plus the bond that perfectly replicates the option. The replicating portfolio can be exactly determined, without anticipation, solving a partial differential equation. The idea of replicating portfolios has important consequences. Whenever a financial instrument (security or derivative instrument) process can be exactly replicated by a portfolio of other securities, absence of arbitrage requires that the price of the original financial instrument coincide with the price of the replicating portfolio. Most derivative pricing algorithms are based on this principle: to price a derivative instrument, one must identify a replicating portfolio whose price is known.

---

[4] F. Black and M. Scholes, "The Pricing of Options and Corporate Liabilities," *Journal of Political Economy* 82 (1973): 637–654; and R. C. Merton, "Theory of Rational Option Pricing," *Bell Journal of Economics and Management Science* 4 (1973): 141–183.

[5] In this context, **arbitrage-free** means that after eliminating uncertainty about a portfolio of option and the underlying stock, the rate of return on this portfolio must be the risk-free interest rate.

Black and Scholes assume that stock price movements are described by the following continuous-time stochastic process:

$$dS = \mu S dt + \sigma S dW \tag{11.13}$$

where μ and σ are the constant drift and diffusion parameters of the geometric Brownian motion. Suppose that f is the price of a call option on stock price S. The variable f must be some function of stock price S and time t. Hence, from Itô's lemma discussed earlier in this chapter, we have

$$df = \left(\frac{\partial f}{\partial S} \mu S + \frac{\partial f}{\partial t} + \frac{1}{2} \frac{\partial^2 f}{\partial S^2} \sigma^2 S^2 \right) dt + \frac{\partial f}{\partial S} \sigma S dW \tag{11.14}$$

The discrete versions of equations (11.13) and (11.14) are

$$\Delta S = \mu S \Delta t + \sigma S \Delta W \tag{11.15}$$

$$\Delta f = \left(\frac{\partial f}{\partial S} \mu S + \frac{\partial f}{\partial t} + \frac{1}{2} \frac{\partial^2 f}{\partial S^2} \sigma^2 S^2 \right) \Delta t + \frac{\partial f}{\partial S} \sigma S \Delta W \tag{11.16}$$

where ΔS and Δf are changes in S and f in a small time interval Δt. Recall from the discussion of Itô's lemma that the Wiener processes underlying f and S are the same. In other words, the ΔW ($= \varepsilon \sqrt{\Delta t}$) in equations (11.15) and (11.16) are the same. It follows that by constructing a portfolio that includes both the stock and the call option, the Wiener process can be eliminated.

The appropriate portfolio comprising the stock and the call option is

$$-1 = \text{Call option}$$

$$+\frac{\partial f}{\partial S} = \text{Number of shares}$$

The holder of this portfolio is short one call option and long an amount $\frac{\partial f}{\partial S}$ shares of the underlying stock. Hence, the value of the portfolio, which we denote by Π, is given by

$$\Pi = -f + \frac{\partial f}{\partial S} S \tag{11.17}$$

The change $\Delta \Pi$ in the value of the portfolio in the time interval Δt is given by

$$\Delta \Pi = -\Delta f + \frac{\partial f}{\partial S} \Delta S \tag{11.18}$$

Substituting equations (11.15) and (11.16) into equation (11.18) yields

$$\Delta \Pi = \left(-\frac{\partial f}{\partial t} - \frac{1}{2} \frac{\partial^2 f}{\partial S^2} \sigma^2 S^2 \right) \Delta t \tag{11.19}$$

Because this equation does not involve ΔW, the portfolio must be riskless during the time interval Δt. Hence, the portfolio must earn the risk-free interest rate. If it earned more than the risk-free rate, arbitrageurs could make a riskless profit by shorting the risk-free securities and using the proceeds to buy the portfolio; if it earned less than the risk-free rate, they could make a riskless profit by shorting the portfolio and buying risk-free securities. Therefore, we have

$$\Delta \Pi = r \Pi \Delta t \tag{11.20}$$

where r is the risk-free interest rate. Substituting from equations (11.19) and (11.20), we obtain

$$\left(-\frac{\partial f}{\partial t} - \frac{1}{2} \frac{\partial^2 f}{\partial S^2} \sigma^2 S^2 \right) \Delta t = r \left(f - \frac{\partial f}{\partial S} S \right) \Delta t \tag{11.21}$$

so that

$$\frac{\partial f}{\partial t} + r S \frac{\partial f}{\partial S} + \frac{1}{2} \sigma^2 S^2 \frac{\partial^2 f}{\partial S^2} = r f \tag{11.22}$$

Equation (11.22) is the familiar Black-Scholes stochastic differential equation. Although we have derived the formula using a call option, it has many solutions, corresponding to all the different derivatives that can be defined with S as the underlying variable.[6] The particular derivative that is obtained when the equation is solved depends on the boundary conditions that are used. These specify the values of the derivative at the boundaries of

---

[6]The derivation of Black-Scholes is valid for European styles call and put options written on individual stocks, stock index, and currency.

possible values of S and t. In the case of a European call option,[7] the key boundary condition is

$$f = \max(S - X, 0) \quad \text{when } t = T$$

In the case of a European put option, it is

$$f = \max(X - S, 0) \quad \text{when } t = T$$

Solving equation (11.22) with the boundary conditions gives the Black-Scholes option pricing formula:

$$c = S_0 N(d_1) - Xe^{-rT} N(d_2)$$

$$p = Xe^{-rT} N(-d_2) - S_0 N(-d_1)$$

where

$$d_1 = \frac{\ln(S_0/X) + (r + \sigma^2/2) T}{\sigma \sqrt{T}}$$

$$d_1 = \frac{\ln(S_0/X) + (r - \sigma^2/2) T}{\sigma \sqrt{T}} = d_1 - \sigma \sqrt{T}$$

and $N(x)$ is the cumulative probability distribution function for a variable that is normally distributed with a mean of zero and a standard deviation of one (i.e., it is the probability that such a variable will be less than x). S_0 is the stock price at time zero, X is the strike price, r is the continuously compounded risk-free interest rate, σ is the stock return volatility, and T is the time to maturity of the option.

To illustrate the Black-Scholes option pricing model, suppose we have an options trader (Trader A) who expects volatility of the underlying stock return to be 30% per annum. Assuming that the risk-free interest rate is 6% per annum, Trader A computes the prices of six-month European call and put options written on a stock currently trading at $45 and with a strike price of $43.

---

[7]A European call option is one in which the option can only be exercised at the expiration date.

First, Trader A computes d_1 and d_2:

$$d_1 = \frac{\ln(S_0/X) + (r + \sigma^2/2)\,T}{\sigma\sqrt{T}} = \frac{\ln(45/43) + (0.06 + 0.30^2/2)\,0.5}{0.30\sqrt{0.5}} = 0.4618$$

$$d_1 = \frac{\ln(S_0/X) + (r - \sigma^2/2)\,T}{\sigma\sqrt{T}} = d_1 - \sigma\sqrt{T} = 0.2497$$

Following Black-Scholes, he then assumes that the underlying stock return follows a Normal distribution, which gives

$$N(d_1) = N(0.4618) = 0.6779$$

$$N(d_2) = N(0.2497) = 0.5986$$

Since the Normal distribution is symmetric around the mean, $N(-d_1) = 1 - N(d_1) = 0.3221$ and $N(-d_2) = 1 - N(d_2) = 0.4014$.

Substituting $S_0 = 45$, $X = 43$, $r = 0.06$, $\sigma = 0.30$, $N(d_1)$ and $N(d_2)$ into the Black-Scholes option pricing formula gives the prices of six-month European call and put options:

$$c = S_0 N(d_1) - Xe^{-rT} N(d_2) = 45 \cdot (0.6779) - 43 \cdot e^{(-0.06)(0.5)} \cdot (0.5986) = \$5.53$$

$$p = Xe^{-rT} N(-d_2) - S_0 N(-d_1) = 43 \cdot e^{(-0.06)(0.5)} \cdot (0.4014) - 45 \cdot (0.3221) = \$2.26$$

According to Trader A's expectation of 30% volatility, the six-month call and put options should be trading at $5.53 and $2.26, respectively. We should note that the prices of call and put options are sensitive to the volatility estimate. If two traders in the market have a different volatility estimate for the same underlying asset, they will have different option prices. For example, if we had another trader (Trader B) with a volatility expectation of 50% per annum, she would think the call and put options should be trading at $7.86 and $4.59 (following the same procedure described above). At that point in time, if the market prices of call and put options were $6.00 and $3.50, respectively, there would be a trade. Trader A would be willing to sell call option and Trader B would be willing to buy at the market price of $6.00 because Trader A would think the call is expensive, whereas Trader B would think the call is cheaper than their own estimates. Similarly, Trader A would be willing to sell put option at the market price of $3.50 and Trader B would be willing to buy it. These different volatility expectations generate demand and supply pressures that move the option prices in the market.

The Greeks

The Black-Scholes formula gives the value of European call and put options under some specific assumptions. Clearly, this is useful for computing the arbitrage-free value of an option. However, a derivatives trader needs methods for determining how the option premium changes as the variables or the parameters in the formula change in the market. Since market conditions change quite frequently, traders and risk managers must constantly monitor the sensitivity of their options portfolio with respect to changes in stock price, volatility, interest rate, and time.

Delta: Sensitivity to Underlying Price Change   In the Black-Scholes framework, **delta** determines how much the theoretical price would change if the underlying asset price moved by an infinitesimal amount:

$$\text{delta} = \frac{\partial C(S_t, t | r, \sigma, T, X)}{\partial S_t} = N(d_1)$$

Suppose that the delta of a call option on a stock is 0.7. This means that when the stock price changes by a small amount, the option price changes by about 70% of that amount. Assume that the stock price is $100 and the option price is $10. Suppose an investor who has sold 20 option contracts, that is, options to buy 2,000 shares. The investor's position could be hedged by buying $0.7 \times 2,000 = 1,400$ shares. The gain (loss) on the option position would then tend to be offset by the loss (gain) on the stock position. For example, if the stock price goes up by $1 (producing a gain of $1,400 on the shares purchased), the option price will tend to go up by $0.7 \times \$1 = \$0.70$ (producing a loss of $1,400 on the options written); if the stock price goes down by $1 (producing a loss of $1,400 on the shares purchased), the option price will tend to go down by $0.70 (producing a gain of $1,400 on the options written).

In this example, the delta of the investor's option position is $0.7 \times (-2,000) = -1,400$. In other words, the investor losses $1,400 \cdot \Delta S$ on the short option position when the stock price increases by ΔS. The delta of the stock is 1.0 and the long position in 1,400 shares has a delta of 1,400. Hence, the delta of the investor's overall position is zero. The delta of the stock position offsets the delta of the option position. A position with a delta of zero is referred to as being **delta neutral**.

Suppose a financial institution has sold for $600,000 a European call option on 100,000 shares of a stock. Assume that the stock price is $45, the strike price is $43, the risk-free rate is 6% per annum, and the volatility is 30% per annum, and the time to maturity is six months.

As presented above, the Black-Scholes price of the option is about $553,000. The financial institution has, therefore, sold the option for $47,000 more than its theoretical values. It is faced with the problem of hedging its exposure.

Based on the values $S_0 = 45$, $X = 43$, $r = 0.06$, $\sigma = 0.30$, and $T = 0.5$ (26 weeks), the initial value of delta is $N(d_1) = 0.678$. This means that as soon as the option is written, $3,051,000 must be borrowed to buy 67,800 shares at a price of $45. Assume that the hedge is assumed to be adjusted or rebalanced weekly. Since the interest rate is 6% per annum (or about 0.12% per week), interest rate costs totaling $3,520 are incurred in the first week.

Suppose the stock price falls to $44 by the end of the first week. Delta is recomputed at the end of the first week using $S_0 = 44$, $X = 43$, $r = 0.06$, $\sigma = 0.30$, and $T = 0.48$ (25 weeks), and is equal to 0.638. A total of 3,996 shares must be sold to maintain the hedge (67,800 – 63,803 = 3,996). This realizes $175,863 in cash and the cumulative borrowings at the end of the first week are reduced to $2,875,137.

Vega: Sensitivity of Volatility Vega is the rate of change of the value of a call (put) option with respect to the volatility of the underlying asset:

$$\text{vega} = \frac{\partial C(S_t, t | r, \sigma, T, X)}{\partial \sigma} = S_0 \sqrt{T} N'(d_1)$$

Rho: Sensitivity to Interest Rate Rho determines how much the price of a call (put) option would change as a result of changes in the interest rate:

$$\text{rho} = \frac{\partial C(S_t, t | r, \sigma, T, X)}{\partial r} = XTe^{-rT} N(d_2)$$

Theta: Sensitivity to Time Theta is the rate of change of the value of a call (put) option with respect to time when all else remains the same:

$$\text{theta} = \frac{\partial C(S_t, t | r, \sigma, T, X)}{\partial t} = -\frac{S_0 N'(d_1)\sigma}{2\sqrt{T}} - r X e^{-rT} N(d_2)$$

where d_1 and d_2 are defined above and

$$N'(x) = \frac{1}{\sqrt{2\pi}} e^{-x^2/2}$$

KEY POINTS

- Stochastic differential equations give meaning to ordinary differential equations where some terms are subject to random perturbation.
- Following Itô and Stratonovich, stochastic differential equations are defined through their integral equivalent: The differential notation is just a shorthand.
- Itô processes are the sum of a time integral plus an Itô integral.
- Itô processes are closed with respect to smooth maps: A smooth function of an Itô process is another Itô process defined through the Itô formula.
- Stochastic differential equations are equations established in terms of Itô processes.
- Linear equations can be solved explicitly as the sum of the solution of the associated deterministic equation plus a stochastic cumulative term.

Index

Printed and bound by CPI Group (UK) Ltd, Croydon, CR0 4YY

23/04/2025

14660922-0002